"Many people find Esther a strange and difficult text. But with careful attention to its historical and literary features, Andrew Steinmann shows how even a book which never names God offers an important theological and pastoral resource. This will be an important resource for all who wish to think through the importance of this book."

David Firth, Trinity College Bristol

"Steinmann's commentary provides an erudite and welldocumented historical account of the events in the book of Esther. The author's linguistic remarks, attention to intertextuality, and thoughtful theological reflections make this work accessible to all, from layperson to scholar."

Hélène Dallaire, Denver Seminary

"This is a superb commentary in every way! Andy Steinmann unpacks Esther's historical, literary, canonical, and Christological features—thus making this treasured Old Testament book eminently accessible, understandable, and applicable."

Reed Lessing, Concordia University, St. Paul

CHRISTIAN STANDARD COMMENTARY

ESTHER

CHRISTIAN STANDARD
COMMENTARY

ESTHER

—

Andrew E. Steinmann

REFERENCE

1 2 3 4 5 6 • 26 25 24

Printed in China

RRD

Dedication

In Memoriam:
Esther Josephine Catharine Bavis Masters
August 13, 1898–April 25, 1972)

TABLE OF CONTENTS

SERIES INTRODUCTION

The Christian Standard Commentary (CSC) aims to embody an "ancient-modern" approach to each volume in the series. The following explanation will help us unpack this seemingly paradoxical practice that brings together old and new.

The *modern commentary* tradition arose and proliferated during and after the Protestant Reformation. The growth of the biblical commentary tradition largely is a result of three factors: (1) *The recovery of classical learning* in the fifteenth–sixteenth centuries. This retrieval led to a revival of interest in biblical languages (Greek, Hebrew, and Aramaic). Biblical interpreters, preachers, and teachers interpreted Scripture based on the original languages rather than the Latin Vulgate. The commentaries of Martin Luther and John Calvin are exemplary in this regard because they return to the sources themselves (*ad fontes*). (2) *The rise of reformation movements* and the splintering of the Catholic Church. The German Reformation (Martin Luther), Swiss Reformation (John Calvin), and English Reformation (Anglican), among others (e.g., Anabaptist), generated commentaries that helped these new churches and their leaders interpret and preach Scripture with clarity and relevance, often with the theological tenets of the movements present in the commentaries. (3) *The historical turn in biblical interpretation* in the seventeenth and eighteenth centuries. This turning point emphasized the historical situation from which biblical books arise and in which they are contextualized.

In light of these factors, the CSC affirms traditional features of a *modern commentary*, evident even in recent commentaries:

- Authors analyze Old and New Testament books in their original languages.
- Authors present and explain significant text-critical problems as appropriate.
- Authors address and define the historical situations that gave rise to the biblical text (including date of composition, authorship, audience, social location, geographical and historical context, etc.) as appropriate to each biblical book.
- Authors identify possible growth and development of a biblical text so as to understand the book as it stands (e.g., how the book of Psalms came into its final form or how the Minor Prophets might be understood as a "book").

The CSC also exhibits recent shifts in biblical interpretation in the past fifty years. The first is the literary turn in biblical interpretation. Literary analysis arose in biblical interpretation during the 1970s and 1980s, and this movement significantly influenced modern biblical commentaries. Literary analysis attends to the structure and style of each section in a biblical book as well as the shape of the book as a whole. Because of this influence, modern commentaries assess a biblical book's style and structure, major themes and motifs, and how style impacts meaning. Literary interpretation recognizes that biblical books are works of art, arranged and crafted with rhetorical structure and purpose. Literary interpretation discovers the unique stylistic and rhetorical strategies of each book. Similarly, the CSC explores the literary dimensions of Scripture:

- Authors explore each book as a work of art that is a combination of style and structure, form and meaning.
- Authors assess the structure of the whole book and its communicative intent.
- Authors identify and explain the literary styles, poetics, and rhetorical devices of the biblical books as appropriate.
- Authors expound the literary themes and motifs that advance the communicative strategies in the book.

As an *ancient commentary,* the CSC is marked by a theological bent with respect to biblical interpretation. This bent is a tacit recognition that the Bible is not only a historical or literary document but is fundamentally the Word of God. That is, it recognizes Scripture as fundamentally both historical *and* theological. God is the primary speaker in Scripture, and readers must deal with him. Theological interpretation affirms that although God enabled many authors to write the books of the Bible (Heb 1:1), he is the divine author, the subject matter of Scripture, and the One who gives the Old and New Testaments to the people of God to facilitate their growth for their good (2 Tim 3:16–17). Theological interpretation reads Scripture as God's address to his church because he gives it to his people to be heard and lived. Any other approach (whether historical, literary, or otherwise) that diminishes emphasis on the theological stands deficient before the demands of the text.

Common to Christian (patristic, medieval, reformation, or modern) biblical interpretation in the past two millennia is a sanctified vision of Scripture in which it is read with attention to divine agency, truth, and relevance to the people of God. The *ancient commentary* tradition interprets Scripture as a product of complex and rich divine action. God has given his Word to his people so that they may know and love him, glorify him, and proclaim his praises to all creation. Scripture provides the information and power of God that leads to spiritual and practical transformation.

The transformative potential of Scripture emerges in the *ancient commentary* tradition as it attends to the centrality of Jesus Christ. Jesus is the One whom God sent to the world in the fullness of time and whom the OT anticipates, testifies to, and witnesses to. Further, he is the One the NT presents as the fulfillment of the OT promise, in whom the church lives and moves and has her being, who the OT and NT testify will return to judge the living and the dead, and who will make all things new.

With Christ as the center of Scripture, the *ancient commentary* tradition reveals an implicit biblical theology. Old and New Testaments work together as they reveal Christ; thus, the tradition works within a whole-Bible theology in which each Testament is read in dialectic relationship, one with the other.

Finally, the *ancient commentary* tradition is committed to spiritual transformation. The Spirit of God illumines the hearts of readers so they might hear God's voice, see Christ in his glory, and live in and through the power of the Spirit. The transformational dimensions of Scripture emerge in *ancient commentary* so that God's voice might be heard anew in every generation and God's Word might be embodied among his people for the sake of the world.

The CSC embodies the *ancient commentary* tradition in the following ways:

- Authors expound the proper subject of Scripture in each biblical book, who is God; further, they explore how he relates to his world in the biblical books.
- Authors explain the centrality of Jesus appropriate to each biblical book and in the light of a whole-Bible theology.
- Authors interpret the biblical text spiritually so that the transformative potential of God's Word might be released for the church.

In this endeavor, the CSC is ruled by a Trinitarian reading of Scripture. God the Father has given his Word to his people at various times and in various ways (Heb 1:1), which necessitates a sustained attention to historical, philological, social, geographical, linguistic, and grammatical aspects of the biblical books that derive from different authors in the history of Israel and of the early church. Despite its diversity, the totality of Scripture reveals Christ, who has been revealed in the Old and New Testaments as the Word of God (Heb 1:2; John 1:1) and the One in whom "all things hold together" (Col 1:15–20) and through whom all things will be made new (1 Cor 15; Rev 21:5). God has deposited his Spirit in his church so that they might read spiritually, being addressed by the voice of God and receiving the life-giving Word that comes by Scripture (2 Tim 3:15–17; Heb 4:12). In this way, the CSC contributes to the building up of Christ's church and the Great Commission to which all believers are called.

AUTHOR'S PREFACE

Writing a commentary on a biblical book is always a challenge, no matter which book of the canon is in view. However, it is perhaps most difficult to write a theologically oriented commentary on a book such as Esther, which exhibits no overt theological content and appears to studiously avoid mention of either the God of Israel or the gods of the nations. Nevertheless, I felt honored when Ray Clendenen asked me to write the Christian Standard Commentary on Esther. This book, though not a large historical narrative book like Samuel, Kings, or Chronicles, nevertheless contains much to ponder and enjoy and offers insights into God's ways without ever mentioning him. I am indebted to those who aided me in this work: Concordia University Chicago—especially the Klinck Library staff who helped me track down several hard-to-find secondary sources; Gary Millar, my fellow CSC associate editor whose helpful review comments served to enhance the commentary; and Andrew King, the CSC series general editor, whose helpfulness in bringing this volume to fruition is much appreciated. As always, the support of my wife Rebecca is a constant in my life that has contributed much to my work in ways she may never fully understand. The dedication of this book to my grandmother—another Esther—is a way for me to acknowledge that all of us owe much to those who came before us and shaped our lives as they cared and nourished us physically, intellectually, spiritually, and morally. Finally, any errors in this book are mine, but anything correct belongs ultimately to our gracious triune God. Soli deo gloria!

ABBREVIATIONS

AB	Anchor Bible
ABD	*Anchor Bible Dictionary*. Edited by David Noel Freedman. 6 vols. New York: Doubleday, 1992.
AJA	*American Journal of Archaeology*
AJSL	*American Journal of Semitic Languages and Literatures*
ANF	*The Ante-Nicene Fathers*. Edited by A. Roberts and J. Donaldson. 10 vols. Repr., Peabody, MA: Hendrickson, 1994.
AsJT	*The Asia Journal of Theology*
AT	The Alpha Text of Esther (Greek)
BA	*Biblical Archaeologist*
Bib	*Biblica*
BN	*Biblische Notizen*
BSac	*Bibliotheca Sacra*
BT	*The Bible Translator*
CBQ	*The Catholic Biblical Quarterly*
ConJ	*Concordia Journal*
ESV	English Standard Version
GW	God's Word
HUCA	*Hebrew Union College Annual*
IBHS	Bruce Waltke and Michael O'Connor, *An Introduction to Biblical Hebrew Syntax*. Eisenbrauns: Winona Lake, IN, 1990.
ICC	The International Critical Commentary
JANER	*Journal of Ancient Near Eastern Religions*
JBL	*Journal of Biblical Literature*
JETS	*Journal of the Evangelical Theological Society*
JHebS	*Journal of Hebrew Scriptures*
JNES	*Journal of Near Eastern Studies*
JSOT	*Journal for the Study of the Old Testament*

JSOTSup	Journal for the Study of the Old Testament Supplement Series
JSS	*Journal of Semitic Studies*
JTS	*Journal of Theological Studies*
LCL	Loeb Classical Library
MT	The Masoretic Text of the Old Testament (Hebrew/Aramaic)
NAC	New American Commentary
NCBC	New Century Bible Commentary
NET	The NET Bible/New English Translation
NIV	New International Version
NPNF[1]	*The Nicene and Post-Nicene Fathers.* Series 1. Edited by P. Schaff. 14 vols. Repr., Peabody, MA: Hendrickson, 1994.
NRSV	New Revised Standard Version
OG	The Old Greek Text of Esther (Septuagint)
OTE	*Old Testament Essays*
SBLDS	Society of Biblical Literature Dissertation Series
TANAKH	*TANAKH, The Holy Scriptures: The New JPS Translation according to the Traditional Hebrew Text* N.P.: Jewish Publication Society, 1985.
TOTC	Tyndale Old Testament Commentary
VT	*Vetus Testamentum*
WBC	Word Biblical Commentary
ZAW	*Zeitschrift für die Alttestamentliche Wissenschaft*

ESTHER

INTRODUCTION OUTLINE

INTRODUCTION

It is perhaps ironic that while women play a relatively small role in the overall narrative of the Old Testament, two of the most beloved books of the Hebrew Scriptures—Ruth and Esther—are named after women who play central roles in those respective books. A comparison of these two women leads to other ironic contrasts: Ruth is a Moabite whose home becomes Israel whereas Esther is an Israelite whose home is Persia. The narrative of Ruth is largely about Yahweh: Ruth's conversion to belief in Israel's God, God's provision of a son for Ruth and Boaz, and Ruth's role as an ancestor of David furthering the messianic thread running through the Old Testament. In contrast, the narrative in the Hebrew text of Esther never mentions Yahweh or any other god, is completely devoid of overt references to religious practices (either by Esther and Mordecai or the Persians), and the book is full of what appear to be secular feasts, celebrations, and commemorations.

Esther is, therefore, an Old Testament anomaly: a book of Scripture recounting an apparent secular tale of secularized Jews living on foreign soil. It is largely unmentioned in the New Testament—with Mark 6:23 providing the only close verbal tie to Esther (see Esth 5:3, 6; 7:2). Yet what appears on the surface of the text of Esther can be deceptive. Religious practices are mentioned but veiled; for instance, the casting of lots (3:7; 9:24) and fasting (4:3, 16; 9:31). Its narrative culminates in the festival of Purim, the only Old Testament annual celebration not derived from the Pentateuch and a festival part of Jewish worship to this day. Esther relates the rescue of the Judeans throughout the great

Persian Achaemenid Empire, thereby preserving the "holy seed" and the messianic line (Isa 6:13). The depth of Esther is revealed by the author's skilled use of irony, plot twists and turns, and his portrayal of the courage of Esther and faithfulness of Mordecai. This can lead perceptive readers only to one conclusion: God is not absent at all; he is still involved intimately in human affairs even when persons, empires, or storytellers fail to unambiguously acknowledge his presence.

1   AUTHOR AND DATE OF COMPOSITION

In English Bibles the book of Esther is grouped among the historical books. As is true of most writers of those books, the author of Esther does not identify himself by name. However, there are indications within the text that enable us to identify the author as a Judean living in Persia. These include:

1. He has knowledge of both Judean and Persian customs.

2. He accurately represents Persian names in Hebrew and employs Persian loan words.[1]

3. Near the end of the book he emphasizes the establishment of the feast of Purim.

4. He is knowledgeable about the city of Susa, the geographical setting of the book.

5. He never mentions Judah or Jerusalem.

We can also draw some conclusions about when Esther was written.[2] The events in Esther take place between 483 and 473 BC. This leads to the conclusion the earliest possible date of composition is 473 BC. However, 9:28 indicates that Purim had become a regular, annual feast among Jews and had been celebrated for some years before the book was written. In addition, chap. 10 summarizes the reign of Ahasuerus and indicates Mordecai's role as prime minister. When combined with the book's opening verse, these details imply Esther was written after Ahasuerus's death in 465 BC. On the other hand, with the conquest of the Persian

---

[1] Edwin Yamauchi, *Persia and the Bible* (Grand Rapids: Eerdmans, 1990), 237–8.

[2] Critical scholars who doubt Esther's historicity often date the book to a later period after Alexander the Great. For a summary of these positions, see Yamauchi, *Persia and the Bible*, 226–8.

Empire of Alexander the Great in 331 BC, Greek customs and language quickly spread across much of the ancient Near East (although Greek culture had already been seeping eastward for some centuries before this). Yet the author employs no Greek loan words and demonstrates no knowledge of Greek customs, allowing the reader to conclude it is unlikely Esther was written after 331 BC. Esther was composed early in this intervening period (465–331 BC), about 460 BC (see also the discussion of 9:19 in the commentary). Evidence for this date includes:

1. Dual dating of months, listing both the ordinal number of the month and the Babylonian name. These demonstrate the author assumes his readers are still becoming familiar with the Babylonian names for months (2:16; 3:7 [twice], 13; 8:9, 12; 9:1), placing the composition of Esther after the book of Zechariah but before those of Ezra and Nehemiah.[3]

2. Esther 9:19 speaks of the custom of celebrating Purim on a different date in the provinces than in Susa, assuming the practice is contemporary with the intended readers of the book, signaling the author was writing for Jews in the Persian Empire, not for Jews of a later period.

3. Since it appears Judith, a book patterned after Esther, was written during the reign of Artaxerxes II (404–359 BC), Esther must have been written earlier.[4]

4. "The number of Persian words in Esther and its numerous Aramaisms suggest the story's composition during a period not far removed from the events it describes."[5]

---

[3] For the use of dual-date formulas in Esther (both ordinal number for the month and the Babylonian name of the month), see Albert D. Friedberg, "A New Clue in the Dating of the Composition of the Book of Esther," *VT* 50 (2000): 561–5. While Friedberg's analysis was challenged (Gerhard Larsson, "Is the Book of Esther Older Than Has Been Believed?" *VT* 52, no. 1 (2002): 130–1), it was ably defended in a rejoinder (Albert D. Friedberg and Vincent DeCaen, "Dating the Composition of the Book of Esther: A Response to Larsson," *VT* 53, no. 3 (2003): 427–9). However, David Talshir and Zipora Talshir, "The Double Month Naming in Late Biblical Books: A New Clue for Dating Esther?" *VT* 54 (2004): 549–55, argued the use of Babylonian names for months in Hebrew was not common until late in the Second Temple period, thus making Esther a late book. This is singularly unconvincing since the Babylonian month names are used at 1 Macc 4:52, 59; 7:43; 9:3; 10:21; 16:14 *without the ordinal for the month*, and 1 Maccabees appears to have been composed in Hebrew in the second century BC, far from late in the Second Temple period.

[4] Shemaryahu Talmon, "'Wisdom' in the Book of Esther," *VT* 13 (1963): 449.

[5] Sandra Beth Berg, *The Book of Esther: Motifs, Themes, and Structures,* SBLDS 44 (Missoula, MT: Scholars, 1979), 2.

2 DATES OF THE EVENTS IN ESTHER

The book is set within the ancient Persian Empire ruled by a line of kings known to history as the Achaemenids, since they claimed descent from Achaemenes (c. 700–675 BC). These kings were:

1. Cyrus (the Great)   538–530 BC
2. Cambyses   529–522 BC
3. Darius I   521–486 BC
4. Xerxes (Ahasuerus) 485–465 BC
5. Artaxerxes I   464–424 BC
6. Darius II   423–405 BC
7. Artaxerxes II   404–359 BC
8. Artaxerxes III   358–338 BC
9. Arses   337–336 BC
10. Darius III   335–331 BC

The events in Esther take place during the reign of Xerxes, one of the most powerful men to rule the Persian Achaemenid Empire. This king's name in Old Persian was *Khshayarshan,* meaning either "ruling over heroes" or "he who rules over men."[6] Attempts by Hebrew speakers led to his name becoming *Aḥašwērôš* in Hebrew. This is reflected in some English Bible versions as *Ahasuerus* (e.g., CSB 1:1). The Greek attempt to pronounce his name led to his being called *Xerxes.* Since much of our knowledge of the Achaemenid kings has been preserved by the ancient Greek historians such as Herodotus, this king is best known in the English-speaking world as Xerxes, and many modern English Bible versions use this form of his name. Ahasuerus is mentioned briefly by name in Ezra (Ezra 4:6).[7]

To date the events in Esther, we must be familiar with the basic chronology of Ahasuerus's reign.[8] When Darius I died in late 486 BC

---

[6] Yamauchi, *Persia and the Bible,* 187; A. R. Millard, "Persian Names in Esther and the Reliability of the Hebrew Text," *JBL* 96, no. 4 (1977): 481–8, has examined the Persian names in MT Esther in contrast to Septuagint Esther and concluded that the MT and its later scribes accurately preserved the Persian names whereas they are often altered and garbled in the Septuagint.

[7] Ahasuerus is also mentioned at Dan 11:2, although not by name. There Daniel's prophecy speaks of a fourth king—Ahasuerus who "will arise" over Persia after the reign of Cyrus (the first three being Cambyses, Gaumata [who briefly attempted to usurp the throne], and Darius I).

[8] Much of the following discussion is drawn from Andrew E. Steinmann, *From Abraham to Paul: A Biblical Chronology* (St. Louis: Concordia, 2011), 193–5.

(probably in November), Egypt was in open rebellion against Persian rule. Ahasuerus would have ruled the last months of 486 BC and the first months of 485 BC before coming to his first official year on the throne in Nisan 485 BC.[9] During these early months of Ahasuerus's reign, a formal letter indicting the Judeans in Jerusalem (Ezra 4:6) was written, accusing them of complicity in the Egyptian revolt.[10] Since the earliest known Egyptian inscriptions relating to Ahasuerus's reign date to 484 BC, he must have been successful in subduing the rebellion during his first regnal year (i.e., Nisan [March/April] 485–Adar [February/March] 484 BC).

After pacifying Egypt, Ahasuerus was free to turn his attention toward the Greeks who aided the Egyptians and supported their uprising. This would have been the setting for the 180-day banquet during his third year (Esth 1:3). The banquet probably served as a step in the planning of his later western campaign. It was a way of garnering the support of his nobles, officers, and influential courtiers. Since the city of Susa was not usually the Persian royal residence in the summer months, the banquet probably took place in late winter. Esther 1:5 notes that Ahasuerus provided a seven-day feast for everyone present in Susa, likely in conjunction with the new year corresponding to the beginning of Ahasuerus's fourth official year on the throne. The year began on 1 Nisan (Saturday, April 3), 482 BC.[11] This would place the 180-day banquet from 4 Tishri (Sunday, October 4) 483 BC to 30 Adar (Friday, April 2) 482 BC. The seven-day feast was 1–7 Nisan (Saturday, April 3–Friday, April 9) 482 BC. During his fourth year it appears as if Ahasuerus suppressed a revolt in Babylon, explaining why the Greek invasion was delayed until Ahasuerus's fifth year.[12]

Ahasuerus began his Greek invasion in May 480 BC from Sardis, located in western Turkey. He failed to complete his conquest of

---

[9] The Persian regnal year began with the first month of spring (Nisan in the Jewish calendar—approximately March/April in the Gregorian calendar).

[10] The letter was written "[a]t the beginning of the reign of Ahasuerus" (בְּתְחִלַת מַלְכוּתוֹ; Ezra 4:6), not in Ahasuerus's first year.

[11] Dates from the lunar calendar (used by ancient Judeans, Babylonians, Persians, and others) can be converted to dates on the Julian calendar using the tables in Richard A. Parker and Waldo H. Dubberstein, *Babylonian Chronology 626 B.C.-A.D. 75* (Eugene, OR: Wipf and Stock, 2007).

[12] Ctesias places Babylon's revolt before Ahasuerus's Greek campaign. Arrian places it afterward. Since Ahasuerus dropped the traditional title "King of Babylon" from his regal designations from his fifth year onward, the evidence supports Ctesias.

Greece, largely due to the defeat of his fleet at the Battle of Salamis. He returned to Sardis in December 480 BC without having pacified Greece. Following this, he turned his attention to a search for a new queen (2:1–4). According to 2:12 all of the young girls who were considered by Ahasuerus underwent twelve months of preparation. Since Esther was presented to the king in Tebeth 479/478 BC (2:16),[13] she entered into the preparations no later than Shebat (February) 479 BC. From this point onward, the rest of the chronology of Esther can be constructed from references in the book itself:[14]

LATE 486/EARLY 487		LETTER TO AHASUERUS	EZRA 4:6
25 Elul 483– 30 Adar 482	Sat., Oct. 3, 483– Fri., Apr. 2, 482	180-day banquet	Esth 1:3
1–7 Nisan 482	Sat., Apr 3– Fri. Apr. 9, 482	Seven-day feast	Esth 1:5
Shebat–Tebeth 479	Feb.–Dec. 479	Twelve-month preparation	Esth 2:12
Tebeth 479/478	Dec. 479/Jan. 478	Esther presented to Ahasuerus	
1 Nisan 474	Fri., Apr. 5, 474	Haman casts the Pur	Esth 3:7
13 Nisan 474	Wed., Apr. 17, 474	Haman issues edict	Esth 3:12
23 Sivan 474	Mon., June 25, 474	Mordecai issues edit	Esth 8:9
13 Adar II 473	Thu., Apr. 5, 473	Judeans defend themselves	Esth 3:13; 8:12; 9:1
14 Adar II 473	Fri., Apr. 6, 473	Purim celebrated	Esth 9:15, 17

3   ESTHER'S HISTORICAL SETTING

3.1   The Importance of Herodotus for Knowledge of the Persian Empire

Herodotus, an ancient Greek writer (c. 484–425 BC), was called "The Father of History" by the Roman orator Cicero. His only extant work, *The Histories of the Persian Empire* (hereinafter *Histories*), is often considered the first true attempt at historiography. Before Herodotus no one attempted an orderly and thorough study of the past, including

---

[13] During Ahasuerus's seventh year Tebeth ran from December 22, 479 BC to January 20, 478 BC.

[14] Dates from Steinmann, *From Abraham to Paul*, 194–5.

attempts to analyze the causes of events and their effect on persons and on future events. He has also been called "The Father of Lies" by critics who believed his history is little more than exaggerated tales.

Herodotus was born about 485 BC in the Greek city of Halicarnassus (modern Bodrum, Turkey). At the time Halicarnassus was one of the satrapies in the Persian Empire. He was born into a wealthy Greek family, affording him a good education in the best schools available. Herodotus traveled extensively around the eastern Mediterranean, and after the Peace of Callias between the Greek Delian League and Persia in 449 BC, he also traveled broadly throughout the Persian Empire. He visited Palestine and Syria, Babylon, Egypt, the Greek islands of Rhodes, Cyprus, Delos, Paros, Thasos, Samothace, Crete, Samos, Cythera, and Aegina. He sailed through the Hellespont and on the Black Sea as far north as the mouth of the Danube River. Throughout his travels he took notes on local oral histories, myths, and legends. When not traveling, Herodotus lived in Athens where he gave public readings of the histories he collected. He received fees for his public appearances, and in 445 BC the citizens of Athens awarded him the sum of ten talents for his contributions to Athenian culture. About that time he completed his only known work, *Histories*. In 443 BC, Herodotus joined a group of fellow Athenians who set out to colonize the city of Thurii in the south of the Italian peninsula. Many believe he died there about 425 BC. However, some believe he died in Athens between 425 and 413 BC in the plague that also took the life of the Athenian statesman Pericles.[15]

After his death, Herodotus's *Histories* was divided into nine books—each one named after one of the Muses. Their content can be described this way:

> The first five books look into the past to try to explain the rise and fall of the Persian Empire. They describe the geography of each state the Persians conquered and tell about their people and customs. The next four books tell the story of the war itself, from the invasions of Greece by the Persian emperors Darius and Xerxes to the Greek triumphs at Salamis, Plataea and Mycale in 480 and 479 B.C.[16]

---

[15] Joshua J. Mark, "Herodotus," *Ancient History Encyclopedia,* last modified March 27, 2018, http://www.ancient.eu/herodotus.

[16] "Herodotus," https://www.history.com/topics/ancient-history/herodotus, last updated June 23, 2023.

Histories reveals Herodotus to be a skilled storyteller who engaged his readers with his narratives using dramatic scenes inhabited by noteworthy characters. At times he employed dialogue (although clearly not verbatim quotations) to make history's participants appear more lifelike and three-dimensional.

Even in antiquity the authenticity of Herodotus's *Histories* was challenged. Both Ctesias (fifth century BC) and Plutarch (c. AD 46–120) expressed doubts about his portrayal of persons, places, and events. In the early twentieth century scholars questioned whether Herodotus actually visited Egypt and Babylonia. Such doubts can be traced back to Herodotus's own narrative technique. He did not allow a good anecdote to go unused, even if he did not consider it to be historically accurate. At times he reports several stories that appear to contradict each other.

Nevertheless, Herodotus has proven to be generally accurate in his historical portrayals—though like all historians he could make mistakes. It is now widely accepted he visited Egypt, and he is our most important source for information concerning the twenty-sixth dynasty (sixth century BC). His knowledge of Egypt even included details about such as the construction of a ship, which he called a *baris*.[17] Excavations at Babylon in the early twentieth century demonstrate Herodotus's description of the city was accurate. He did, however, make errors concerning the size of the city, the height of its walls, and the number of gates the walls contained. Another example of vindication of Herodotus's reportage is described this way:

> [Herodotus's] claim of fox-sized ants in Persia who spread gold dust when digging their mounds . . . has been rejected for centuries until, in 1984 CE, the French author and explorer Michel Peissel, confirmed that a fox-sized marmot in the Himalayas did indeed spread gold dust when digging and that accounts showed the animal had done so in antiquity as the villages had a long history of gathering the dust. Peissel also explains that the Persian word for "mountain ant" was very close to their word for 'marmot' and so it was established that Herodotus was not making up his giant ants but, since he did not speak Persian and had to rely on

---

[17] Herodotus, *Histories*, 2.96.1–3. See "Nile shipwreck discovery proves Herodotus right—after 2,469 years," *The Guardian*, https://www.theguardian.com/science/2019/mar/17/nile-shipwreck-herodotus-archaeologists-thonis-heraclion, posted March 17, 2019.

translators, was the victim of a misunderstanding in translation. This same scenario could apply to other observations and claims found in Herodotus' histories though, certainly, not all.[18]

Herodotus is our most important ancient source for information about the Persian Empire up to 479 BC. Much of what he reported about the Achaemenid dynasty is accurate, but he (or his sources) could make mistakes or display their prejudices. He accurately preserved the account of Cyrus the Great's rise to become Persian king. His description of Cambyses's invasion of Egypt, however, appears to have been received from anti-Persian sources and portrays the Persian king in a less-than-flattering manner.[19] Herodotus is thorough in narrating the rise of Darius to become Persia's king as well as his defeat of Pseudo-Smerdis, a false claimant to the throne. In this regard, his information corresponds closely to the same information contained in the Behistun Inscription.[20]

Herodotus's account of Xerxes's (Ahasuerus's) invasion of Greece in 480 BC has for the most part been vindicated by later research, including topographical surveys and archaeological findings. He includes vivid and accurate accounts of the battles at Thermopylae, Salamis, and Plataea.[21] But Herodotus greatly exaggerated the size of Xerxes's army. In addition, Herodotus's account of the evacuation of Athens as Xerxes advanced upon the city is seemingly contradicted by the Decree of Themistocles.[22] Nevertheless, W. Kendrick Pritchett

---

[18] Mark, "Herodotus." Mark's comments are based on Michel Peissel, *The Ants' Gold: The Discovery of the Greek El Dorado in the Himalayas* (New York: HarperCollins, 1984). See also "Himalayas Offer Clue to Legend of Gold-Digging 'Ants,'" *New York Times,* November 25, 1996, https://www.nytimes.com/1996/11/25/world/himalayas-offer-clue-to-legend-of-gold-digging -ants.html.

[19] Edwin Yamauchi, "Herodotus," Vol. 3: 180–1 in *ABD.*

[20] The Behistun Inscription is a trilingual (Old Persian, Elamite, and Akkadian) inscription and monument on Mount Behistun in western Iran. It was authored by Darius I and contains a brief biography (including Darius's ancestry) as well as his account of nineteen battles he fought against pretenders to the throne following the deaths of Cyrus and Cambyses.

[21] For these battle accounts, see *Histories* 7.205–26 (Thermopylae), 8.78–97 (Salamis), and 9.28–75 (Plataea).

[22] The Decree of Themistocles was found as an inscription on a stone discovered in Troezen, Greece, and first published in 1960. It records a resolution of the Athenian assembly proposed by Themistocles. If the decree's assertions are accurate, the Greek defensive battles at Thermopylae and Artemisium were intended only to be holding actions designed to give time to evacuate Athens and Attica. In contrast, Herodotus describes these battles as full-scale attempts to defeat the Persian invasion.

argues, "Herodotus has in fact been proven to be correct in so many cases where he had earlier been doubted, that when a late document is found which flatly contradicts him, this document has to be considered *a priori* suspect."[23]

Because of the importance of Herodotus's *Histories,* it is a valuable resource in understanding the Persian background and setting of Esther. It will be referenced throughout this commentary whenever it offers insight into the customs and conventions of the Persian royal court.

3.2 The Reign of Ahasuerus

Ahasuerus was the son of Darius I and Atossa, the daughter of Cyrus the Great. Ahasuerus, who was born about 518 BC, was not the oldest of Darius's sons, but he was the eldest of Atossa's four sons. Ahasuerus's father Darius was not a descendant of Cyrus but from a collateral line of the Achaemenids.

For about twelve years before his accession to the throne Ahasuerus served as viceroy of Babylonia. Upon Darius's death in November 486 BC, Ahasuerus assumed the Persian throne. The first challenge faced by Ahasuerus was the revolt of Egypt against Persian rule. Egypt had been conquered by Cambyses and was in revolt before Ahasuerus assumed the throne. Ahasuerus led a campaign to Egypt in 485, and by January 484 he had successfully pacified Egypt. Early in his reign Ahasuerus also had to suppress two revolts in Babylon. The first one took place for about two months in 484 when a certain Belshimmani killed the Persian satrap in Babylon and declared himself king. A second, more serious revolt occurred in August 482 when Shamash-Eriba claimed the title "king of Babylon and the lands." This revolt was crushed before the spring of 481. In response to these revolts, Ahasuerus and subsequent kings rarely used the title "king of Babylon and the lands" after this time. In addition, to reduce Babylon's prominence, the great ziggurat of Babylon was destroyed and other temples desecrated. Herodotus reports an eighteen-foot statue of Marduk made of solid gold was looted from Babylon by Ahasuerus.[24]

---

[23] W. Kendrick Pritchett, "Herodotos and the Themistokles Decree," *AJA* 66 (1962): 43.

[24] Herodotus, *Histories* 1.183. For an English text of Herodotus (with facing Greek text) see A. D. Godley, *Herodotus, with an English Translation* LCL. Cambridge: Harvard University,

Ahasuerus's best-known military campaign was his invasion of Greece with what was most likely the largest military force assembled in antiquity. Among the more notable battles and events during this campaign were these:

1. The Battle of Thermopylae (August/September 480 BC) where Leonidas and his Spartans made a gallant, though ultimately unsuccessful, effort to block the Persian advance southward into Greece.

2. The burning of Athens by the Persian forces (September 480 BC). Athens had been evacuated.

3. The decisive defeat of the Persian fleet by the much smaller Greek allied fleet at the Battle of Salamis (September 480 BC).

Ultimately, Ahasuerus's invasion of Greece was a failure and only inflamed the Greeks' hatred for the Persians.

Upon his return to Persia, the rest of Ahasuerus's reign was occupied with domestic matters—especially continued construction in the great Persian city of Persepolis which his father began. Ahasuerus's reign saw increased taxation across the empire not only to fund his fruitless Greek campaign but also to pay for a growing imperial bureaucracy and the lavish construction in Persepolis. Ahasuerus himself seems to have been rather self-indulgent. While he had only one official wife at any one time, he kept a harem of more than 360 concubines from the provinces throughout the empire. Ancient historians mention a number of love affairs with wives of his relatives and his court officials.[25] This inward focus and intemperate pleasure-seeking appears to have had deleterious effects on the western edge of the empire, and at the very end of his reign Asiatic Greeks in Anatolia and its islands revolted, seceding from the empire and joining the Delian League.

Intrigue within the Persian court led to Ahasuerus's assassination in early August 465. Artabanus, the captain of the royal bodyguard, plotted a palace coup in which he hoped to remove the Achaemenids from the throne. He killed Ahasuerus in his bedchamber and then

---

1920, available online at http://www.perseus.tufts.edu/hopper/text?doc=Perseus%3atext%3a 1999.01.0126.

[25] Jon L. Berquist, *Judaism in Persia's Shadow: A Social and Historical Approach,* reprint (Eugene, OR: Wipf and Stock, 2003), 91.

attempted to kill the king's sons.[26] Ahasuerus was succeeded by his third son Artaxerxes I (Longimanus).

3.3   The Historicity of Esther

Critical scholars have long expressed the opinion the book of Esther is of little historical value. A typical view is that of Adele Berlin, who states, "The story itself is implausible as history and, as many scholars now agree, it is better viewed as imaginative."[27] They have often classified its genre with terms more suited for fiction than history: novella, historical novel, or farce.[28] Yet, as Forrest S. Weiland demonstrated, Esther displays features which indicate the author was presenting his book as true historical narrative, though he wrote with a keen eye to telling the story with a literary flair that incorporates comedic, satiric, and ironic elements.[29] Among the indications in the text of Esther that mark it as historical narrative are these:

1. The use of the narrative past tense (i.e., preterite aspect) of the verb *to be* to introduce temporal clauses, [30] as is typical of historical accounts in the Hebrew text of the Old Testament (1:1; 2:7–8; 3:4; 5:1–2).

2. Frequent use of chronological references (e.g., 1:1, 3; 2:6, 16; 3:7, 13; 8:9; 9:1, 17–19.) Moreover, some of these references use dual dating for the month, listing it both by ordinal number and by its name (2:16; 3:7, 13; 8:9; 9:1). For instance, 2:16 mentions "the tenth month, the month of Tebeth." In earlier biblical books month names are seldom used, and it was common to refer to months by the ordinal number.[31] In Esther, however, the dual naming of months is common, signaling the author's original audience needed the ordinal number to help them identify the month, since the names used were adopted

---

[26] Diodorus Siculus, *Biblotheca Historica* 11.69. See also Ctesias, *Persica* 20, and Aristotle, *Politics* 5.1311b. The ancient sources give differing and sometimes conflicting reports of the intrigue surrounding the assassination of Ahasuerus.

[27] Adele Berlin, *Esther: The Traditional Hebrew Text with the New JPS Translation,* The JPS Bible Commentary (Philadelphia: Jewish Publication Society, 2001), xv.

[28] See the discussion in Forrest S. Weiland, "Historicity, Genre, and Narrative Design in the Book of Esther," *BSac* 159 no. 634 (2002): 153–4.

[29] Weiland, "Historicity," 155–64.

[30] I.e., ויהי (*wayehi*).

[31] Using names of months was so uncommon in earlier biblical books that we have only eight references to four months (Abib [Exod 13:4; 23:15; 34:18; Deut 16:1]; Ziv [1 Kgs 6:1, 37]; Ethanim [1 Kgs 8:2], and Bul [1 Kgs 6:38]).

from the Babylonian names of the months to which Jews would have been regularly exposed only during the Babylonian captivity and later.[32] This points to the text of Esther as historical narrative, originally intended for an audience that had not yet become familiar with the Babylonian month names.[33]

3. Reference to written records, which the reader is invited to search (10:2; cf. 2:23; 6:1). Weiland concludes, "Obviously Esther's author considered his narrative just as historical as the authors of Kings and Chronicles considered theirs."[34] Yet the author also took great care to present this narrative with literary style that compels readers to engage the narrative and its message. Weiland summarizes:

> The author of Esther has artistically intertwined both history and drama. He designed his narrative in a way that accurately and effectively reflected the dramatic significance of the events he recorded. Several textual indicators support the notion that he purports to have written about historical events in the reign of Xerxes. . . . At the same time, other narrative features reveal that he encased his story in a highly dramatic form. These include the heroic roles of Esther and Mordecai, the satirical portrait of the king, the type-casting of Haman as the archetypal villain, the ironic turn of events, and the employment of poetic justice that give the book its comic design.[35]

The book records the names of many persons, both major and minor characters. Many of these can be demonstrated to be genuine Persian names.[36] Furthermore, it presents accurate geographical and architectural descriptions of Susa and the royal palace.[37] For these reasons Esther should be classified as skillfully executed historical narrative. This is how the author intended this book to be received by his audience.

---

[32] For instance, Tebeth is a Hebrew reflection of the Babylonian month Tebetu.

[33] See Friedberg, "A New Clue in the Dating of the Composition of the Book of Esther."

[34] Weiland, "Historicity," 158.

[35] Weiland, "Historicity," 164.

[36] A. R. Millard, "Persian Names in Esther and the Reliability of the Hebrew Text," *JBL* 96 (1977): 481–8; Edwin Yamauchi, "Mordecai, the Persepolis Tablets, and the Susa Excavations." *VT* 42 (1992): 273–4.

[37] Yamauchi, "Mordecai, the Persepolis Tablets, and the Susa Excavations," 274.

Critics, of course, have raised specific objections to the book's historical accuracy.[38] Most of these objections are easily dismissed either as misunderstandings of the text or as logically invalid.

One of the objections argues verses 1:1; 8:9; and 9:30 states that Ahasuerus ruled an empire divided into "127 provinces," which would contradict sources which indicate Ahasuerus's father Darius had divided the empire into twenty-two satrapies. This is simply a misunderstanding of these verses. It is clear from 3:12 that the author understood the difference between satrapies (large governmental districts) and provinces (smaller subdivisions of a satrapy), since he distinguished between satraps and officials of the provinces.[39]

Another objection commonly raised involves the author's statements at 1:19 and 8:8 claiming the laws of Persia were unalterable (see also Dan 6:8, 12 [MT 6:9, 13]). This is simply a biblical notion for which there is not corroborative evidence yet. Nevertheless, J. Stafford Wright noted that a passage from the ancient Greek historian Diodorus Siculus may well indicate that Persian royal decrees were unalterable.[40]

Moreover, some have raised the issue of Mordecai's implied age. If he was taken into captivity by Nebuchadnezzar (Esth 2:5–6), he would have been well over a century old—too old to be the contemporary of his cousin Esther who is depicted as a young woman of marriageable age (2:7). However, it is not certain that 2:5–6 is stating that Mordecai was taken into captivity by Nebuchadnezzar. These verses could be read as stating Mordecai's great-grandfather Kish was the one taken into captivity. If that is the case, then Mordecai would have been about Esther's age during the reign of Ahasuerus.

Another difficult issue at the center of challenges to Esther's historicity is the identity of Ahasuerus's wife and queen. According to

---

[38] For lists of these objections and discussions of them see Ran Zadok, "On the Historical Background of the Book of Esther," *BN* 24 (1984): 18; David M. Howard Jr., *An Introduction to the Old Testament Historical Books* (Chicago: Moody, 1993), 367–9; Victor P. Hamilton, *Handbook on the Historical Books* (Grand Rapids, MI: Baker Academic, 2004), 532; F. B. Huey Jr., "Esther," pages 773–839 in *The Expositor's Bible Commentary with the New International Version*, edited by Frank E. Gaebelein (Grand Rapids, MI: Zondervan, 1988), 4.788–92. For a typical critical rejection of the historicity of Esther, see the otherwise fine work of Fox on characterization in Esther: Michael Fox, *Character and Ideology in the Book of Esther*, 2nd ed. (Grand Rapids: Eerdmans, 2001), 131–9.

[39] Note שָׂרֵי הַמְּדִינוֹת (= officials of the provinces) versus אֲחַשְׁדַּרְפְּנִים (= satraps).

[40] J. Stafford Wright, "The Historicity of the Book of Esther," in *New Perspectives on the Old Testament*, edited by J. Barton Payne (Waco, TX: Word, 1970), 39.

Herodotus (*Histories* 7.114; 9:112), Ahasuerus's wife was Amestris, neither Vashti (Esth 1–2) nor Esther. It is certain that Esther cannot be identified with Amestris, even though the English forms of the two names are similar. Importantly, Herodotus's treatment of Ahasuerus's reign covers only the first part of his rule, down to sometime in 479 BC. He presents Amestris as Ahasuerus's wife during this time. Ahasuerus's seventh year ran from March 31, 479 BC to April 18, 478 BC.[41] The tenth month when Esther was first brought to Ahasuerus ran from December 22, 479 to January 20, 478. Herodutus's narrative of the reign of Ahasuerus had terminated before this, probably in the seventh or eighth month.[42] Thus, Amestris cannot be Esther.[43]

Wright and, later, William H. Shea, made a convincing case Amestris can be identified with Vashti.[44] While the names look different in English, a series of phonological equivalences in the names makes it possible the Greek reflection of this woman's Old Persian name corresponds to its Hebrew reflection *Waštī*. The initial *alpha* (A) in Amestris can be explained as a prosthetic vowel added for euphony (ease of pronunciation) in Greek.[45] Therefore, even though these names look

---

[41] This was according to the ancient lunar calendar followed throughout most of the ancient Near East. Like the Babylonians before them, the official Persian royal years began in Nisan (Babylonian: *Nisanu*; Old Persian: *Adukanish*). That year had a thirteenth month (i.e., an intercalated month), second Adar, making it longer than a solar year. See Parker and Dubberstein, *Babylonian Chronology*, 31.

[42] Herodotus's narrative of Ahasuerus's reign ends at *Histories* 9.113.

[43] Critical scholars who view Esther as legendary often are confused on the chronology of Herodotus's account as well as what the book of Esther claims about Ahasuerus's wives. For instance, Fox, *Character and Ideology,* 132, states that Amestris "was still [Xerxes's] wife in 479, the year Xerxes spent in Ionia after his defeat at Salamis (IX 112)—this was the year *after* he supposedly married Esther—and Ametris remained his wife in old age." However, Esther was not presented to Ahasuerus until the month of Tebeth in his seventh year—late 479 or early 478—when Ahasuerus was no longer in Sardis. In addition, Esther nowhere portrays Vashti as being divorced from Ahasuerus. She was banished from his sight (1:19; i.e., she no longer had the privilege of royal audiences with the king as Esther later had; cf. 2:22; 4:11; 5:2; 8:4). In addition, her royal position (queen; Hebrew מַלְכָּה) was to be given to someone else. In effect, she was placed into the harem with Ahasuerus's other wives and concubines.

[44] Much of the ensuing discussion uses insights gleaned from J. Stafford Wright, "The Historicity of the Book of Esther," and William H. Shea, "Esther and History." *ConJ* 13 (1987): 234–48.

[45] Use of prosthetic vowels is common, especially in attempts to reflect foreign words. Hebrew uses a prosthetic vowel in the pronunciation of Ahasuerus's name: אֲחַשְׁוֵרוֹשׁ, whereas Greek Ξέρξης does not use a prosthetic vowel. Note the use and omission of a prosthetic vowel in the similar English words *especially* and *specially*.

different to English readers, they are phonological cousins and may well be different ways of reflecting the same name from Old Persian.[46]

The information given to us by Herodotus concerning Amestris fits well with Esther's report of Vashti. Vashti's offense reported in chap. 1 would have taken place in the king's third year on the throne (v. 3) before Ahasuerus left for the west and his campaign in Greece.[47] Amestris/Vashti would have been left in Susa when Ahasuerus mounted his western campaign, still queen, since no wife for Ahasuerus had yet been found to replace her. Following his failed invasion of Greece, Ahasuerus's time in Sardis in 479 led to his desire to find a new wife. Herodotus (*Histories* 9.108–111) reports that he fell in love with the wife of Masistes, his brother. When she rejected him, he then fell in love with her daughter Artaynta. Ahasuerus presented Artaynta a brightly colored robe that Amestris had woven for him. Eventually Ahasuerus had Artaynta married to his son Darius, but in time Amestris discovered the first affair. When the king, now back in Persia, was throwing a banquet on his birthday, she requested that Masistes's wife be given to her. (Herodotus claims that the Persian king was obliged to grant all requests brought to him on his birthday.) Ahasuerus turned the woman over to Amestris, who had her mutilated.

This account fits well with the narrative of Esther. Amestris's gift of the colorful robe may have been designed to ingratiate herself once again with Ahasuerus. It backfired when Ahasuerus used it in an attempt to woo Artaynta. In an attempt to eliminate a rival who might replace her as queen, Amestris had Masistes's wife mutilated. With Amestris/Vashti still slated to be replaced and with both Masistes's wife and daughter eliminated as possible rivals, the way was clear for Esther to win the king's heart and be elevated to the position of queen.

Herodotus makes no further mention of Amestris except to report in her old age (presumably when her third son Artaxerxes I reigned as king) she had fourteen sons of Persian nobles buried as a sacrifice to a god of the underworld.[48] That she exercised power—perhaps as queen

---

[46] Note also that the names *Xerxes* and *Ahasuerus* look quite different in English, though each represents a different attempt to reflect the Old Persian name *Khshayarshan*.

[47] Ahasuerus's third year was April 14, 483 through April 2, 482 BC. Parker and Dubberstein, *Babylonian Chronology*, 31.

[48] *Histories* 7.114.

mother—says nothing about her status in Ahasuerus's court after his seventh year.[49]

Others have claimed, based again on Herodotus's statements, the Achaemenid kings married wives only from the seven most prominent Persian families. Esther, being a Jew whose ethnic identity was unknown to Ahasuerus (2:20), would not have been made a royal wife. On this matter, Herodotus was clearly wrong. Artaxerxes I, Ahasuerus's son and successor, had at least two wives/concubines who were of non-Persian lineage.[50]

Also, the height of the gallows constructed by Haman (fifty cubits or about seventy-five feet/twenty-two meters; 5:14; 7:9) is sometimes said to be too tall to have been constructed in a relatively short time. The Hebrew word *ʿēṣ* is the general word for *tree* or *wood*, and whether this designates gallows or a simple pole is not clear (see commentary on 2:23). Some dispute whether this structure was a gallows for execution by hanging or simply a post upon which Mordecai's corpse was to be hung.[51] Moreover, erecting a high pole would not require much time, and the height might include the height of a hill or tall building on which it was erected, making the pole itself much shorter.[52] Alternatively, the phrase "fifty cubits" high may have been a commonly used hyperbolic phrase, a way of saying "extremely high."[53]

Critics of Esther's historicity also point out it is unlikely that a foreigner, especially a Jew, would rise to the position of prime minister as Mordecai does in Esther to succeed another non-Persian prime

---

[49] There is another passage in which a certain Amestris is mentioned in relation to Otanes, a commander in the Persian army (*Histories* 7.61). The Greek text reads, Ὀτάνεα τὸν Ἀμήστριος πατέρα τῆς Ξέρξεω γυναικός, which is ambiguous and could be rendered as "Otanes, son of Amestris [and] father of Xerxes's wife" or as "Otanes, son of Amestris, the father of Xerxes's wife." Robert L. Hubbard, "Vashti, Amestris and Esther 1,9," *ZAW* 119 (2007): 260–6, argues that this Amestris is the father of Otanes and the father of Ahasuerus's wife, since when introducing military commanders Herodotus always introduces them with the formula X son of Y (as here) where Y is the father or with the formula X son of Y and Z (a formula not used in this passage), where Y is the father and Z is the mother. Hubbard also notes that the Greek rendering of Old Persian names is often inaccurate; therefore, this Amestris may have had a similar but different actual name than Ahasuerus's wife.

[50] Zadok, "On the Historical Background of the Book of Esther," 19.

[51] At 9:13–14 there is reference to hanging the corpses of Haman's sons who had already been executed, and at 9:25 the same hanging is ordered for Haman's corpse.

[52] Jacob Hoschander, *The Book of Esther in the Light of History* (Philadelphia: Dropsie College, 1923), 205.

[53] Berlin, *Esther*, 55; Mervin Breneman, *Ezra, Nehemiah, Esther*, NAC 10 (Nashville: B&H, 1993), 341; Frederick Bush, *Ruth, Esther*, WBC 9 (Dallas: Word, 1996), 60.

minister, Haman the Agagite. Yet history is full of unlikely occurrences. What would be the likelihood two out of three consecutive
United States presidents would be father and son? Yet that is the case
for George H. W. Bush and George W. Bush. Events are not governed
by what is considered probable to happen, and such an objection is
an attempt to substitute someone's judgment about what was likely
to happen for the actual events themselves, which can at times defy
expectations. Moreover, it is possible Ahasuerus purposely chose foreigners as his prime ministers. For instance, he may have been wary
of elevating an upper-class Persian to the office second only to his
own for fear that such a person might conspire against him in order
to usurp the throne. Considering the reality of palace intrigue eventually leading to Ahasuerus's assassination, it is not at all inconceiv-
able Ahasuerus would place foreigners who would be unlikely to find
the support of Persia's elite in positions of leadership to prevent their
ascension to the throne as a result of a palace coup.

Finally, some object that a Persian king would be unlikely to tolerate the massacre of thousands of his own people by one of the sub-
jugated ethnic groups within the Persian Empire as in 9:1–19. Once
again, this objection relies on what is considered likely. Moreover,
nowhere does Esther depict the massacre of Persians. It refers to the
deaths of the "enemies" of the Jews (*'ōybēhem*; 8:13; 9:1, 5, 16, 22)
and "those who hated them" (*śōn'ēhem*; 9:1, 5, 16). The only identifi-
able nationality among those who were killed were Agagites: the sons
of Haman, who were foreigners (9:10, 12–14, 25).

4   THEME AND PURPOSE OF ESTHER

Since Esther demonstrates no overt theological interest, determining
its theme and purpose as a book of Holy Scripture is more difficult
than for other portions of the Bible. For this reason some commentators—both Christian and Jewish—concluded the purpose of Esther
is to relate the origin of and authorization for the annual celebration
of the feast of Purim.[54] The author appears to go out of his way to
note the origin of the word *Purim* (3:7; 9:24–26), and the festival's
origin is placed near the end of the book (9:18–32). The festival is the

---

[54] Berlin, *Esther*, xv-xvi; Carey A. Moore, *Esther: Introduction, Translation, and Notes,* AB 7B
(Garden City, NY: Doubleday, 1971), xx, li. This is partially affirmed by Breneman, *Ezra, Nehemiah, Esther*, 299.

celebration of the Jews in the Persian Empire gaining "relief from their enemies" (9:22) and a way of commemorating this event for future generations (9:26–28). This theme of security for Jews throughout Ahasuerus's realm comes to a climax at the end of the book: the Jews have gained a measure "of peace and security" (9:30; 10:3). The relative insecurity of the Jews is highlighted throughout the book: Esther was instructed by Mordecai not to reveal her ethnic identity (2:10, 20), and Haman plotted to do away with all Jews (3:6; 7:4). Purim is an artifact pointing to a continuing fulfillment of a promise inherited from Abraham and Isaac—those who bless God's people "will be blessed," but those who curse them "will be cursed" (Gen 12:3; 27:29; Num 24:9).

If the theme of Esther is security for God's people, what is the purpose of the book? This can be determined by considering two important emphases the book's narrative features.

4.1   Happenstance as a Driver of the Narrative

A number of events included in the narrative of Esther seem to the casual reader to be happenstances beyond the control of the persons they affected. Esther happened to please Hegai, so he accelerated her beauty treatments and gave her servants to aid her (2:8–9); Mordecai just happened to overhear the plot to assassinate Ahasuerus (2:21–23); when Haman cast lots to determine when to hold his pogrom against the Jews, the answer happened to fall "on the twelfth month," eleven months in the future (3:7); when Ahasuerus had a sleepless night, his servants chose to read the account of how the plot to kill the king was thwarted (6:1–2); when Ahasuerus returned to the banquet, he happened to see Haman on the queen's couch and assumed Haman was molesting her (7:8).

To the careful reader these coincidences are too numerous to be happenstance. They point to a control of human events exercised out of sight of the reader, unmentioned by the narrator, and only hinted at in the words of Mordecai (4:14). Thus, Esther testifies indirectly to God's providence and protection of his people.

4.2   Reversal as a Prominent Feature of the Narrative

Several scholars noted in telling the story of Esther the author conspicuously highlights reversals in the status of Haman, Mordecai, and the

Jews in the Persian Empire.[55] This literary technique is called *peripety*, a relating of a sudden turn of events leading to an unexpected outcome. Several reversals are presented below:[56]

SITUATION	REVERSAL
Haman's High Rank	*Mordecai's High Rank*
After all this took place, King Ahasuerus honored Haman, son of Hammedatha the Agagite. He promoted him in rank and gave him a higher position than all the other officials. The entire royal staff at the King's Gate bowed down and paid homage to Haman, because the king had commanded this to be done for him. But Mordecai would not bow down or pay homage. (3:1–2)	All the officials of the provinces, the satraps, the governors, and the royal civil administrators aided the Jews because they feared Mordecai. For Mordecai exercised great power in the palace, and his fame spread throughout the provinces as he became more and more powerful. (9:3–4) Mordecai the Jew was second only to King Ahasuerus. He was famous among the Jews and highly esteemed by many of his relatives. He continued to pursue prosperity for his people and to speak for the well-being of all his descendants. (10:3)
Haman's Vestiture	*Mordecai's Vestiture*
The king removed his signet ring from his hand **and gave it to** Haman son of Hammedatha the Agagite, the enemy of the Jews. (3:10)	**The king removed his signet ring** he had recovered from Haman **and gave it to** Mordecai, and Esther put him in charge of Haman's estate. (8:2)
Mordecai's Mourning Clothes and Lament	*Mordecai's Royal Clothes and Acclaim*
When Mordecai learned all that had occurred, he tore his clothes, put on sackcloth and ashes, went into the middle of the city, and cried loudly and bitterly. (4:1)	Mordecai went from the king's presence clothed in royal blue and white, with a great gold crown and a purple robe of fine linen. The city of Susa shouted and rejoiced. (8:15)
Jews Lament	*Jews Celebrate*
There was great mourning among the Jewish people **in every province where the king's command and edict reached**. They fasted, wept, and lamented, **and many** lay in sackcloth and ashes. (4:3)	**In every province** and every city where **the king's command and edict reached**, gladness and joy took place among the Jews. There was a celebration and a holiday. **And many** of the ethnic groups of the land professed themselves to be Jews because fear of the Jews had overcome them. (8:17)

---

[55] Fox, *Character and Ideology*, 158–63; J. A. Loader, "Esther as a Novel with Different Levels of Meaning," *ZAW* 90 (1978): 419; Sandra Beth Berg, *The Book of Esther*, 106–7; Bush, *Ruth, Esther*, 323–26; Abraham Winitzer, "The Reversal of Fortune Theme in Esther: Israelite Historiography in Its Ancient Near Eastern Context," *JANER* 11 (2011): 170–218.

[56] Modified from Bush, *Ruth, Esther*, 324. Text in bold highlights similar phrasing in the Hebrew text of Esther.

SITUATION	REVERSAL
Haman Advised to Execute Mordecai	*Haman Advised That Mordecai Will Prevail*
His wife Zeresh and all his friends told him, "Have them build a gallows seventy-five feet tall. Ask the king in the morning to hang Mordecai on it. Then go to the banquet with the king and enjoy yourself." The advice pleased Haman, so he had the gallows constructed. (5:14)	Haman told his wife Zeresh and all his friends everything that had happened. His advisers and his wife Zeresh said to him, "Since Mordecai is Jewish, and you have begun to fall before him, you won't overcome him, because your downfall is certain." While they were still speaking with him, the king's eunuchs arrived and rushed Haman to the banquet Esther had prepared. (6:13–14)
Haman Constructs a Gallows for Mordecai	*Haman Hangs on the Gallows Made for Mordecai*
His wife Zeresh and all his friends told him, "Have them build **a gallows seventy-five feet tall**. Ask the king in the morning to hang Mordecai on it. Then go to the banquet with the king and enjoy yourself." The advice pleased Haman, so he had the gallows constructed. (5:14)	Harbona, one of the king's eunuchs, said, "There is **a gallows seventy-five feet tall** at Haman's house that he made for Mordecai, who gave the report that saved the king." The king said, "Hang him on it." They hanged Haman on the gallows he had prepared for Mordecai. Then the king's anger subsided. (7:9–10)
Haman Seeks His Own Honor	*Haman Forced to Honor Mordecai*
Haman entered, and the king asked him, "**What should be done for the man the king wants to honor**?" Haman thought to himself, "Who is it **the king would want to honor** more than me?" Haman told the king, "For the man the king wants to honor: Have them bring a royal **garment** that the king himself has worn and a **horse** the king himself has ridden, which has a royal crown on its head. Put **the garment and the horse** under the charge of one of the king's most noble officials. **Have them clothe the man the king wants to honor, parade him on the horse through the city square, and call out before him, 'This is what is done for the man the king wants to honor.'**" (6:6–9)	So Haman took **the garment and the horse. He clothed Mordecai and paraded him through the city square, calling out before him, "This is what is done for the man the king wants to honor."** Then Mordecai returned to the King's Gate, but Haman hurried off for home, mournful and with his head covered. (6:11–12)

Another reversal involves an ironic twist on the Persian king's ostensibly immutable decrees (1:19).[57] In order to overcome the decree issued by Haman in Ahasuerus's name, Esther requests Ahasuerus issue a decree reversing the decree of Haman (8:3, 5). Such a decree— this one also supposedly irreversible—is issued (8:8). In each case the

---

[57] Winitzer, "The Reversal of Fortune Theme," 175–6.

Hebrew verbal roots *'br* ("pass over/across") or *šûb* ("turn, return") are used.[58] It would appear that the decrees of the Persian king are not inflexible but remain subject to a higher authority.

The author's use of similar wording to draw his readers' attention to these reversals demonstrates the intentional narrative art employed in Esther. Moreover, in at least two cases the author deliberately notes the reversal of circumstances:

> On the day when the Jews' enemies had hoped to overpower them, just *the opposite happened*.[59] (9:1; emphasis added)

> That was the month when their sorrow *was turned into*[60] rejoicing and their mourning into a holiday.

It is interesting to observe the Hebrew verbs in both cases are in the passive voice, (the *Niphal* stem), and do not reveal the outside agent affecting the action. Just who is it that made the opposite happen? Who turned sorrow into joy and mourning into a holiday?

For the perceptive reader, the cumulative effect of this series of reversals combined with the all-too-improbable series of events that appear to be happenstance leads to a consideration divine providence lay behind this improbable concatenation of events. Subtly urging the reader to this conclusion are the two fasts recorded in Esther: the fasting that followed the news of Haman's edict (4:3) and the fast requested by Esther (4:15–17). In the postexilic books of the Old Testament, fasting is mentioned in connection with calling on God's assistance in times when the Jewish community faced danger (Ezra 8:21–22, [see 8:31]; Dan 9:3). Thus, it appears as if the appeal to God implied by these fasts was heard in heaven.

Moreover, the use of peripety, a turning point in the story, to demonstrate God's defense of and providential care for his people is a common literary trope in the Old Testament.[61] Examples include Joseph's rise from slave to "lord of" Egypt (Gen 39–45; see esp. Gen 45:8–9); Israel's deliverance from Pharaoh's army at the Red Sea (Exod 14–15; see esp. Exod 15:9–10); Hannah's elevation in her rivalry with

---

[58] Other uses of the term include 1:19: (לֹא־יַעֲבוֹר 1:19), "cannot be revoked"; 8:3: לְהַעֲבִיר, "to revoke"; 8:5: לְהָשִׁיב, "to change"; 8:8: אֵין לְהָשִׁיב, "is not to be changed."

[59] Hebrew: וְנַהֲפוֹךְ הוּא.

[60] Hebrew: נֶהְפַּךְ לָהֶם.

[61] J. A. Loader, "Esther as a Novel with Different Levels of Meaning," *ZAW* 90 (1978): 419.

Peninnah (1 Sam 1–2; see esp. 1 Sam 2:5); David's victory over Goliath (1 Sam 17); Shadrach, Meshach, and Abednego's rescue from the fiery furnace and the execution of their accusers (Dan 3); and Daniel's deliverance from the lion's den and the downfall of his opponents (Dan 6). The multiple uses of peripety in Esther imply God's activity here also.

Therefore, the use of apparent (but not real) happenstance combined with peripety serves to direct readers to the message of the book of Esther. *The book's purpose is to demonstrate that even when God's actions are veiled and hidden, he nevertheless is working to defend and provide for his people and to bring about the salvation of all mankind in the promised Savior.* Mordecai's challenge to Esther should be read in this light: " If you keep silent at this time, relief and deliverance will come to the Jewish people from another place, but you and your father's family will be destroyed. Who knows, perhaps you have come to your royal position for such a time as this." (Esth 4:14)

How could Mordecai be so confident the Jewish people would be delivered, perhaps through Esther's actions from her royal position as queen? In fact, Mordecai's words point to his faith in God's promises: God would bless those who bless Israel and curse those who curse them (Num 24:9; see also Gen 12:3; 27:29). Moreover, God had promised all nations would "be blessed through" Israel (Gen 12:3; 18:18; 22:18; 26:4; 28:14; see Gal 3:8). Since this last promise is ultimately fulfilled in Christ (Gal 3:14), God's protection for Israel was certain. His determination to save the world through his promised Messiah could only be fulfilled through Israel. Therefore, Israel would be delivered from Haman so God's chosen people of the Old Testament could bring forth the world's Redeemer.

5   LITERARY FEATURES OF ESTHER

The previous section already explored two literary features of Esther underlying its theme and purpose: the use of apparent (though not actual) happenstance and the use of peripety. Several other literary characteristics of Esther will be highlighted here.

5.1   The Author's Use of Hebrew

The Hebrew of Esther shares grammatical and stylistic features with other late books of the Old Testament, especially Chronicles, Ezra, and Nehemiah. For this reason, many scholars see it as an example of the development of a form of Hebrew often labeled *Late Biblical Hebrew* as opposed to many preexilic biblical books that exhibit the characteristics of what has been termed *Standard* (or *Early*) *Biblical Hebrew*. Language change, however, is often on a continuum, so it is not surprising one can find in Esther both features of Standard Biblical Hebrew and the first examples of expressions that will become common in later Mishnaic Hebrew.[62]

The author also appears to be more comfortable with Aramaic modes of expression than Hebrew. This is apparent in his preference for sentence word order: subject-verb-object instead of the more common Hebrew narrative word order sequence of verb-subject-object. His preference for word order is partly due to his relatively uncommon use of the Hebrew narrative past tense (the preterite aspect) which requires the verb to appear at the head of its clause.[63] In addition, the writer of Esther made frequent use of Hebrew past tense (perfect aspect) verbs.[64]

Another feature of the Hebrew text of Esther is the extensive use of the passive voice in relating the narrative.[65] Normally, biblical Hebrew

---

[62] Ronald L. Bergey, "Post-Exilic Hebrew Linguistic Developments in Esther: A Diachronic Approach," *JETS* 31 (1988): 161–8.

[63] In Esther the *preterite* aspect is used only 159 times in 167 verses (0.95 occurrences per verse). Compare this to preexilic biblical books that are primarily narrative: 1,141 uses in 618 verses in Judges (1.85 occurrences per verse), 138 uses in 85 verses in Ruth (1.62 occurrences per verse); 2,392 uses in 1,506 verses in Samuel (1.59 occurrences per verse), or 2,267 uses in 1,536 verses in Kings (1.48 occurrences per verse). Esther is much more aligned with Chronicles, another postexilic book: 1,455 uses in 1,765 verses (0.82 occurrences per verse).

[64] A total of 158 times or 0.95 occurrences per verse. Compare Judges (0.74 occurrences per verse), Ruth (0.87 occurrences per verse), Samuel (0.77 occurrences per verse), and Kings (0.88 occurrences per verse). Chronicles is rather sparing in using perfect aspect verbs (0.60 occurrences per verse).

[65] Berlin, *Esther*, xxvi. Some examples include "Let it be recorded" (1:19), "The decree the king issues will be heard" (1:20), "what was decided against her" (2:1), "Esther/[S]he was taken" (2:8, 16), "what was happening to her" (2:11), "When the virgins were gathered" (2:19), "When Mordecai learned of the plot" (2:22), "the report was investigated and verified, both men were hanged" (2:23), "he/Haman was filled with rage" (3:5; 5:9), "let an order be drawn up" (3:9), "The royal scribes were summoned . . . and the order was written. . . . It was written in the name of King Ahasuerus and sealed" (3:12), "Letters were sent" (3:13), "the law was issued" (3:15), "all that had occurred" (4:1), "It will be given to you" (5:3, 6; 9:12), "It will be done (5:6; 7:2; 9:12), "They found the written report" (6:2), "This is what is done for the man the king wants to honor." (6:9, 11), "my people and I have been sold" (7:4), "let a royal edict be written" (8:5), "the royal scribes were summoned. Everything was written" (8:9), "their sorrow was turned into rejoicing" (9:22), "These days are remembered and celebrated" (9:28).

avoids passive voice. Its occurrence in biblical Hebrew is much less frequent than in English, which also eschews using passive voice. Since passive voice verbs hide the agent committing the action, the extensive use of passive voice in Esther reinforces the reader's impression concerning apparent happenstance—without explicitly identifying divine or human agent, events simply occur. Finally, the author was fond of introducing names of characters appearing in the narrative, even those who play minor roles. In just ten chapters he names forty people:

1. Ahasuerus/Xerxes—a Persian king (1:1)

2. Vashti—a Persian queen (1:9)

3. Mehuman, eunuch and personal servant of the king (1:10)

4. Biztha, eunuch and personal servant of the king (1:10)

5. Harbona, eunuch and personal servant of the king (1:10)

6. Bigtha, eunuch and personal servant of the king (1:10)

7. Abagtha, eunuch and personal servant of the king (1:10)

8. Zethar, eunuch and personal servant of the king (1:10)

9. Carkas, eunuch and personal servant of the king (1:10)

10. Charshena, the king's legal advisor (1:14)

11. Shethar, the king's legal advisor (1:14)

12. Admatha, the king's legal advisor (1:14)

13. Tarshish, the king's legal advisor (1:14)

14. Meres, the king's legal advisor (1:14)

15. Marsena, the king's legal advisor (1:14)

16. Memucan, the king's legal advisor (1:14)

17. Hegai, eunuch in charge of the harem (2:3)

18. Mordecai, Esther's cousin and eventual prime minister to Ahasuerus (2:5)

19. Jair, Mordecai's father (2:5)

20. Shimei, Mordecai's grandfather (2:5)

21. Kish, Mordecai's great-grandfather (2:5)

22. Hadassah/Esther (2:7)

23. Shaashgaz, eunuch, keeper of the king's concubines (2:14)

24. Abihail, Esther's father and Mordecai's uncle(2:15)

25. Bigthan, eunuch who plotted to assassinate Ahasuerus (2:21)

26. Teresh, eunuch who plotted to assassinate Ahasuerus (2:21)

27. Haman, prime minister to Ahasuerus (3:1)

28. Hammedatha, Haman's father (3:1)

29. Hathach, eunuch who attended to Esther (4:5)

30. Zeresh, wife of Haman (5:10)

31. Parshandatha, son of Haman (9:7)

32. Dalphon, son of Haman (9:7)

33. Aspatha, son of Haman (9:7)

34. Poratha, son of Haman (9:8)

35. Adalia, son of Haman (9:8)

36. Aridatha, son of Haman (9:8)

37. Parmashta, son of Haman (9:9)

38. Arisai, son of Haman (9:10)

39. Aridai, son of Haman (9:10)

40. Vaizatha, son of Haman (9:10)

The inclusion of all these names, most of them connected to the Persian court or to Mordecai's family, demonstrate the author's familiarity with both Mordecai and the intricacies of the organization of the Persian royal court. Perhaps they indicate the author had access to Persian court records.

5.2 Use of Irony in Esther

A literary feature reinforcing the author's use of peripety is frequent use of irony.[66] Carey A. Moore notes,

---

[66] Stan Goldman, "Narrative and Ethical Ironies in Esther," *JSOT* 15 (1990): 15–31.

The author is especially interested and effective in his use of irony. For example, Vashti was deposed for being disobedient (i 17–19)—Esther was disobedient twice and yet was rewarded (v 1–2, 8); Haman obeyed the king's command, humiliating though it was (vi 11–12)—Mordecai deliberately disobeyed a royal command, yet was handsomely rewarded (iii 2, viii 1–2); the city wept while the king and Haman drank (iii 15); Haman, thinking that he was prescribing royal honors for himself, was actually prescribing them for Mordecai, his bitter enemy (vi 6–9); Haman was hanged on a gallows which he had intended for Mordecai (vii 9–10).[67]

These ironies heighten the effect of the reversals noted in Esther. Not only do Mordecai and the Jews reverse their situation and overcome their enemies, but their rise also presents an almost biting and satirical comment on the supposed power of Ahasuerus and his subordinates.

5.3   Feasts in Esther

Irony in Esther works hand in hand with another feature of Esther: the frequent mention of celebrations and banquets. This is obvious by the frequent use of the Hebrew term *mišteh*, meaning "feast, celebration, banquet." This term occurs twenty times in Esther and only twenty-six times in the rest of the Old Testament.[68] Ten feasts or celebrations are mentioned in the book:

1. Ahasuerus's 180-day feast for his officers and nobles (1:3–4)

2. A seven-day banquet for all the people in Susa (1:5–8)

3. Vashti's feast for the women (1:9)

4. The banquet celebrating Esther's elevation to the status of queen (2:18)

5. The king and Haman sitting down to drink following Haman's issue of the decree permitting Jews to be attacked (3:15)

6. Esther's first banquet for Ahasuerus and Haman (5:1–8)

---

[67] Moore, *Esther*, lvi.
[68] Esther 1:3, 5, 9; 2:18; 5:4–6, 8, 12, 14; 6:14; 7:2, 7–8; 8:17; 9:17–19, 22. Elsewhere: Gen 19:3; 21:8; 26:30; 29:22; 40:20; Judg 14:10, 12, 17; 1 Sam 25:36; 2 Sam 3:20; 1 Kgs 3:15; Ezra 3:7; Job 1:4–5; Prov 15:15; Eccl 7:2; Isa 5:12; 25:6; Jer 16:8; 51:39; Dan 1:5, 8, 10, 16.

7. Esther's second banquet for Ahasuerus and Haman (7:1–10; mentioned at 5:8, 12, 14; 6:14)

8. Jews celebrating the defeat of their enemies (8:17)

9. Jews outside of Susa celebrating on the fourteenth day of Adar (9:17)

10. Jews in Susa celebrating on the fifteenth day of Adar (9:18)

Clearly, Esther is not only a book in which God's acts are hidden; it is also a book in which human acts, especially eating, drinking, and merrymaking, are foregrounded.

The author of Esther delineates the first eight feasts as two sets of four feasts each to form a framework for the narrative. The first four culminate with Esther's ascension to the position of Ahasuerus's queen (feast 4 above), replacing Vashti. The second four culminate with the Jews' defeating their enemies under the auspices of Mordecai, who had ascended to the position of prime minister, replacing Haman (8 above). In both sets of four feasts, the first two feasts (1, 2, 5, and 6 above) present the background elements that lead to the fall of someone close to Ahasuerus as a result of actions at the third feast: Vashti was deposed because she refused to leave her feast (3 above) to have her beauty put on display by Ahasuerus (1:10–12). Haman was executed in part as a result of his actions at the second feast (7 above).

The author's use of the framework of feasts emphasized it was the combination of the rise of two persons—Esther first and then Mordecai—that made possible the deliverance of the Jews throughout the Persian Empire. The work of Mordecai (9:3–4, 20, 23, 29, 31; 10:2–3) and Esther (9:12–13, 29, 31–32) together led to the yearly feast of Purim, mentioned as two festivals: one on the fourteenth day of Adar in the provinces (9:17; 9 above) and one on the fifteenth day of Adar in Susa (9:18; 10 above).

5.4   Esther's Relation to Other Old Testament Books

5.4.1   Genesis

The rise of Esther and Mordecai as important advisers to Ahasuerus cannot help but remind avid Bible readers of the rise of Joseph in Egypt. The writer of Esther also had this in mind, though his allusions to the Joseph story are subtle and easily missed. A number of terminological and grammatical constructions present in the Joseph narrative of Genesis recur in the text of Esther. These include: [69]

ESTHER	GENESIS
"*Let* the king *appoint commissioners* in each province of his kingdom,[70] so that they *may gather all* the beautiful young virgins to the harem at the fortress of Susa. Put them under the supervision of Hegai, the king's eunuch, keeper of the women, and give them the required beauty treatments. Then the young woman who pleases the king will become queen instead of Vashti." *This suggestion pleased the king,*[71] and he did accordingly. (2:3–4)	"Let Pharaoh do this: *Let* him *appoint overseers* over the land and take a fifth of the harvest of the land of Egypt during the seven years of abundance. *Let* them *gather all* the excess food during these good years that are coming. Under Pharaoh's authority, store the grain in the cities, so they may preserve it as food. The food will be a reserve for the land during the seven years of famine that will take place in the land of Egypt. Then the country will not be wiped out by the famine." *The proposal pleased* Pharaoh and all his servants. (Gen 41:34–38)
When they had *warned* him *day after day* and *he still would not listen* to them,[72] they told Haman in order to see if Mordecai's actions would be tolerated, since he had told them he was a Jew. (3:4)	Although she *spoke* to Joseph *day after day,* *he refused* to go to bed with her. (Gen 39:10)
The king *removed his signet ring from his hand and gave it* to Haman son of Hammedatha the Agagite,[73] the enemy of the Jews. (3:10)	*Pharaoh removed his signet ring from his hand and put it* on Joseph's hand, clothed him with fine linen garments, and placed a gold chain around his neck. (Gen 41:42)
"Go and assemble all the Jews who can be found in Susa and fast for me. Don't eat or drink for three days, night or day. I and my female servants will also fast in the same way. After that, I will go to the king even if it is against the law. *If I perish, I perish.*" (4:16)	"May God Almighty cause the man to be merciful to you so that he will release your other brother and Benjamin to you. As for me, *if I am deprived of my sons, then I am deprived.*" (Gen 43:14)

---

[69] Similar wording or syntax in the Hebrew text is highlighted in italics. See Joyce G. Baldwin, *Esther: An Introduction and Commentary*, TOTC (Leicester: Intervarsity, 1984), 26–27; Berlin, *Esther*, xxxvii.

[70] The words for "commissioners" in Esther and "overseers" in Genesis are identical in Hebrew.

[71] The words for "suggestion" in Esther and "proposal" in Genesis are identical in Hebrew.

[72] The phrases "would not listen" in Esther and "refused" in Genesis are identical in Hebrew.

[73] "The phrases "his hand" and "gave it" in Esther are identical with Gen 41:42.

ESTHER	GENESIS
"Put the garment and the horse under the charge of one of the king's most noble officials. Have them *clothe* the man the king wants to honor, parade him on the horse through the city square, and *call out before him*,[74] 'This is what is done for the man the king wants to honor.'" (6:9)	Pharaoh *removed his signet ring* from his hand and *put it* on Joseph's hand, *clothed* him with fine linen garments, and placed a gold chain around his neck. He had Joseph ride in his second chariot, and servants *called out before him*, "Make way!" (Gen 41:42–43)
So Haman took the garment and the horse. He clothed Mordecai and paraded him through the city square, *calling out before him*, "This is what is done for the man the king wants to honor." (6:11)	
The king *removed his signet ring* he had recovered from Haman *and gave it* to Mordecai, and Esther put him in charge of Haman's estate. (8:2)	
"For how could I bear to see the disaster that would come on my people? *How could I bear to see the destruction* of my relatives?" (8:6)	"For how can I go back to my father without the boy? *I could not bear to see the grief* that would overwhelm my father." (Gen 44:34)

While individually each of these literary parallels is unremarkable, their cumulative effect leads to the conclusion Esther's author either consciously or unconsciously identified a parallel between Esther and Mordecai on one hand and Joseph on the other. Since the author of Esther sought to veil God's actions (compare 4:14 with Gen 45:7–8; 50:20), it is possible he deliberately included these parallels to Joseph's story without directly referencing it. This would not be uncommon in the use of earlier OT texts in historically later contexts since most allusions do not include a citation formula as they do in the NT. This is another way the author artfully leads perceptive readers to understand although God is never mentioned in Esther, the events and their results were controlled by him.

5.4.2 *Samuel*

Another indirect way in which the author of Esther recalls an earlier biblical book is through the rivalry of Mordecai and Haman. When Mordecai is introduced to the reader, he is called "Mordecai son of Jair, son of Shimei, son of Kish, a Benjaminite" (2:5). In a number

---

[74] The phrases "call out before him" and "calling out before him" in Esther and "called out before him" in Genesis are identical in Hebrew.

of other instances, he is called "Mordecai the Jew" (5:13; 6:10; 8:7; 9:29, 31; 10:3). When Haman is first mentioned, he is called "Haman, son of Hammedatha the Agagite" (3:1), an appellation used at other important junctures in the narrative (3:1, 10; 8:5; 9:24).[75] The clearest reference to the book of Samuel, however, occurs when Haman is characterized as "the enemy of the Jews" (3:10; 8:1; 9:10).

Why would Haman be the enemy of the Jews? The key is found in the way Mordecai and Haman are introduced. Mordecai is a Benjaminite, from the same tribe as Israel's first king, Saul. His great-grandfather even bore the same name as Saul's father, Kish (1 Sam 9:1, 3; 10:11, 21; 14:51; 2 Sam 21:14). But Haman is an Agagite, a descendant of Agag. The Amalekite king Agag had been captured by Saul when the Lord, through Samuel, directed Saul to destroy the Amalekites (1 Sam 15:1–33). The Amalekites had been enemies of God's people since the time of Moses when they attacked Israel in the desert (Deut 25:17–19). The animosity behind that Amalekite attack on Israel stemmed from the rivalry of Esau and Israel's forefather Jacob since the Amalekites were descended from Esau's grandson Amalek (Gen 36:12). After Israel's army defeated the Amalekites in Exod 17:8–16, Moses prophesied, "The Lord will be at war with Amalek from generation to generation" (Exod 17:16). Saul's capture of Agag, forebear of Haman, was a partial fulfillment of that prophecy. Haman's animus against Mordecai in particular and every Jew in general (Esth 3:6) represented a family grudge held since the capture of his ancestor Agag and Agag's execution at the hands of the prophet Samuel (1 Sam 15:33)

For the reader familiar with events behind this account from the book of Samuel, the refusal of Mordecai to bow or pay homage to Haman becomes an act of faith and confidence in God. Mordecai sided with the Lord in the long-standing war against Amalek, continuing the fight his Benjaminite predecessor Saul had failed to finish.

Most importantly, these subtle references to the book of Samuel and to God's promise in Exod 17:14 leave no doubt about the ultimate outcome of Haman's plan. Haman would be defeated because the Lord was still at war with Amalek, and the Almighty always obtains victory.

---

[75] Interestingly, he is called simply "Haman the Agagite" only once, when Esther asked Ahasuerus that the plot Haman had devised be undone; see 8:3.

An additional echo of the book of Samuel occurs at Esth 9:16 where the Jews "gained relief from their enemies." The combination of the Hebrew *nôaḥ*, meaning "rest, relief," and *'ōyēb*, meaning "enemy," calls to mind 2 Sam 7:1, 11 and through it also Deut 12:10–11; 25:19.

The connection to Deut 25:19 celebrates the fulfillment of God's command to destroy the Amalekites when he had given his people rest. Although Israel's kings did not complete the task, it was accomplished though the execution of Haman and his sons (Esth 9:6–14).

Moreover, when God gave King David, and therefore Israel, rest from enemies all around in 2 Sam 7:1–6, David proposed to build a house for the Lord, a place chosen by God for his name to dwell in fulfillment of Deut 12:10–11 (see Ezra 6:12; Neh 1:9). In response, God did not allow David to build the house but instead promised David a house—an everlasting dynasty (2 Sam 7:16). This promise is ultimately fulfilled in Christ, who would not arrive until centuries past Esther's era.[76] The Jews' celebration of their victory thus appropriates messianic overtones from the author's connection with 2 Sam 7. The preservation of the Jews was not simply for their sake alone but for the sake of the redemption of the entire human race (Gen 18:18; 22:18; 26:4; 28:14; Gal 3:8).

5.4.3 Daniel

Daniel 1–6, set during the exile with prophecies related to the postexilic period, like Esther, relates the rise of Judeans as important officials for a pagan king. There is little indication the author of Esther intentionally evoked Daniel in the same way as he echoed texts in Genesis and Samuel, however.

Although there are fewer shared references between these two books and even fewer verbal parallels, both books describe the common challenge of Jews living among a predominately pagan culture, inviting the readers to compare and contrast the lives of Esther and Mordecai with the lives of Daniel and his companions: Azariah, Hananiah, and Mishael. The parallels include:

---

[76] For the messianic import of this promise to David and David's understanding of it, see Andrew E. Steinmann, "What Did David Understand about the Promises in the Davidic Covenant?" *BSac* 171 (2014): 19–29.

1. Parties with wine where intoxication leads to rash and injudicious acts (Esth 1; Dan 5).

2. Mordecai and Daniel are advisors to their respective kings (Esth 2:19, 21; 3:2–3, 4:2, 6; 5:9, 13; 6:10, 12; Dan 2:49).

3. Mordecai and Daniel are honored with special garments given by a king (Esth 6:7–11; Dan 5:29).

4. Both books refer to the immutability of Persian kings' decrees (Esth 1:19; Dan 6:8, 12, 15).

5. The books highlight professional jealousy that leads to persecution of Jews. In Daniel the persecution is explicitly based on religion, while in Esther the persecution is based on more personal animosity (Esth 3; 5:9–7:12; Dan 3; 6).

6. Both texts demonstrate that God's faithful people can serve in positions of authority even under rulers who are not among believers and profess faith in pagan gods (although this is much more subtly expressed in Esther than in Daniel).[77]

6 ESTHER AND THEOLOGY

Probably more than any other book of Scripture except Song of Songs, it is difficult to speak of theology in Esther. The book not only contains no overt theological statements, but the author has studiously avoided any mention of Israel's God and Jewish religious practice. Yet there is a consensus in recent decades among evangelical scholars that certain theological themes are found in Esther.

6.1 God's Sovereignty and Providence

Many point to God's sovereignty coupled with his providence as a major theme woven through the many reversals found in the book.[78] Eugene H. Merrill observes,

---

[77] Andrew E. Steinmann, *Daniel* (St. Louis: Concordia, 2008), 39–40.

[78] William Dumbrell, *The Faith of Israel: A Theological Survey of the Old Testament*, 2nd ed. (Grand Rapids: Baker Academic, 2002), 301; Paul R. House, *Old Testament Theology* (Downers Grove, IL: Intervarsity, 1998), 493–5; Huey, "Esther," 793–4; Peter Y. Lee, "Esther," in *A Biblical-Theological Introduction to the Old Testament: The Gospel Promised*, edited by Miles V. Van Pelt (Wheaton, IL: Crossway, 2016), 487–91; Iain Provan, "Hearing the Historical Books,"

Another way of describing the theology of the book is under the
rubric of divine sovereignty. Under Xerxes, the Persian Empire
had become [one of] the most powerful political entit[ies] of all
history to that time. Encapsulated within that mighty kingdom
were the impotent remnants of the Jewish Diaspora, descendants
of the nation whose forebears had also known isolation and then
persecution in Egypt a millennium earlier. Just as Moses had
been raised up then to become the deliverer of Israel, so now
God would effect another deliverance, this time through a Jewish
maiden who against all odds would sit on a Persian throne as the
agent of Almighty God.[79]

As Merrill describes, this is not simply God's sovereignty but also
divine providence—his deliverance of his people. Throughout Esther
the hidden hand of God exercises sovereign power over humanity to
provide for the Jews and, ultimately, for all people. In Esther there is
no narrative pointing the readers to God's sovereignty as the sole focus
of the author. Instead, God's sovereign rule is exercised not as only a
demonstration of his power and authority but as a means to provide
and care for the Jews as well as humans in general.

Indeed, in chap. 2 as Esther rises to become the Persian queen,
the insightful reader will already feel God's presence as the real power
behind Ahasuerus's throne. Yet again in chap. 3, with Haman's use of
lots to determine the day on which to attack the Jews, there is another
opportunity for the Almighty to exercise his sovereign control over
events. It is not immediately obvious to readers how this provides for
the welfare of the Jews. However, as the narrative unfolds, it becomes
clear that a date at the end of the year affords time for Mordecai and
Esther to foil Haman's plot. In chap. 4 Mordecai and the Jews in Susa

---

in *Hearing the Old Testament: Listening for God's Address*, edited by Craig G. Bartholomew and
David J. H. Beldman (Grand Rapids: Eerdmans, 2012), 274; Paul R. Redditt, "Esther, Book Of,"
in *Dictionary for Theological Interpretation of the Bible*, edited by Kevin J. Vanhoozer, Craig G.
Bartholomew, Daniel J. Trier, and N. T. Wright (Grand Rapids: Baker, 2005), 196, reprinted as
"Esther," in *Theological Interpretation of the Old Testament*, edited by Kevin J. Vanhoozer, Craig
G. Bartholomew, and Daniel Trier (Grand Rapids: Baker Academic, 2008), 145–6; Thomas R. Sch-
reiner, *The King in His Beauty: A Biblical Theology of the Old and New Testaments* (Grand Rap-
ids: Baker Academic, 2013), 222–5; Bruce K. Waltke, *An Old Testament Theology: An Exegetical,
Canonical, and Thematic Approach* (Grand Rapids: Zondervan Academic, 2007), 769.

[79] Eugene H. Merrill, "The Book of Esther," in *The World and the Word: An Introduction to
the Old Testament*, edited by Eugene H. Merrill, Mark Rooker, and Michael A. Grisanti (Nashville:
B&H Academic, 2011), 359.

fast, which is one of the few hints of religious practice in the book. In antiquity fasts almost always included time for prayer and supplication of God. Here is a signal that Esther, Mordecai, and the Jews were acknowledging their dependence on God to furnish their deliverance from Haman (see also 4:14).

Esther 5 continues this intertwining of God's sovereignty and providence. The author already documented Esther's ability to gain the "favor" of others (2:9, 15, 17). Here it is highlighted as she gained Ahasuerus's favor for her request to derail Haman's evil scheme. God also used Ahasuerus's predilection for magnanimity toward those he liked. He even used Haman's overinflated ego and his animosity against Mordecai to accomplish his purposes as Haman is blithely carried along by events toward his own destruction. Later, in chaps. 7 and 8, Esther, though personally delivered from Haman's plot, persists in pursuing the welfare of her people—even at the risk of irritating Ahasuerus with additional requests. Here the astute reader senses God exerting his control of human history through Esther, and later Mordecai, as they receive the king's permission to do what is necessary to defend their people (Esther 9).

6.2   God's Promises

A corollary of God's providence is the surety of the promises he made to his people. Evangelical scholars point in two ways to God's continuing fulfillment of his previous promises.

6.2.1   *Victory over Amalek*

Some scholars point to Esther as a fulfillment of Moses's prophecy of God's victory over "Amalek from generation to generation" (Exod 17:16).[80] The Esther author introduces this topic by the way he introduces Mordecai and Haman. Mordecai is a Benjaminite, from the same tribe as Israel's first king, Saul. His great-grandfather bore the same name as Saul's father, Kish (1 Sam 9:1, 3; 10:11, 21; 14:51; 2 Sam 21:14). Haman is an Agagite, a descendant of Agag. The Amalekite king Agag was captured by Saul when the Lord, through Samuel, directed Saul

---

[80] Dempster, *Dominion and Dynasty*, 222; Stephen G. Dempster, *Dominion and Dynasty: A Biblical Theology of the Hebrew Bible,* NSBT 15 (Downers Grove, IL: Intervarsity, 2004), 222; Waltke, *An Old Testament Theology*, 769–70.

to destroy the Amalekites (1 Sam 15:1–33). The Amalekites had been enemies of God's people since the time of Moses. They attacked Israel in the desert shortly after the exodus from Egypt (Deut 25:17–19). The animosity that lay behind the Amalekite attack on Israel stemmed from the rivalry of Esau and Jacob, since the Amalekites were descended from Esau's grandson Amalek (Gen 36:12). After Israel's army defeated the Amalekites, Moses prophesied, "The LORD will be at war with Amalek from generation to generation" (Exod 17:16). Saul's capture of Agag was a partial fulfillment of that prophecy.

For the reader familiar with Israel's interactions with Amalekites like King Agag, Mordecai is perceived as siding with the Lord in the war against Amalek; he continued the fight his Benjaminite predecessor Saul engaged in. Haman's actions are also explained in light of 1 Samuel 15. His hatred for Mordecai and by extension for every Jew (Esth 3:6) reflected a family grudge held since the capture of his ancestor Agag and Agag's execution at the hands of the prophet Samuel (1 Sam 15:33).

Most importantly, this veiled reference to the book of Samuel and to Moses's prophecy in Exodus is a reminder God keeps his promises to his people. He provides for their ultimate victory over those who would harm and even annihilate them.

6.2.2 The Messianic Promise

Some evangelical writers on Esther also view the book as indirectly pointing to God's promise of a Messiah.[81] Key to this observation are Mordecai's actions to thwart Haman not in self-interest or to benefit the Jews in Susa but for the Jews throughout the Persian Empire. The Jews were the bearer of the promise of the coming Messiah who would deliver all humanity from sin, death, and the devil. Jesus himself noted that "salvation is from the Jews" (John 4:22). For the book of Esther, this means the survival of the Jews is paramount for God's plan for all humankind. As Frederic Bush notes,

> [T]he end to which the providence of God and the loyalty and sagacity of human characters direct their efforts is also important theologically, for that end is the deliverance of the Jewish people. By placing his own beliefs (very ironically!) in the mouth of

---

[81] Bush, *Ruth, Esther*, 334–5; Lee, "Esther," 487–8.

Haman's wife Zeresh (6:13), the author expresses his conviction that this people is invincible. This is no ancient form of "manifest destiny" or the like, for both the larger context of the book and the other OT deliverance stories (Joseph and the Exodus) that his theme and language reflect place this deliverance fully within the context of the faith of the OT. A central tenet of that faith, maintained throughout the OT, is God's promise to the patriarch Abraham that through him and his descendants all the families of the earth would be blessed (Gen 12:3). Hence, the deliverance of the Jews has implications for more than the people affected. . . . Those who share the faith stance of the NT and affirm that the OT hope of blessing has begun to be actualized in the coming of Jesus, the Jewish Messiah, read this story of the deliverance, then, with special thanks for the grace of God, because the preservation of the Jews (important as that is in its own right) assured the coming of the (Jewish) Savior of the world, making possible the salvation of both Jews and Gentiles.[82]

According to Jesus and the apostles, the entire Old Testament witnesses to the Christ (Luke 1:69–71; 24:25–27, 44; John 1:45; Acts 3:24–26; 10:37–43; 26:22–23; 28:23; Rom 1:2–7; 3:21; 1 Pet 1:10–11). The deliverance of Esther, Mordecai, and their fellow Jews is part of that testimony to God's commitment to his ancient messianic promise.

6.3   Vocation

Evangelicals also occasionally point to the role humans play (or fail to play) as servants of God in Esther. For instance, F. B. Huey, Jr. believes Esther teaches that faithfulness—presumably of Esther and Mordecai—is rewarded by God and so the book also stresses "the value of standing for one's convictions even in the midst of a dangerous situation."[83] In contrast, Bruce K. Waltke argues the book portrays Mordecai and Esther as only nominally God's covenant people.[84] He points out neither expresses thanks or praise to God for deliverance, neither pray, and their request is mainly for personal deliverance from Haman's threat. Waltke concludes, "In sum, neither Esther nor

---

[82] Bush, *Ruth, Esther*, 335.

[83] Huey, "Esther," 794.

[84] *Waltke, An Old Testament Theology*, 767–8.

Mordecai nor the Jews show love for God or for their neighbors, the identifying marks of the true covenant people of God."[85]

These contradictory views result from viewing the author's portrayal of the actions of Esther and Mordecai (and Ahasuerus and Haman) through the wrong theological lens. After all, it is unclear whether Esther and Mordecai prayed or engaged in other personal acts of devotion as part of their normal piety. The author simply does not broach the subject. Indeed, the lack of any overt theology in Esther gives readers little guidance as to how to understand the actions of Esther and Mordecai as faithful Jews under God's Old Testament covenant. I therefore propose the author's portrayal of these two main characters, as well as the actions of Ahasuerus and Haman, may be better viewed through another lens, that of vocation. For faithful believers, service to one's neighbor in the various roles in which God places them is a holy calling (Eph 2:10; Col 3:23–24). Serving as a faithful and conscientious son or daughter, father or mother, citizen or ruler, or in any of a myriad of other roles allows one to be God's instrument for others' welfare—even when one's piety is not on display. This was articulated most clearly during the Reformation by Martin Luther. Robert Kolb explains Luther's view of this scriptural teaching:

> Believers recognize that God has placed them in the structures of human life created by God and has called them to the tasks of caring for other creatures, human and otherwise, as agents of God's providential presence and care. Luther called people in the exercise of their response-abilities "masks of God," through whom God, for example, milks cows so that his human creatures may be nourished."[86]

In Esther, the author leads us to see persons as fulfilling or failing to fulfill their God-given vocations. In chap. 2 Mordecai lives out his vocation as Ahasuerus's servant when he foiled the plot to assassinate the Persian ruler. In contrast, chap. 3 portrays Ahasuerus as neglecting his role as king by abdicating his responsibility to rule wisely and justly

---

[85] Waltke, *An Old Testament Theology*, 768.

[86] Robert Kolb, "Called to Milk Cows and Govern Kingdoms: Martin Luther's Teaching on the Christian's Vocations." *ConJ* 39 (2013): 135. Kolb's use of "response-abilities" is purposeful. He sees the Christian's vocation as a response to God's grace in Christ and a rightful use of God-given abilities.

when he allowed Haman to decide an entire, unnamed ethnic group in the empire might be extirpated. Haman used his position as an instrument of his bigotry (itself a sin), thereby also rejecting his vocation as a high government official. Esther, in contrast, used her position as queen not only to deliver herself and Mordecai from Haman's plot, but also in chaps. 7–8, to speak up for her fellow Jews and to persist in seeing that they were able to defend themselves against any who would attack them.

In this way, the book of Esther teaches about godly use of one's opportunities. Though readers may never serve in high offices as imperial prime ministers or in influential positions like being the spouse of a world leader, the portrayal of Mordecai and Esther communicates that in everyday tasks the faithful can serve God and neighbor in ways often seen only as secular and ordinary.

7   ESTHER AS A PART OF THE OLD TESTAMENT CANON

Since Esther never mentions God and appears to be nearly devoid of references to any religious practices,[87] it is not surprising Esther's place in the canon has been questioned from time to time.[88] Nevertheless ancient evidence reveals Esther had been accepted as part of the Jewish canon. The apocryphal book of Ben Sira (i.e., Sirach/Ecclesiasticus) appears to have known Esther and employed its vocabulary as it did other canonical books.[89] Still, no scroll of Esther was discovered in the caves at Qumran, and the writings of the sectarians revealed in those caves make no mention of it. Whether the Qumran sect accepted Esther's canonicity has been debated by scholars.[90]

The New Testament quotes many Old Testament books as Scripture, and most of those not quoted are known to the New Testament writers.[91] The lone exception is Esther. This may be due to the nature of Esther with its lack of obvious theological content. The New Testament writers may have found no occasion to reference it (though see

---

[87] The only possible references to any practices tied to religion and piety are those of casting lots (3:7; 9:24) and fasting (4:3, 16; 9:31).

[88] Louis A. Brighton, "The Book of Esther—Textual and Canonical Considerations," *ConJ* 13 (1987): 200–204.

[89] Andrew E. Steinmann, *The Oracles of God: The Old Testament Canon* (St. Louis: Concordia, 1999), 42–43.

[90] Steinmann, *The Oracles*, 62–3.

[91] Steinmann, *The Oracles*, 91–5.

Mark 6:23; Esth 5:3). Regardless, the first-century Jewish historian Flavius Josephus knew of Esther (*Antiquities* 11.184–274), and he most likely included it in his canon.[92]

In the second and third centuries AD, the Jewish sages of the Talmud recognized Esther as part of the canon (*Baba Bathra* 14b); they placed it in the third section of the Scriptures.[93] During this same era, early Christian lists of Old Testament canonical books present a mixed picture concerning Esther: it is missing from the list of Melito of Sardis (second century), but present in the Bryennnios List (second century) and the list of Origen (early third century).[94] During the fourth century, both Athanasius and Gregory of Nazianzus omitted Esther from their lists of canonical books. On the other hand, Cyril of Jerusalem and Epiphanius of Salamis included Esther, as did the rulings of the Council of Laodicea (c. 360). Amphilochius of Iconium's list omitted Esther but noted that others include Esther.[95] It would appear, then, some in the early centuries of the Christian church's history doubted whether Esther ought to be included in the canon, while others affirmed its canonical status. Certainly, some of this ambivalence was due to Esther's content. Nevertheless, Esther retained a place in the Christian Old Testament canon, and its place in the Jewish canon was never questioned.

Among later Christians, the most well-known challenge to Esther's canonical status came from Martin Luther. In his *Bondage of the Will* he stated,

> [T]hough I could rightly reject [Ecclesiasticus], for the time being I accept it so as not to waste time by getting involved in a dispute about the books received in the Hebrew canon. For you poke more than a little sarcastic fun at this when you compare Proverbs and The Song of Solomon (which with a sneering innuendo you call the "Love Song") with the two books of Esdras, Judith, the story of Susanna and the Dragon, and Esther (which despite their inclusion of it in the canon deserves more than all the rest in my judgment to be regarded as non-canonical).[96]

---

[92] Steinmann, *The Oracles*, 115–6. See *Against Apion* 37–43.

[93] Steinmann, *The Oracles*, 143. The Jewish canon (that is, the Old Testament) was divided into three sections: The Torah (that is, the Pentateuch), the Prophets, and the Writings.

[94] Steinmann, *The Oracles*, 147–57.

[95] Steinmann, *The Oracles*, 158–62.

[96] Jaroslav Jan Pelikan, Hilton C. Oswald, and Helmut T. Lehmann, eds., *Luther's Works:*

Nevertheless, he did not excise Esther from the canon and included it in his translation of the Old Testament with a preface such as he wrote for other biblical books.

8   TEXTS AND VERSIONS OF ESTHER

The ancient text of Esther has come down to us in three distinct variations. One version is found in the traditional Hebrew Masoretic Text (MT), and two versions are in the Greek Septuagint manuscripts: the Old Greek (OG) and the Alpha Text (AT). Both OG and AT contain six additions not found in MT. These appear to be later embellishments.[97] It is generally agreed the OG is a somewhat free translation of a Hebrew text similar to MT.[98] The OG contains a colophon: "In the fourth year of the reign of Ptolemy and Cleopatra, Dositheos, who said he was a priest and Levite and his son Ptolemy brought the above book of Purim, which they said was genuine. It had been translated by Lysimachus, son of Ptolemy, a member of Jerusalem's community." This indicates one of three possible dates for its origin in the fourth year of the reign of Ptolemy and Cleopatra: 113 BC, 77 BC, or 48 BC.[99]

The AT, which is extant in only five Greek manuscripts from the tenth to thirteenth centuries AD, is much shorter than either MT or OG. There is little agreement about the origin of AT. Some believe it

---

American Edition 55 Vols. (St. Louis: Concordia, 1955–86), 33.110. According to Luther's *Table Talk* (i.e., *Tischreden*) Luther denied the canonicity of Esther. However, the *Table Talk* consists of notes taken by Luther's students around his dinner table and are neither necessarily reliable nor are they from the pen of Luther himself.

[97] One primary piece of evidence for this is that the six additions are almost identical in both AT and OG, whereas throughout the rest of Esther AT and OG are different. See Karen H. Jobes, "Esther: To the Reader," pages 424–5 in Pietersma, Albert and Benjamin G. Wright eds., *A New English Translation of the Septuagint and the Other Greek Translations Traditionally Included under That Title* (New York: Oxford University, 2007), 425; Fox, *Character and Ideology*, 265–6.

[98] Jobes, "Esther: To the Reader," 424–425; Fox, *Character and Ideology*, 265.

[99] The colophon in Greek (Addition F:11): ἔτους τετάρτου βασιλεύοντος Πτολεμαίου καὶ Κλεοπάτρας εἰσήνεγκεν Δωσίθεος ὃς ἔφη εἶναι ἱερεὺς καὶ Λευίτης καὶ Πτολεμαῖος ὁ υἱὸς αὐτοῦ τὴν προκειμένην ἐπιστολὴν τῶν Φρουραι ἣν ἔφασαν εἶναι καὶ ἑρμηνευκέναι Λυσίμαχον Πτολεμαίου τῶν ἐν Ιερουσαλημ ("In the fourth year of the reign of Ptolemy and Cleopatra, Dositheos, who said he was a priest and a Levite, and Ptolemy his son brought the above letter about Phrourai, which they said existed, and Lysimachus son of Ptolemy, one of those in Jerusalem, translated it.") The rulers mentioned in the colophon could be Cleopatra III and her son Ptolemy IX Philometor Soter II (116–107 BC) or Ptolemy XII Auletes and his sister and wife Cleopatra V Tryphaena (c. 80–58 BC) or Ptolemy XIII Theos Philopator and his older sister and wife Cleopatra VII Philopator (51–c. 47 BC).

to be a revision of OG. Others propose it is a Greek translation of a Hebrew text of Esther different from MT. Still others believe it to be a rewritten version of Esther in the style of a midrash.[100]

Scholars are not agreed concerning which of the versions of the text—MT or AT—is older and how these two different forms of the Esther story arose, and there is little agreement determining how all three versions are related to one another. Most English translations are based on the MT, and it has been the authoritative text of Esther for both Jews and Christians throughout the centuries. Despite the arguments of some scholars, there is little reason to believe AT preserves a form of Esther older than MT. [101] Moreover, AT makes explicit references to God in several places:

---

[100] Jobes, "Esther: To the Reader," 424. The Göttingen Septuagint presents critical texts of both OG and AT, with AT appearing below OG on each page. See Robert Hanhart, *Esther,* Septuaginta: Vetus Testamentum Graecum Vol. VIII, 3 (Göttingen: Vandenhoeck & Ruprecht), 1983. For English translations of both Greek versions, see *The New English Translation of the Septuagint* (Oxford: Oxford University, 2007), 426–40. The Old Greek version is printed in the left-hand column and the Alpha Text in the right-hand column of each page.

[101] Jobes, "Esther: To the Reader," 424 notes, "Current theories propose that it is (a) a revision of the o' text [i.e., OG], (b) a second, independently made, translation of the MT, (c) a translation of another Hebrew text of Esther of uncertain relationship to the MT, or (d) a Midrashic re-write of the Esther story." Tov argues that AT was a condensation and reworking of OG (Emanuel Tov, *The "Lucianic" Text of the Canonical and the Apocryphal Sections of Esther: A Rewritten Biblical Book* [Jerusalem: Magnes, 1982]). Jobes argues that AT is a translation of a Hebrew text similar to MT but has been radically reworked, especially in Esther 8–10 (Karen H. Jobes, *The Alpha-Text of Esther: Its Character and Relationship to the Masoretic Text,* SBLDS 153 (Atlanta: Scholars, 1996). DeTroyer argues that AT is derived from both MT and OG (Kristin De Troyer, "On Crowns and Diadems from Kings, Queens, Horses and Men," in Bernard A. Taylor, ed., *IX Congress of the International Organization for Septuagint and Cognate Studies, Cambridge, 1995* [Atlanta: Scholars, 1997]). Fox argues AT and MT were both produced from a Hebrew text containing the current text of Esther minus some later expansions including 2:12–15, 21–23; 9:1–10:3. While Fox's view can be considered the consensus view among critical scholars, narrating the story of Esther as a whole makes little sense if the text originally ended with chap. 8. At that point the story is incomplete: Did the Jews rise up against their enemies as permitted in the decree promulgated by Mordecai (see 8:11), or was this also an expansion to the text (as argued by Fox, *Character and Ideology*, 262)? Moreover, why tell the story if it had no relevance for later generations? Fox argues that in the original Hebrew text only Esther and Mordecai were active in delivering the Jews and that the rest of the Jewish population were only spectators. The book's point was that "Jews become influential by being of value to the crown. . . . The power of the state is essentially reliable." But relying on the power of the state—especially a state by a single person and his elite courtiers—is a dangerous lesson. Moreover, without the account of the origin of Purim in Esther 9, the story becomes little more than an extended anecdote with little reason to be preserved. To that end, AT includes a brief version of both the Jews killing their enemies and the institution of Purim. Thus, it must be argued these are later expansions added to AT under the influence of OG.

"[T]hen surely God will be a helper and deliverance for them" (4:14).

"[P]roclaim a religious service and earnestly petition God" (4:16).

"God gave her courage as she called on him" (7:2).

It is much more likely the AT is secondary to the MT, and adding these references to God is an indication of this. These references to him appear to be the AT's author/translator attempting to correct the MT's neglect of mentioning God's role in saving the Jews from Haman's plot. It is improbable the MT as a revision of AT removed all references to God—something completely unnatural for a Jewish author to do.

As for OG, it is a highly paraphrastic translation. It appears as if the translator decided to make God's role more explicit than in the Hebrew original. He added the following explicit references to the Almighty:

"[T]o fear God and do his ordinances" (2:20).

"[C]all upon the Lord" (4:8).

"[T]he Lord deprived the king from sleep that night" (6:1).

"[B]cause a living god is with him" (6:13).

9   THE GREEK ADDITIONS TO ESTHER

Greek Esther contains six additions not found in the Hebrew text that are designated sections A–F. They can be characterized this way:

SECTION	LOCATION	CONTENT
A	Before chap. 1	Mordecai has a dream vision about Israel in chaos; Mordecai hears two eunuchs plotting to assassinate the king. (17 vv. OG; 18 vv. AT)
B	Between 3:13 and 3:14	Haman's letter giving instructions to destroy Judeans (7 vv.)
C	After chap. 4	Mordecai and Esther's prayers during the fast requested by Esther (30 vv.)
D	After C	God gives Esther favor in the eyes of the king as she comes before him with a request. (16 vv.)
E	Between 8:12 and 8:13	Letter of the king rescinding Haman's letter (17 vv.)
F	After chap. 10	Mordecai explains his dream now that it has been fulfilled. (11 vv. OG; 10 vv. AT)

These additions are obviously paired as a chiastic arrangement: section F explains the dream in section A. Section E counters Haman's work in section B. Section D portrays the answer to the prayers in section C, the center of the chiasm. Because none of these were found in the Hebrew text, Jerome removed them from their contexts and gathered them in an appendix to Esther. When chapter and verse numbers were added to Jerome's Latin Vulgate, these became Esth 10:4–16:24.

The paired sections accomplish a number to things some readers thought were missing from Esther. Most obviously, they mention God, who is never mentioned in the Hebrew text.[102] Additions A and F serve to elevate the status of Mordecai as a prophet who receives visions and explains them, thereby also diminishing Esther's status. Addition A also fills in a gap in the narrative of Hebrew Esther, explaining how Mordecai learned of the plot to assassinate Ahasuerus. Additions B and E fill in what may have been perceived as a gap—the content of Haman's decree and the decree that rescinded Haman's actions. Additions C and D add overt religious practices (prayer).

Opinions differ concerning the overall effect of additions A–F (as well as additional mentions of God in OG and AT, see the discussion above). André Barucq thought they expressed what the author of MT had allowed readers to infer.[103] On the other hand, Carey A. Moore believes they transform Esther:

> [T]he Additions do significantly change the emphases in the Greek version. First, Esther and Mordecai were the heroes of the story in the MT; but in the Greek version, God is. Second, whereas the author of the Hebrew text was primarily interested in providing the "historical" background for cultic considerations, i.e. for establishing the historical basis for the celebrating of Purim, the authors of the Additions concentrated more on the religious aspects, i.e. on God's concern for his people and his deliverance of them.[104]

Indisputable evidence indicates the additions were not part of the original text of Esther. Since the additions appear in similar forms

---

[102] In the additions he is mentioned at A: 8, 10; C: 8, 14, 23, 29, 30; D: 2, 8; E: 16, 18, 21; and F: 1, 6, 7, 8, 9, 10.

[103] André Barucq, *Judith, Esther*, 2nd ed., La Sainte Bible (Paris: Cerf, 1959), 87.

[104] Carey A. Moore, *Daniel, Esther and Jeremiah: The Additions: A New Translation with Introduction and Commentary* AB 44. (New York: Doubleday, 1977), 158–9.

in both AT and OG, it is argued they were added after both AT and OG were produced in Greek. Moreover, since they seem to address perceived problems with the book of Esther as part of Scripture, they may have been added to make Esther more palatable to those who objected to Esther's place in the canon. None of the additions appear in Semitic language translations based on the Hebrew text: Syriac, Talmud, Targums. Origen (c. AD 184–253) commented that neither the prayers of Esther and Modecai nor the letters written by Haman and Mordecai (i.e., Additions A, D, and F) were contained in the Hebrew text of Esther.[105] When Jerome (c. AD 347- 420) translated the Latin Vulgate, he placed the additions at the end of Esther because they were not found in the Hebrew text in his day. Finally, it ought to be noted the additions appear to conflict with the MT at a number of points, indicating their secondary nature.[106] As Moore comments, "[V]irtually all modern scholars agree that the two royal letters (Additions B and E) are much too florid and rhetorical in character to be anything but Greek in origin."[107]

The composition of these versions appears to have been at different times and in different languages. Addition A, Mordecai's dream, was written in Hebrew.[108] Moore observes,

> There are three occurrences of *kai idou*, "and behold!" which presupposes the Heb. *Wəhinnêh*, a recognized literary device for introducing either a dream or the various component elements of a dream.[109] Moreover, five times in ten verses a sentence begins with *kai*, "and," which presupposes the Heb. conjunction.[110]

---

[105] Origen, *Letter to Africanus*, 3: "Concerning the Book of Esther: neither the prayer of Mordecai nor that of Esther, both constructed to edify the reader, is found in the Hebrew; neither are the letters, including the one written to Haman about the uprooting of the Jewish nation, nor the one of Mordecai in the name of Artaxerxes rescuing the nation from death."

[106] For example, addition A reports the following items concerning Mordecai that contradict MT Esther: Mordecai was a prominent man serving in Artaxerxes's court. He personally reported a plot against the king's life to the king. He was given an immediate reward. See Carey A. Moore, "On the Origins of the LXX Additions to the Book of Esther," *JBL* 92 (1973): 386.

[107] Moore, *Daniel, Esther, and Jeremiah: The Additions*, 154.

[108] Moore, "On the Origins," 388, offers the opinion that A:11–17 was composed in Greek. R. A. Martin, "Syntax Criticism of the LXX Additions to the Book of Esther," *JBL* 94 (1975): 65–72, concludes that there are features in Addition A indicating it is characterized by a balance of features characteristic of translation Greek and features characteristic of composition Greek, perhaps supporting Moore's findings that addition A is a Hebrew composition with a Greek insertion.

[109] A:4, 5, 7. Compare Gen 37:7 (three times), 9; 40: 9, 16; 41:1, 2, 3, 5, 6, 7.

[110] A:4, 5, 6, 8, 9.

The corresponding addition, addition F, the interpretation of the dream, was either composed in Greek or is a very translation of a Semitic language composition.[111] Additions B and E, the two letters, were clearly composed in Greek.[112] Moore observes,

> [T]heir literary style, which is best characterized as florid, rhetorical, and bombastic, is free of all Hebraisms and is quite unlike Greek translations of other Semitic decrees in the Bible; . . . the two letters in B and E abound in grammatical constructions characteristic of "good" Greek, such as participial and infinitival constructions, genitive absolutes, and the noun and its article separated by qualifying prepositional phrases.[113]

Additions C and D, Esther's prayers and God's response to them, appear to have been composed in Hebrew or Aramaic.[114]

When these various additions were composed is a matter of speculation. Josephus, who generally relied on the Septuagint for his work, included information from additions B, C, D, and E but not A or F when retelling the story of Esther.[115] Thus, he provides evidence that additions B, C, D, and E were composed before AD 93–94 and by that time had been inserted into Septuagint Esther. However, additions A and F had not yet been inserted into Greek Esther. Therefore, whether they had been composed by Josephus's day or at a later time is an open question.

OUTLINE OF ESTHER

1   Introduction: Ahasuerus and His Kingdom (1:1–2)
2   Esther Rises to Become Queen (1:3–2:23)
    2.1   Three Banquets in Susa (1:3–9)
        2.1.1   Ahasuerus's Banquet for His Officials and Courtiers (1:3–4)
        2.1.2   Ahasuerus's Banquet for the People of Susa (1:5–8)

---

[111] Martin, "Syntax Criticism," 69. Moore, "On the Origins," 388, argues that addition F was composed in a Semitic language (i.e., Hebrew or Aramaic).

[112] Moore, "On the Origins," 383–6; Martin, "Syntax Criticism," 69.

[113] Moore, "On the Origins," 384.

[114] Martin, "Syntax Criticism," 69. Moore, "On the Origins," 391–3, believes addition C to be a Semitic composition but is less certain as to whether addition D was composed in a Semitic language or in Greek.

[115] Josephus, *Antiquities*, 11.184–296 [11.6.1–13].

COMMENTARY

SECTION OUTLINE

1   INTRODUCTION: AHASUERUS AND HIS KINGDOM (1:1–2)

¹ These events took place during the days of Ahasuerus, who ruled 127 provinces from India to Cush. ² In those days King Ahasuerus reigned from his royal throne in the fortress at Susa.

The beginning of the book of Esther introduces the historical setting of the events, briefly introducing Ahasuerus and his kingdom. This introduction corresponds to the book's conclusion (10:1–3), which depicts Ahasuerus's kingdom under the guidance of Mordecai. A transformation in the power structure inside the Persian royal administration can be traced from the introduction through the body of the book to its conclusion. These introductory verses give the impression Ahasuerus oversees the empire. When reading the main body of the book, however, the reader is lead to the conclusion Ahasuerus is not in charge. Instead, he is one who is subject to the desires of others: he follows their advice and suggestions without ever questioning their reasons or motives.[1] Finally, at the end of the book someone clearly is in charge.

---

[1] Michael Fox, *Character and Ideology in the Book of Esther*, 2nd ed. (Grand Rapids, MI: Eerdmans, 2001), 173 notes, "Thus the all-powerful Xerxes in practice abdicates his responsibility

While Ahasuerus remains king (10:1), Mordecai is the prime mover in the empire (10:2–3).

1:1 The opening phrase of Esther in Hebrew *(wayehî bîmê)* is identical to the opening of narratives in Gen 14:1; Ruth 1:1; and Isa 7:1, clearly marking the writer's intention of presenting Esther as historical narrative, not fiction.

There is no doubt the king called "Ahasuerus" in Hebrew is identified with the Persian king better known as Xerxes to English readers. In Old Persian his name was *Khshayarshan.* In Hebrew this was realized as *ʾaḥašwērôš* but in Greek as *Xerxēs.* He is also mentioned in Ezra 4:6. While the Septuagint and Josephus identify Ahasuerus with Artaxerxes, that is clearly a mistake. The names Xerxes and Artaxerxes are preserved in six ancient languages other than Old Persian. In every case the Persian name *Artaxshasta* (Gk.: *Artaxerxes*; Hb. *Artaḥshasta*) is always realized in those languages with a *t* from the Artax- prefix.[2] In contrast, the name *Khshayarshan* (*Xerxes/Ahasuerus*) contains no *t* sound.

Ahasuerus's empire was divided into "127 provinces," while the Persian Empire was divided by Ahasuerus's father Darius I into twenty-two satrapies; the units listed appear to be subdivisions of the larger satrapies.[3] The reference to provinces with the larger number is probably to make the kingdom appear vaster and more magnificent. The word "province" *(mədînâ)* is frequently used in Esther to remind readers of the extent of Ahasuerus's realm. The term occurs thirty-nine times in the book and only fourteen more times in the rest of the Old Testament.

The extent of Ahasuerus's kingdom is listed according to its easternmost and westernmost extremes. In the east was "India." In Hebrew this is *hōdû,* a cognate of the word *Hindû,* designating the area drained by the Indus River in modern-day Pakistan and India. In the west the empire included "Cush," the region of Nubia south of Egypt, including much of modern Sudan.

---

and surrenders effective power to those who know how to press the right buttons—namely, his love of 'honor,' his anxiety for his authority, and his desire to appear generous."

[2] William H. Shea, "Esther and History," *ConJ* 13 (1987): 234, , "Esther and History," 234, n. 4. The languages are Akkadian, Aramaic, Egyptian, Elamite, Greek, and Hebrew.

[3] The author of Esther is well aware of the difference between a satrapy, governed by a satrap, and a province headed by a governor. See 3:12; 8:9; 9:3. Note also the description of Judah as a province in the Persian Empire (Ezra 2:1).

1:2 The setting is further defined by Ahasuerus reigning "from his royal throne." While some understand this phrase to be a reference to Ahasuerus having secured his throne after suppressing revolts in Egypt and Babylon, this is improbable.[4] Instead, it places the action at a time when Ahasuerus was ruling from the city of Susa. Four cities served as the seat of government for the Achaemenids: Susa, Persepolis, Babylon, and Ecbatana. Susa was generally used as the winter residence for the Persian kings.

Ahasuerus's father Darius I had built a large upper city on a mound in Susa. This is apparently what the author calls "the fortress at Susa" as opposed to the lower city. The Hebrew word for fortress (*bîrâ*) is used only in the postexilic Old Testament books (2 Chr 17:12; 27:4; Neh 1:1; 2:8; 7:2; Dan 8:2) and derives from the Akkadian loanword *birtu*.

---

[4] Joyce G. Baldwin, *Esther: An Introduction and Commentary*, TOTC (Leicester: Intervarsity, 1984), 56. For rejection of this view, see Frederic Bush, *Ruth, Esther*, WBC 9 (Dallas: Word, 1996), 346; Fox, *Character and Ideology*, 16; Moore, *Esther*, 5.

SECTION OUTLINE

2   Esther Rises to Become Queen (1:3–2:23)
  2.1   Three Banquets in Susa (1:3–9)
     2.1.1   Ahasuerus's Banquet for His Officials and Courtiers
              (1:3–4)
     2.1.2   Ahasuerus's Banquet for the People of Susa (1:5–8)
     2.1.3   Vashti's Banquet for the Women of Susa (1:9)
  2.2   Vashti Refuses the King's Command (1:10–12)
  2.3   Ahasuerus Issues a Decree Concerning Vashti and All Wives
         in His Kingdom (1:13–22)
  2.4   Ahasuerus's Search for a New Queen (2:1–23)
     2.4.1   The King's Courtiers Suggest a Search for a New
              Queen (2:1–4)
     2.4.2   Mordecai and Esther Introduced (2:5–7)
     2.4.3   Esther Taken into the King's Harem (2:8–11)
     2.4.4   The Procedure for Choosing a New Queen (2:12–14)
     2.4.5   Esther Chosen as the New Queen (2:15–18)
     2.4.6   Mordecai and Esther in the King's Service (2:19–23)

2   ESTHER RISES TO BECOME QUEEN (1:3–2:23)

The first major section of Esther chronicles her rise as Ahasuerus's most favored wife, queen of the Persian Empire. This is the first of three key accomplishments by Jews in Esther—the second is the rise of Mordecai to become prime minister (3:1–8:17). The third is Jewish triumph over their enemies (9:1–32). Esther and Mordecai play key roles in each of these achievements. In this section Esther is portrayed as playing a passive role (e.g., 2:15). In fact, the author emphasizes what she *did not do:* she "did not reveal her ethnicity or her family" connections (2:10, 20). By depicting Esther in this way, the author contrasts two women who did not do things: Vashti, Ahasuerus's original queen who did not obey Ahasuerus's summons (1:12), and Esther who did not reveal her Jewish ethnicity. The ironic twist is that Vashti's behavior was active defiance of Ahasuerus's order whereas Esther's behavior was in obedience to Mordecai's wishes.

2.1   Three Banquets in Susa (1:3–9)

While the book of Esther is filled with banquets, parties, and celebrations—ten altogether—three of the banquets are presented in short order at the beginning of the book. Two of these banquets foreground Ahasuerus's desire to appear to be a magnanimous and generous ruler, thereby hoping to receive honor from his guests and subjects as they are impressed by his wealth and, presumably, led to acknowledge his authority and supreme dignity. As Michael Fox notes, "Xerxes tries to buy honor by ostentatious generosity. His marathon banquets lavish hospitality upon those who come to witness his glory."[1] The third banquet—the one hosted by Vashti—is noted only briefly by the author. In contrast to the other two which describe the king's grandiose display of his wealth, this banquet is hardly mentioned, occupying one lone verse with no authorial ornamentation. Yet from this third banquet arose a perceived challenge to Ahasuerus's authority and dignity.

2.1.1   Ahasuerus's Banquet for His Officials and Courtiers (1:3-4)

[3] *He held a feast in the third year of his reign for all his officials and staff, the army of Persia and Media, the nobles, and the officials from the provinces.* [4] *He displayed the glorious wealth of his kingdom and the magnificent splendor of his greatness for a total of 180 days.*

Date: 25 Elul (Saturday, October 3), 483 BC to 30 Adar (Friday, April 2), 482 BC

The banquet described in these verses sustains connections to Ahasuerus's plans for a campaign to conquer Greece on the western frontier of his kingdom. He may have been raising support for his ambitions by courting the favor of his nobles and officials. Susa was not usually the royal residence during the hot Persian summer months, so it is probable this banquet took place in late winter. Esther 1:5 appears to confirm this by noting Ahasuerus provided a seven-day feast for everyone present in Susa. The second banquet may have coincided with the new year commencing Ahasuerus's fourth regnal year on 1 Nisan (Saturday, April 3), 482 BC. This would place this first 180-day banquet at the end of the previous year.

1:3 The first feast is set in Ahasuerus's "third year." The official years of the Persian kings began on the first day of the first lunar month of spring, the month of Nisan. Thus, Ahasuerus's third year began in spring 484 BC and ended on the last day of the last winter

---

[1] Fox, *Character and Ideology*, 172.

month (Adar) in 483 BC. This verse notes that Ahasuerus invited "his officials and staff," which are further divided into groups.

"[T]he army of Persia and Media" is listed first and would have been especially important if this banquet was intended to raise support for a military incursion into Greece.[2] The phrase *Persia and Media* is the common order throughout chap. 1 for these two ethnically related nations (1:3, 14, 18, 19).[3] Before Cyrus the Great, the Medes had dominated the Persians. Cyrus was of both Persian and Median descent. He overthrew his maternal grandfather, the Media king, and afterward the Persian Achaemenids ruled the combined nations of Media and Persia. The word for "nobles," *partǝmîm*, is a loanword from Old Persian (*fratama*) and demonstrates the author's knowledge of Persia.[4]

1:4 The 180-day feast may not necessarily denote ongoing eating and drinking. Instead, it may represent the intervening time during which various officials from the outlying provinces could visit the court and partake of the king's largesse.

2.1.2   *Ahasuerus's Banquet for the People of Susa (1:5–8)*

[5] At the end of this time, the king held a week-long banquet in the garden courtyard of the royal palace for all the people, from the greatest to the least, who were present in the fortress of Susa. [6] White and blue linen hangings were fastened with fine white and purple linen cords to silver rods on marble columns. Gold and silver couches were arranged on a mosaic pavement of red feldspar, marble, mother-of-pearl, and precious stones.

[7] Drinks were served in an array of gold goblets, each with a different design. Royal wine flowed freely, according to the king's bounty. [8] The drinking was according to royal decree: "There are no restrictions." The king had ordered every wine steward in his household to serve whatever each person wanted.

---

[2] Some take this phrase to be a reference to administrators (see Berlin, *Esther*, 8), but חַיִל is commonly used to denote an army in the Old Testament (e.g., Exod 14:4; Deut 11:4; Jer 32:2).

[3] However, see 10:2 where the phrase is "Media and Persia" as at Dan 8:20. In Daniel the Medes are always mentioned before the Persians (Dan 5:28; 6:8, 12, 15).

[4] George Glenn Cameron, "Persepolis Treasury Tablets Old and New," *JNES* 17 (1958): 162, 166 n. 17.

Date: 1–7 Nisan (Saturday, April 3–Friday, April 9), 482 BC

1:5 This second banquet is described in more lavish terms than the first. It is prepared "[a]t the end of this time," that is, at the conclusion of the 180-day banquet. In this instance, the invitees included everyone "in the fortress of" Susa, "from the greatest to the least," encompassing all of Ahasuerus's servants, including the most menial of them. The word for "palace" is *bîtan*, and although related to the Hebrew word for house (*bāyit*), it is a loanword from Akkadian.

1:6–8 The description of Ahasuerus's lavish provisions is without parallel in the Bible. Esther 1:6 is the only verse in the Bible describing the physical environment of a scene.[5] The lavish "hangings" of white and blue fabric on silver rods, "gold and silver couches," and "a mosaic pavement" testify to the opulent way Ahasuerus's palace was furnished. Even those of lowest rank could enjoy this royal garden, testifying to the special nature of this banquet. Beside the word for "marble," the author uses three distinct terms, not used elsewhere in the OT, to describe the stone pavement. The first is *bahaṭ*, translated as "red feldspar" in CSB but often identified as porphyry (ESV, NIV, NRSV), a purplish-red stone. Porphyry does not appear to have been in widespread use before the Roman era, and early uses of it were for bowls.[6] The second term, "*dar*," is translated "mother-of-pearl" in CSB on the assumption it is a cognate of the Arabic word for *pearl*. The third word, *sōḥāret*, is translated "precious stones."[7]

The lavish furnishings include a description of the "goblets," each one individually designed. The expense incurred by commissioning so many custom-made drinking vessels serves to further depict the king's wealth, as does the generous supply of wine. The interpretation of 1:8 has been disputed because of the presence of the word *dāt*, a loanword from Old Persian frequently used in Esther and often denoting a "royal decree." Some have questioned how a decree could allow each

---

[5] Shimon Bar-Efrat, *Narrative Art in the Bible*, JSOTSup 70 (Sheffield: Sheffield Academic, 1989), 195.

[6] David Lees, "Hapax Legomena in Esther 1.6: Translation Difficulties and Comedy in the Book of Esther," *BT* 68 (2017): 93.

[7] There is no support for the notion that these three words describe types of carpet as suggested by Lees, "Hapax Legomena." In fact, the word for marble, שֵׁשׁ (*šēš*), is used twice in this verse: once to describe the columns and another time to describe one of the elements of the pavement, making it difficult to see it as a term for a fabric carpet. Moreover, the word for "pavement" (*riṣpat* is used elsewhere only of stone surfacing (2 Chr 7:3; Ezek 40:17, 18; 42:3).

person to drink as desired instead of mandating how much to drink.[8] However, the decree seems to suspend any rule of drinking (such as drinking at prescribed times) and allows each person discretion as to when and how much to drink.

2.1.3 *Vashti's Banquet for the Women of Susa (1:9)*

[9] *Queen Vashti also gave a feast for the women of King Ahasuerus's palace.*

1:9 Parallel to Ahasuerus's feast, Vashti banqueted with "the women of King Ahasuerus's palace." The author introduces Vashti with no description other than she reigned as queen. Moreover, in contrast to the detailed description of Ahasuerus's feast, Vashti's feast is barely described, noting only that it was separate from the one in the garden with the men. Yet this verse, though it suspends the use of ornate language, is important for setting the stage for subsequent events. Ahasuerus's summons of his queen (1:11) necessarily implied she, as hostess of her own party, was compelled to neglect her female guests to impress the king's male guests with her beauty. The brevity of the description of Vashti's banquet as opposed to the extensive portrayal used to describe Ahasuerus's banquet mirrors the low regard Ahasuerus and his male guests had for the women of the Persian realm.

2.2 Vashti Refuses the King's Command (1:10–12)

[10] *On the seventh day, when the king was feeling good from the wine, Ahasuerus commanded Mehuman, Biztha, Harbona, Bigtha, Abagtha, Zethar, and Carkas—the seven eunuchs who personally served him—*[11]*to bring Queen Vashti before him with her royal crown. He wanted to show off her beauty to the people and the officials, because she was very beautiful.* [12]*But Queen Vashti refused to come at the king's command that was delivered by his eunuchs. The king became furious and his anger burned within him.*

---

[8] See the discussions in Baldwin, *Esther,* 59; Berlin, *Esther*, 10; Bush, *Ruth, Esther*, 348–9; Fox, *Character and Ideology*, 17; Carey A. Moore, *Esther: Introduction, Translation, and Notes*, AB 78 (Garden City, NY: Doubleday, 1971).

Date: 7 Nisan (Friday, April 9), 482 BC

1:10–11 We are told that the king was "feeling good from the wine." The Hebrew phrase is literally "as the heart of the king was good with wine" (*kətôb lēb hammelek bayyāyin*). A "good" heart can imply joyfulness (1 Kgs 8:66; 2 Chr 7:10; Prov 15:15); nevertheless, in this case the expression implies excessive use of alcohol produced impaired judgment (cp. 1 Sam 25:36), leading to a perceived crisis for the king. Ironically, the only other occurrence of such a heart state in Esther is the good mood Haman possessed after feasting with Ahasuerus and Esther, an event which presaged his downfall (Esth 5:9).

The king's mood led to his command to the seven eunuchs.[9] The term *eunuch* (Hb. *sārîs*) indicates a castrated man.[10] These particular eunuchs had access to the king's harem, a privilege extended only since their physical state rendered it impossible for them to be sexually involved with the women in the harem. The overreaching pomp and ritual of the command is signaled not only by sending seven eunuchs on the seventh day of the feast but also by the author's listing of their names.[11] This list is later reinforced by referring to the "command that was delivered by the eunuchs" (1:12, 15). Vashti was ordered to appear before Ahasuerus "with her royal crown" (*bəketer malkût*). This, combined with his desire to show off her beauty, emphasized that Ahasuerus wanted to use her as an object he owned and controlled—like the other possessions on display in his palace (see 1:6–7). The Hebrew word for "crown," *keter*, occurs only in Esther (see 2:17; 6:8). It may have been a headband of a specific color reserved only for royalty.[12]

1:12 No reason is given concerning Vashti's refusal to appear before the king. Since Ahasuerus's purpose was to display her beauty,

---

[9] Among the seven names, A. R. Millard, "Persian Names in Esther and the Reliability of the Hebrew Text," JBL 96 (1977): 585, notes the following as genuine Persian names: *Mehuman*, from Old Persian *Vahumanah*, meaning "intelligent," and *Carkas*. The *latter* is an Elamite writing of a name in the Persepolis Treasury Tablets that corresponds to Avestan *kahrkasa*, "vulture."

[10] The word at times may indicate a high official (see Gen 37:36). In Esther, however, these men appear to have access to the royal harem; eunuchs were often used for such purposes (see Esth 1:12, 15; 2:3, 14–15, 21; 4:4–5; 6:2, 14; 7:9).

[11] Fox's suggestion (*Character and Ideology*, 19) the author lists the names in order to give his account a measure of historical verisimilitude misses the point (see Bush, *Ruth, Esther*, 349). The author already amply demonstrated his familiarity with the Persian court and had no need to add artificial details to convince readers of this fact.

[12] Alison Salvesen, "*Keter* (Esther 1:11; 2:17; 6:8): 'Something to Do with a Camel'?" *JSS* 44 (1999): 35–46.

however, it may be inferred that she was offended at being treated as a mere object possessed by Ahasuerus and used to display his regal honor. If this is the case, she is to be admired for her refusal to be put on display in the middle of a party attended by drunken men. Vashti may have resented the implication that Ahasuerus's banquet was more important than her banquet and that she should abandon her female guests to be displayed to the drunks in the palace garden.

2.3 Ahasuerus Issues a Decree Concerning Vashti and All Wives in His Kingdom (1:13–22)

13 The king consulted the wise men who understood the times, for it was his normal procedure to confer with experts in law and justice. 14 The most trusted ones were Carshena, Shethar, Admatha, Tarshish, Meres, Marsena, and Memucan. They were the seven officials of Persia and Media who had personal access to the king and occupied the highest positions in the kingdom. 15 The king asked, "According to the law, what should be done with Queen Vashti, since she refused to obey King Ahasuerus's command that was delivered by the eunuchs?"

16 Memucan said in the presence of the king and his officials, "Queen Vashti has wronged not only the king, but all the officials and the peoples who are in every one of King Ahasuerus's provinces. 17 For the queen's action will become public knowledge to all the women and cause them to despise their husbands and say, 'King Ahasuerus ordered Queen Vashti brought before him, but she did not come.' 18 Before this day is over, the noble women of Persia and Media who hear about the queen's act will say the same thing to all the king's officials, resulting in more contempt and fury.

19 "If it meets the king's approval, he should personally issue a royal decree. Let it be recorded in the laws of the Persians and the Medes, so that it cannot be revoked: Vashti is not to enter King Ahasuerus's presence, and her royal position is to be given to another woman who is more worthy than she. 20 The decree the king issues will be heard throughout his vast kingdom, so all women will honor their husbands, from the greatest to the least."

21 The king and his counselors approved the proposal, and he followed Memucan's advice. 22 He sent letters to all the royal provinces, to each province in its own script and to each ethnic group in its own language, that every man should be master of his own house and speak in the language of his own people.

1:13 We are told that Ahasuerus followed his normal practice, consulting with those described as "wise men who understood the times" (*laḥăkāmîm yōdᶜê hāᶜittîm*) and "experts in law and justice" (*yōdᶜê dāt wādîn*). The phrase "understood the times" occurs only one other place in Scripture (1 Chr 12:32). It appears to denote persons who not only possess wisdom but also possess insight regarding how to apply it in contemporary circumstances. These particular experts are described by this alliterative phrase in Hebrew: *dāt* and *dîn*, "law and justice." The use of counselors to determine a legal way for the king to impose his will was not unique to Ahasuerus among the Persian royals. Herodotus relates how a previous king, Cambyses, used counselors to find a way to circumvent the law in order to marry one of his sisters.[13]

1:14 The most trusted counselors are listed by name,[14] in keeping with the author's fondness for lists of names of smaller groups of men.[15] These seven men were unique, enjoying regular access to the king. The practice of restricting this number to seven may also be reflected in the seven counselors who served one of Ahasuerus's successors, Artaxerxes (Ezra 7:14) and the seven Persian counselors mentioned by Herodotus.[16]

1:15 Ahasuerus's question to his advisors was concerned with proper legal authority for acting against Vashti. He highlighted the exact offense: his order delivered through the eunuchs. The mention of the delivery method of the order not only sets Vashti's offense in a public and official context; it also serves the author's purpose of lampooning the affected officiousness of Ahasuerus and his court when communicating with his queen.

1:16–18 Apparently the author chose not to preserve the entire discussion among the seven advisors but simply to give readers the advice offered by Memucan since it was accepted and acted upon. While Ahasuerus inquired about available legal options concerning the queen's refusal to obey him as king, Memucan widened the scope

---

[13] Herodotus, *Histories*, 3.31.2–5.

[14] Millard, "Persian Names in Esther," 485, notes that *Carshena*, the name of the first counselor is also found in the Persepolis Fortification Tablets.

[15] These include the seven eunuchs who served Ahasuerus (1:10), the two eunuchs who guarded the King's Gate (2:21), and the ten sons of Haman (9:7–10). Larger numbers of men are not listed by name, including the 500 men killed in Susa on 13 Adar (9:6, 12), and 300 men who were killed in Susa on 14 Adar (9:15).

[16] *Histories* 3.84.2.

of her action, describing it as an offense against all Persian officials and all the various peoples throughout the empire. We can only speculate why he did this. Was it because no existing law addressed the specific offense against the king alone? Was it to help the king save face and maintain his honor by diffusing Vashti's affront throughout the king's officials and even the entire populace? Whatever the motive, the result renders the men in Ahasuerus's court to appear insecure and petty.

Memucan's reasoning included his stated assumption as the word of Vashti's refusal to obey the king's officially delivered order would spread among all the women at Ahasuerus's court. Then they would justify disobeying their husbands based on Vashti's rebellion. Ironically, no women spoke at this point in the narrative. Timothy K. Beal notes,

> Interestingly, at the center of his depiction of the wide-reaching subversion which Vashti's refusal threatens, we find Memucan imagining women *speaking*. Thus far in the narrative, no one but the king and Memucan have been quoted saying anything (*'amr*; vv. 10, 13, 15, and 16). Women, including Vashti, have been given no voice. It is ironic, then, that at the center of Memucan's speech, which aims ultimately to reestablish the subordination of women to their "lords," male anxiety about their power to speak finds its way into the discourse.[17]

There is yet another irony. The person who speaks the most in the book is a woman—Esther, whose words are quoted by the author more often than those of any other person, including Ahasuerus.[18] If the men fear women speaking, Esther's words in the text bear additional weight. They will not only catch Haman by surprise but will lead to more than simply the "contempt and fury" (*bizzāyôn wāqāṣep*) that Memucan predicts will result from the women's words.

1:19–20 Since Memucan has expanded the extent of Vashti's offense, he recommends "a royal decree" resulting in a new law. This is the only place in Esther where the unchangeable laws of the empire

---

[17] Tod Linafelt and Timothy K. Beal, *Ruth and Esther*, Berit Olam: Studies in Hebrew Narrative and Poetry (Collegeville: Liturgical Press, 1999), 14.

[18] Esther is quoted eight times for a total of 227 words: 4:11, 16; 5:4, 8; 7:3–4, 6, 8:5–6; 9:13. Ahasuerus is quoted twelve times for a total of 181 words: 1:15; 3:11; 5:3, 5–6; 6:3–4, 6, 10; 7:2, 5, 8; 8:7–8; 9:12). Even more odd is that Mordecai is quoted only once (4:13), speaking a mere eight words.

are mentioned, a biblical stance found in no other ancient source to date (see Dan 6:8, 12, 15). Critics have often pointed to this assertion about the Persian laws as suspect and permitting an unworkable legal order.[19] Nevertheless, rendering certain laws unchangeable may not have been as unworkable as some suggest. Moreover, consistency would tend to produce stability in the law, allowing everyone a certain measure of assurance of the parameters governing what was legal and illegal.[20] In addition, irrevocable laws may act as a check on the king's power, making him inclined to think about the implications of a law he would have to enforce and could not revoke should he wish to do so in the future.

Memucan does not use the title *Queen* for Vashti at this point in the narrative. In fact, she will never be called queen again in Esther (see 2:1, 4, 17). In addition to that, her punishment is twofold: she would never be allowed again into the king's presence (see 4:10–11; 5:1–2), and her position would be given to another woman. The replacement was required to be "more worthy" (*haṭṭôbâ*) than she. This adjective forms a play on words with the earlier description of Vashti as "beautiful" (*ṭôbat*; 1:11). The king's act was effected by a decree of the despot, literally, "a royal word," to contrast with the "the queen's action" (*dəbar hammalkâ*; 1:17), literally, "the word of the queen."

Memucan also advised a decree for the entire realm. The word for "decree," Hebrew *pitgām*, is a loanword from Old Persian, reinforcing the author's familiarity with Persian culture.[21] The CSB quotes Memucan as saying the decree would be for "his vast kingdom," but the Hebrew text is more dramatic, literally saying "throughout his kingdom—since it is vast" (*bəkol malkûtô kî rabbâ hî'*), a phrase expressed by Memucan, acknowledging Ahasuerus's regal splendor and assuaging his wounded honor.

---

[19] Fox, *Character and Ideology*, 22; Moore, *Esther*, 11; Paton, *Esther*, 157. Nevertheless, Berlin (*Esther*, 18) has offered a different view of the Hebrew phrase וְלֹא יַעֲבוֹר, noting that at 3:3 the verbal root עבר means "transgress, disobey." She proposes the law is one issued with such authority that it cannot be disobeyed. There are several problems with this, however. First, at 8:3 the same verb clearly means "revoke, undo". Second, in Daniel the unchangeable law of the Medes and Persians is described several ways: "it cannot be taken away" (לָא תֶעְדֵּא; Dan 6:9–13) and it "cannot be changed" (לָא לְהַשְׁנָיָה; Dan 6:8).

[20] This is similar to the American legal principle of *stare decisis*.

[21] The Old Persian word also became a loanword in Aramaic (Ezra 4:17; 5:7, 11; 6:11; Dan 3:16; 4:14).

1:21–22 Memucan's proposal not only pleased Ahasuerus, but it also gained the support of the other six counselors. Perhaps they were all—like Memucan—looking for a way to bolster the king's ego since his honor had been besmirched by Vashti. The decree was promulgated by "letters," and the author is careful to point out the letters were not written in the usual language for official correspondence, Aramaic, but "to each province in its own script and to each ethnic group in its own language." Not only did the Persians have a general policy of respecting each locality's ethnic identity, but in this case the king's order was implemented by every nationality. By addressing people in their local languages, the decree was made to suit every household. The command decried every man was to "be master of his own household" (*śōrēr bəbêtô*). The verb translated "be master" (Hb. *śōrēr*) derives from the same root as the word for "official" (*śār*; 1:3, 11, 14, 16, 18; 2:18; 3:1, 12; 5:11; 6:9; 8:9; 9:3). In effect, each man functioned as the king's official within his own household. Since many of the men throughout the empire spoke little or no Aramaic, each man was allowed to carry out this command by speaking "in the language of his own people" (*kilšôn 'ammô*).[22]

THEOLOGY

While on the surface this first major incident in Esther appears to be a secular account of an incident in the Persian court, it plays an important role in the author's understated message about God's sovereignty over human actions. The power and glory of the Persian king (1:4) on display through sumptuous furnishings (1:6) and conspicuous consumption (1:7–8) is humiliated by a simple act of the queen's refusing the king's order. The honor and majesty so promiscuously displayed turns into humiliation as the result of one woman's rebuff of the king's eunuchs and their message from him. Despite the official pomposity of the Persian court and its powerful monarch, the entire world order of Persia could be thrown into chaos by God's use of one person, even though it may not yet be clear to the reader God exercised control in Persia through the actions of humans.

---

[22] Since this phrase is omitted in OG, many critics argue that it was a later gloss added to the MT. But this misses the comedy injected into the situation by the deputizing of all men to be the king's officials in his own house. See Theodor Herzl Gaster, "Esther 1:22," *JBL* 69 (1950): 381.

Moreover, the reaction of Ahasuerus and his advisors shows them to be insecure and petty magistrates seeking to assert their control over the women of the empire. They are interested only in preserving their own self-esteem through deposing the queen and persuading the king to issue a grandiose decree. The king and his advisors need to reduce women to objects to be administered by men rather than treating them as persons who should be wed to kind and caring husbands and fathers (see Eph 5:25–28; 6:4; Col 3:19, 21). Their outlandish overreaction to Vashti's action indicts all the women of the royal court before they had done anything wrong. It speaks to the insecurities within the men's frail egos. This, too, is a subtle but powerful theological indictment. These men find their security by the demonstration and declaration of power instead of by seeking security in the only One who can provide it eternally: the God who desires to save all people from their sinful self-absorption (Ezek 33:11; John 6:40; 1 Tim 2:3–4; 2 Pet 3:9).

2.4 Ahasuerus's Search for a New Queen (2:1–20)

The account of how Esther became the new queen occupies most of chap. 2. This section is highly structured, with several echoes reinforcing items the author considers important:

1. Preparation of the maidens for the king (2:1–4, 12–14). Linking word: "beauty treatment/cosmetics" (2:3, 9; *tamrûq*)

2. Esther in the harem/Esther before Ahasuerus (2:8–9, 16–18). Linking phrases: "Esther was taken" (*wattilāqaḥ 'estēr*; 2:8, 16); "gained his favor/won more favor" (*wattiśśā' ḥeśed*; 2:9, 17)

3. Esther and Mordecai (2:10–12, 19–20); Linking concept: Mordecai's action (walking, sitting; 2:11, 19); Linking comment: Esther did not reveal her ethnicity or family at Mordecai's command (2:10, 20)[23]

In addition, there is a parenthetical section (2:5–7) introducing Mordecai and Esther.

---

[23] Jonathan Jacobs, "Characterizing Esther from the Outset: The Contribution of the Story in Esther 2:1–20," *JHebS* 8 (2008): 4–5, https://jhsonline.org/index.php/jhs/article/view/6214.

The main theme of the narrative centers on Esther's replacement of Vashti, mentioned twice: the first, when the plan to find Vashti's replacement is suggested (2:4), and second, when Esther replaced Vasthi (2:17).[24] The contrast between Esther and the other women leads to her eventual selection as queen (2:17). Contrasting descriptions of the other women and Esther, as well as repetition of Esther's pleasing character, distinguishes her from the numerous candidates:

> During the year before each young woman's turn to go to King Ahasuerus, the harem regulation required her to receive *beauty treatments* with oil of myrrh for six months and then with perfumes and cosmetics for another six months. *When the young woman would go to the king, she was given whatever she requested* to take with her from the harem to the palace. (2:12–13)
>
> **The young woman pleased him and gained his favor** so that he accelerated the process of the *beauty treatments* and the special diet that she received. He assigned seven hand-picked female servants to her from the palace and transferred her and her servants to the harem's best quarters. . . .*When her turn came to go to the king, she did not ask for anything* except what Hegai, the king's eunuch, keeper of the women, suggested. **Esther gained favor in the eyes of everyone who saw her.** (2:9, 15)

In addition, the chapter describes a budding partnership between Esther and Mordecai, with Esther on the inside of the palace and Mordecai on the outside until his eventual elevation to Haman's former position of prime minister (8:1–2). The partnership is one of equal participation, signified by the almost equal use of their names in the book: Mordecai is mentioned 58 times by name and Esther 56 times.[25] Moreover, Esther will appear in every subsequent chapter with Mordecai except chaps. 3 and 10. Clearly, the author is signaling Esther's position and contribution to the triumph of her people over their enemies is as important as Mordecai's.

---

[24] Note the similar wording: תִּמְלֹךְ תַּחַת וַשְׁתִּי ("she shall reign in place of Vashti"; 2:4) and וַיַּמְלִיכֶהָ תַּחַת וַשְׁתִּי ("he made her reign in place of Vashti"; 2:17).

[25] Esther is mentioned 55 times by the name "Esther" and once by the name "Hadassah" (2:7).

2.4.1   The King's Courtiers Suggest a Search for a New Queen (2:1–4)

¹ Some time later, when King Ahasuerus's rage had cooled down, he remembered Vashti, what she had done, and what was decided against her. ² The king's personal attendants suggested, "Let a search be made for beautiful young virgins for the king. ³ Let the king appoint commissioners in each province of his kingdom, so that they may gather all the beautiful young virgins to the harem at the fortress of Susa. Put them under the supervision of Hegai, the king's eunuch, keeper of the women, and give them the required beauty treatments. ⁴ Then the young woman who pleases the king will become queen instead of Vashti." This suggestion pleased the king, and he did accordingly.

2:1 This section begins with a vague chronological notice "[s]ome time later" (*'aḥar haddǝbārîm hā'ēlleh*) the king's anger "cooled." It is unclear how much time has passed to implement the plan suggested by his attendants and choose Esther as queen four years after Vashti's deposition (see 1:3 with 2:16).²⁶ Esther 7:10, using the same verb root (*śqq*), seems to indicate Ahasuerus's temper cooled quickly.

The author notes when the king's anger abated, he recalled Vashti, her act, and her punishment (v. 1). From antiquity some held Ahasuerus longed for Vashti again—since "he remembered" her, while others maintained he focused on his rejection of her.²⁷ It is most probable Ahasuerus experienced mixed emotions about Vashti. He may have longingly remembered her beauty, but he also remembered her act which brought him humiliation. Moreover, he recalled his own decree, which meant he was prohibited any access to her. The picture is probably one of frustration since he lost his queen because of her refusal to obey his order as well as because of his own decree.

2:2–4 Sensing Ahasuerus's frustration, his "attendants" proposed a way of implementing the decree declaring Vashti's position would be transferred to another (1:19). The search was made throughout his vast realm for "beautiful young virgins" (*nǝ'ārôt bǝtûlôt ṭôbôt mar'eh*). The emphasis is on replacing Vashti's beauty, using the same Hebrew idiom (lit., "good appearance") that describes her in 1:11. It appears everyone among Ahasuerus's servants was catering to his

---

²⁶ Two of those years saw Ahasuerus's campaign to conquer Greece, and he would have been away from Susa at that time.

²⁷ For the pros and cons of these positions, see the discussion in Linafelt and Beal, *Ruth and Esther*, 18–19.

desire for beautiful things. Thus, the women who will be gathered are valued only for their outward beauty, reinforcing the error made when Ahasuerus treated Vashti as a beautiful object.

The English word *virgin*—a woman who has not experienced sexual intercourse—is not necessarily an accurate reflection of the Hebrew word (*bətûlâ*).[28] Related words in cognate languages such as Akkadian and Ugaritic do not always denote a virginal woman. Instead, they often refer to a woman's age, not her sexual status: she is a young woman of marriageable age, not prepubescent and not beyond her childbearing years. The same is true for Hebrew, which explains the phrase modifying the word *bətûlâ* at Judg 21:12, "who had not been intimate with a man" (*'ăšer lō' yādʿâ ' îš*), which would otherwise seem superfluous (see also Gen 24:16, Judg 11:39).[29] Moreover, the young women vying to become Ahasuerus's queen are called "virgins" at 2:19 *after they have spent a night with the king*, indicating the Hebrew term does not denote sexual inexperience, leading the reader to conclude the emphasis in the search for a new queen is to find beautiful young women of marriageable age. While it was probably assumed many, if not all of them, were virginal when they were originally brought into the harem, the Hebrew text does not explicitly say that they were.

The suggestion to scour the provinces indicates an extensive "search," since there were 127 of them (1:1). The implication was Ahasuerus would be presented with many beautiful women not only from Persia but from exotic faraway places such as Egypt and India. The women were gathered under the supervision of Hegai, first mentioned here (see also 2:8, 15). He is characterized as understanding the king's preferences in women, and Ahasuerus's attendants relied on him to guide the king in his choice of a pleasing partner who would allow him to forget Vashti. The year of "beauty treatments" would allow time for Hegai to influence the king's decision. Ahasuerus, of course, is usually presented as easily persuaded and manipulated by others, as is the case here. He accepts his attendants' suggestion rather than relying on his own plan.

---

[28] Gordon J. Wenham, "*Bᵉtûlāh*, a Girl of Marriageable Age," *VT* 22 (1972): 326–48.

[29] Hebrew: נַעֲרָה בְתוּלָה אֲשֶׁר לֹא־יָדְעָה אִישׁ לְמִשְׁכָּב, "a young virgin who has not known a man's bed." Wenham notes a similar phrase in Akkadian (Wenham, "Girl of Marriageable Age," 328).

2.4.2 Mordecai and Esther Introduced (2:5–7)

⁵ In the fortress of Susa, there was a Jewish man named Mordecai son of Jair, son of Shimei, son of Kish, a Benjaminite. ⁶ Kish had been taken into exile from Jerusalem with the other captives when King Nebuchadnezzar of Babylon took King Jeconiah of Judah into exile. ⁷ Mordecai was the legal guardian of his cousin Hadassah (that is, Esther), because she had no father or mother. The young woman had a beautiful figure and was extremely good-looking. When her father and mother died, Mordecai had adopted her as his own daughter.

This introduction of Mordecai and Esther represents a parenthetical insertion into the narrative, signaled in 2:5 with unusual word order. The verse begins with the subject rather than a verb, causing the reader to pause. Esther 2:8 then initiates a new narrative sequence with the verb *wayəhî* introducing a temporal clause: "When the king's command . . ." This parenthetical insertion provides background information illuminating the significance of the two important characters in the narrative.

2:5–6 Mordecai is identified as a Jewish man, suggesting his ethnic identity is significant to the story. His genealogy lists three generations preceding him. Mordecai's name derives from the Babylonian god Marduk. During this era and later it was not uncommon for Jews to bear Babylonian names. The name *Mordecai* is attested at least twice more as belonging to other Jewish men. One of these is a man who accompanied Zerubbabel to Jerusalem (Ezra 2:2; Neh 7:7), and the other, a man named in an inscription on the portal of a Jewish burial in Alexandria, Egypt, lived from 200 to 150 BC.[30]

The name *Marduka*, the Babylonian equivalent of *Mordecai*, is found in an inscription from the last years of Darius I or the early years of Ahasuerus. This Marduka is described as an accountant from Susa on a mission authorized by the royal court. Carey A. Moore notes,

> This Marduka could be the biblical Mordecai because, in all likelihood, Mordecai was an official of the king *prior* to his being invested in 8:2 with the powers previously conferred on Haman (cf. also 8:15; 9:4; and 10:2). The reason for our saying this is

---

[30] William Horbury, "The Name Mardochaeus in a Ptolemaic Inscription," *VT* 41 (1991): 220-6. The name is preserved in Greek as ΜΑΡΔΟΧΑΙΟΣ.

that Mordecai is regularly described as one who "sat at the King's Gate" (2:19; 5:13; 6:10); and according to Xenophon, *Cyropaedia* VIII.1, 6 and Herodotus, *History* III,120, Persian officials had to stay at the gate of the royal palace.[31]

While there is no way to be certain the man mentioned in the inscription is the Mordecai of the book of Esther, it is intriguing that both men were royal officials living in Susa.

The name of Mordecai's father *Jair* occurs seven other times, most often denoting men from the tribe of Manasseh who lived in Gilead (Num 32:41; Deut 3:14; Judg 10:3, 5; 1 Kgs 4:13; 1 Chr 2:22; 20:5). Mordecai's grandfather's name *Shimei* is a common Old Testament name, occurring forty-three times. The most notable Shimei was the Benjaminite from Saul's family who cursed King David (2 Sam 16:5–13). The name of Mordecai's great-grandfather, *Kish*, was borne by several men in the OT. The most recognizable of them was the father of Saul, Israel's first king (1 Sam 9:1).

Critical scholars often use the reference to someone being "taken into exile" as evidence of the unhistorical nature of Esther. It is often assumed the Kish and Shimei mentioned are distant ancestors of Mordecai, the father of Saul and the Saulide who cursed David. It is also assumed 2:6 refers to Mordecai's own exile to Babylon.[32] This creates a problem for the historicity of Esther, since if Mordecai was exiled with Jeconiah in 597 BC, he would have been more than 100 years old during Ahasuerus's reign, and Esther would have been beyond childbearing age. But there is no need to assume the Shimei and Kish mentioned in Mordecai's genealogy are not his literal grandfather and great-grandfather. The author most likely chose to list three generations preceding Mordecai's because two of the names would have naturally led readers to recall Saul, the king of Israel from the tribe of Benjamin who was ordered to attack the Amalekites. The Shimei and Kish in Mordecai's genealogy need not be of earlier distant generations to function in this way.

While the Hebrew relative pronoun *'ašer* often refers to a person at the head of a list, it not infrequently refers to someone at the end of

---

[31] Carey A. Moore, "Archaeology and the Book of Esther," *BA* 38 (1975): 74.

[32] Fox, *Character and Ideology*, 29; Moore, *Esther*, 20. The CSB translates it, "Kish had been taken," but in a footnote indicates that the Hebrew text says, "He had been taken."

the list (e.g., 2 Sam 4:8).[33] One other example of this use occurs in Esth 2:15: "Esther was the daughter of Abihail, the uncle of Mordecai *who had adopted her as his own daughter*" (emphasis added). Clearly, the phrase in italics refers to Mordecai at the end of the list, not to Esther at the beginning of the list or to Abihail in the middle. Therefore, it seems logical 2:6 refers to Kish, Mordecai's grandfather who was exiled with Jeconiah. In support of this, at the beginning of 2:5 Mordecai is identified as a Jew while Kish at the end of the list is identified as "a Benjaminite."[34] It was the man from the tribe of Benjamin who was exiled (i.e., Kish); but during the exile and beyond, all the descendants of the exiles came to be known as Jews (*yəhûdîm*) because their ancestors came from the former kingdom of Judah (see Neh 3:33–34; 5:1, 8; 6:6; 13:23).

2:7 Esther is introduced through Mordecai, since he "adopted" his younger cousin when she was orphaned.[35] The adoption of Esther is the only mention of a girl being adopted in the Old Testament. While adoption is sometimes a picture used to describe God's choosing his people (e.g., Exod 4:22; Jer 3:19; Hos 11:1), the only other human adoption in the Old Testament is Jacob's adoption of Joseph's sons: Ephraim and Manasseh (Gen 48:5).

We are told that Esther's Hebrew name was "Hadassah," the feminine form of the Hebrew term for the myrtle tree (*myrtus communis*; Neh 8:15; Isa 41:19; 55:13; Zech 1:8, 10, 11). Her Persian name *Esther* derives from the Old Persian word *stâra*, meaning "star."[36] This might have been a reference to the white, star-shaped flowers of the myrtle.

Esther certainly met the qualifications for recruitment into the harem since she is depicted as having "a beautiful figure" (*yəpat tō'ar*) and as "extremely good-looking" (*wəṭôbat mar'eh*), a description

---

[33] Aaron Koller, "The Exile of Kish: Syntax and History in Esther 2.5-6," *JSOT* 37 (2012): 53–54.

[34] Bush, *Ruth, Esther*, 363.

[35] Paul notes that Hebrew phrase לְקָחָהּ מָרְדֳּכַי לוֹ לְבַת, "Mordecai took her to himself for a daughter" and the similar phrase at 2:15 (לְקַח־לוֹ לְבַת, "he took [her] to himself for a daughter") is "strikingly similar to a standard adoption formula employed in Mesopotamia, *ana mārūtti leqû*, "to take into the status of sonship." Shalom M. Paul, "Adoption Formulae: A Study of Cuneiform and Biblical Legal Clauses," *Maarav* 2 (1980): 181–82.

[36] The opinion that the name *Esther* is derived from that of the Babylonian goddess Ishtar is untenable on linguistic grounds. See Ran Zadok, "Notes on Esther," *ZAW* 98 (1986): 107.

reminiscent of the attractiveness of Rachel (Gen 29:17) and her son Joseph (Gen 39:6).

2.4.3   Esther Taken into the King's Harem (2:8-11)

[8] When the king's command and edict became public knowledge and when many young women were gathered at the fortress of Susa under Hegai's supervision, Esther was taken to the palace, into the supervision of Hegai, keeper of the women. [9] The young woman pleased him and gained his favor so that he accelerated the process of the beauty treatments and the special diet that she received. He assigned seven hand-picked female servants to her from the palace and transferred her and her servants to the harem's best quarters.

[10] Esther did not reveal her ethnicity or her family background, because Mordecai had ordered her not to make them known. [11] Every day Mordecai took a walk in front of the harem's courtyard to learn how Esther was doing and to see what was happening to her.

Date: Shebat-Tebeth (February-December) 479 BC

2:8-9 The narrative resumes with the gathering of the "young women" to Susa. Hegai is mentioned twice in verse 8. The first time notes Hegai followed the suggestion of Ahasuerus's attendants (2:3), and the second time (2:8) notes Esther was no exception—she, too, "was taken" into Ahasuerus's harem with the other young women. Esther's rise because she "pleased" Hegai is similar in description to the rise of Joseph in Egypt (Gen 39:4) and Daniel in Babylon (Dan 1:9). The major difference is that Esther's pleasing Hegai is not explicitly connected by the author to God's action. In addition, Esther is depicted as actively working to gain Hegai's favor. The Hebrew idiom *naśā' ḥesed*, "lift up kindness," translated as "gained his favor," occurs only in Esther (also at 2:15, 17) and refers to Ether's activities as she sought the favor of Hegai and later Ahasuerus. Esther is not pictured as a passive participant in the competition process to identify a new queen. Instead, she endeavored to win the favor of Hegai. Her skill in doing so is signaled by Hegai's reaction: he "accelerated" her preparations for presentation to the king, and he "assigned" her choice female attendants and the "best quarters" among the royal harem. Esther is depicted as a clever, resourceful, and ambitious young woman with whom Hegai was impressed. He recognized in Esther the type of woman who would be able to fill the void in Ahasuerus's marital life, so he ensured she was groomed to be the next queen.

2:10–11 Esther's withholding of information about her ethnic and family connections followed Mordecai's instructions. Esther's obedience demonstrated her respect for Mordecai, who served as a surrogate father to her (see 2:7, 15; Exod 20:12; Matt 15:4; Mark 7:10; Luke 18:20; Eph 6:2). She also understood he had a better insight into the workings of Ahasuerus's court and its political intrigue than she had. The text does not explicitly state a reason Mordecai gave Esther this command, but Mordecai's prohibition may be related to his position among Ahasuerus's subjects in Susa.[37]

Mordecai's daily inquiry concerning Esther's welfare demonstrated his parental concern for her and provides the reader a first glimpse into Mordecai's status at the royal court of Susa. Not everyone could gain access to the harem courtyard; that Mordecai could signals that he was not simply an ordinary inhabitant of Susa.

2.4.4   The Procedure for Choosing a New Queen (2:12–14)

[12] *During the year before each young woman's turn to go to King Ahasuerus, the harem regulation required her to receive beauty treatments with oil of myrrh for six months and then with perfumes and cosmetics for another six months.* [13] *When the young woman would go to the king, she was given whatever she requested to take with her from the harem to the palace.* [14] *She would go in the evening, and in the morning she would return to a second harem under the supervision of the king's eunuch Shaashgaz, keeper of the concubines. She never went to the king again, unless he desired her and summoned her by name.*

2:12 The preparations for the young women of the harem were as lavish as Ahasuerus's banquets in chap. 1. Each was to have a turn to "go to King Ahasuerus." The phrase "go to" (Hb. *bô' 'el*) is a euphemism for entering someone's room for purposes of sexual intercourse.[38] It occurs twice more in this context (2:13, 14). The mention

---

[37] The Hebrew term מוֹלֶדֶת (*môledet*) can refer to either one's native land or one's family. For a use in the sense of *family, relatives,* see Gen 43:7.

[38] Bush, *Ruth, Esther,* 253, 365. Many English versions translate this idiom into English as "go in to." Bush notes that such translations "are unfortunate in that they are doubtless understood by English speakers to refer to the act of coitus itself, hence, hardly a euphemism!" While

of "oil of myrrh" also implies these women were being prepared to satisfy the king's sexual appetite, as myrrh is often mentioned in Song of Songs with implications of sexual desire (Song 1:13; 3:6; 4:6, 14; 5:1, 5, 13; see also Prov 7:17, although the context in Prov 7—unlike in Song or Esther—is one of illicit sexual activity).

2:13–14 In order to allow each woman the best opportunity to please the king, the woman was supplied with "whatever she requested" when she was taken to "the palace." While in English this conveys the impression it was a separate building, this phrase (in Hb. *bêt hammelek*, "house of the king") likely refers to the area regularly used by him in the same palace complex as the harem. Some commentators believe this to specifically refer to the king's private quarters.[39] Berlin, however, points out the phrase is used elsewhere of the more public formal rooms of the palace (5:1; 6:4).[40]

The woman's return would be to "a second harem," this one for the king's concubines. The word *second* (*šēnî*) has presented problems for interpreters since it does not fit the sentence grammatically. Some argue the word must indicate the woman "would return *again* to the harem."[41] But there is little evidence the Hebrew ordinal number *second* can be used in the sense of *again*. Many understand the word as translated in CSB: the woman "would return to a second harem."[42] This is supported by the mention of a second eunuch, "Shaashgaz, keeper of the concubines."

The institution of concubinage was a form of marriage. Concubines were wives a man acquired without paying a bride price for them as he would for a regular wife. While concubines had a lower status, they were still considered wives. Since a man acquired a concubine as a wife without the bride price, it was customary her children would not share in any inheritance with the sons of full wives. Nevertheless at times a man may have given gifts to his sons by his concubines before he died in lieu of an inheritance (Gen 25:5–6).

---

this euphemism is most often used with men as the subject of the verb, it can be used of women (Gen 19:34; 2 Sam 11:4).

[39] Bush, *Ruth, Esther,* 365; Lewis Bayles Paton, *A Critical and Exegetical Commentary on the Book of Esther,* ICC (New York: Scribner's, 1916), *Esther,* 179; Moore, *Esther,* 21; Fox, *Character and Ideology,* 276.

[40] Berlin, *Esther,* 29.

[41] E.g., Bush, *Ruth, Esther,* 365–6.

[42] This interpretation is at least as old as OG: εἰς τὸν γυναικῶνα τὸν δεύτερον, "to the second harem."

Finally, the author notes after having her one turn with the king, a woman would not see him again unless "summoned" by name (see 4:11). While life in a king's harem may have provided a number of material comforts most women might never have afforded otherwise, it also could be a cruel institution, depriving a woman of the companionship of a mate as God intended for marriage.

2.4.5   Esther Chosen as the New Queen (2:15–18)

15 Esther was the daughter of Abihail, the uncle of Mordecai who had adopted her as his own daughter. When her turn came to go to the king, she did not ask for anything except what Hegai, the king's eunuch, keeper of the women, suggested. Esther gained favor in the eyes of everyone who saw her.

16 She was taken to King Ahasuerus in the palace in the tenth month, the month Tebeth, in the seventh year of his reign. 17 The king loved Esther more than all the other women. She won more favor and approval from him than did any of the other virgins. He placed the royal crown on her head and made her queen in place of Vashti. 18 The king held a great banquet for all his officials and staff. It was Esther's banquet. He freed his provinces from tax payments and gave gifts worthy of the king's bounty.

Date: Tebeth 479/478 BC (December 479 BC or January 478 BC)

2:15 Esther's lineage and family connections are mentioned by the author immediately before she is taken to the king. Esther was commanded by Mordecai not to reveal her ethnicity or family (2:10), and even after she had been made queen she did not tell anyone (2:20); nevertheless, the omniscient reader already knows her origins. The name of Esther's father, Abihail, was shared by two other Israelite men in the Scriptures (Num 3:35; 1 Chr 5:14).[43]

That Esther did not bring with her anything other than what Hegai suggested depicts her submissive, pliable personality.[44] Nevertheless, it also demonstrates Esther's active choice not only to trust Hegai knew what pleased Ahasuerus but also to "gain favor" with everyone. The

---

[43] Two women in the Scriptures had a similar name, also written *Abihail* in English but slightly different in Hebrew (אֲבִיהַיִל; the men's name is אֲבִיחַיִל).

[44] Fox, *Character and Ideology in the Book of Esther,* 37.

phrase translated "gained favor" (nōśēʾt ḥēn) differs from the one used at 2:9, implying Esther gained a certain popularity with everyone. The phrase used earlier implies that she gained Hegai's support.

2:16–18 Esther here is transported to the palace as the other young women were. The phrase for "palace," *bêt malkûtô* (lit. "his royal house"), differs from the similar phrase used at 2:13. Nevertheless, the two phrases appear to be alternate ways of referring to the area of the palace complex frequented by the king, as shown by the use of both to describe the area where Ahasuerus's throne room was (5:1).[45]

The author, who may have had access to the royal Persian records, identifies the specific month these events took place. The name of the month, "Tebeth," was borrowed from the Babylonian name for the tenth month in the ancient lunisolar calendar generally used in the ancient Near East. This name for the tenth month occurs only here in the OT. During this period of time, the Jews were gradually adopting the Babylonian names for months as demonstrated not only later in Esther (3:12–13; 8:9, 12; 9:1, 15, 17–19, 21) but also by Ezra and Nehemiah (Ezra 6:15; Neh 1:1; 2:1; 6:15).[46]

Ahasuerus is described as loving "Esther more than all the other women" (wayyeʾĕhab hammelek et ʾestēr mikol hannāšîm). Like the English word *love*, the Hebrew word *ʾahēb* can have a variety of meanings. It often denotes a strong emotional bond. It may, however, signal an infatuation (as in the case of Amnon's attraction to Tamar; 2 Sam 13:1) or a preference for one person over another (Deut 21:15–17). Here, since Esther is portrayed as winning "more favor and approval from [Ahasuerus] than did any of the other virgins," the word appears to involve more than simply sexual attraction on Ahasuerus's part. Yet the king's affections may have fallen short of the ideal type of love a husband ought to have toward his wife (Eph 5:25–28) since at this point in their relationship his feelings appear to be based on one night's encounter in Ahasuerus's private quarters.

---

[45] At 5:1 CSB attempts to distinguish between the two phrases, translating בֵּית־הַמֶּלֶךְ as "palace" and בֵּית הַמַּלְכוּת as "royal courtroom." But if this is the case, then Esther was taken to the royal courtroom, not Ahasuerus's private quarters, which appears unlikely.

[46] Before the Babylonian captivity, months were generally referred to by number, though in a few cases the Canaanite name for the month might be given (Exod 13:4; 23:15; 34:18; Deut 16:1; 1 Kgs 6:1, 37–38; 8:2). See Andrew E. Steinmann, From Abraham to Paul: A Biblical Chronology (St. Louis: Concordia, 2011), 13–16.

The process of replacing Vashti was completed when the king placed the "crown" on Esther's head and "made her queen." This implies a formal, public ceremony at which Esther appeared wearing the crown Vashti refused to don when commanded by Ahasuerus to display her beauty to his party guests (Esth 1:11). The author immediately follows the description of Esther's coronation with news of a party for the royal officials, drawing an even more pointed comparison between Esther and Vashti. In this instance, Esther did not need to leave her banquet to be presented at Ahasuerus's banquet as Vashti was previously commanded. She was already at "Esther's banquet" (*mištēh 'estēr*). Once again, the celebration featured the king's generosity, including freedom from taxes and the bestowal of gifts. While a complete freedom from taxes—even for a while—seems strange to modern readers, the Persians were known at times to offer such tax relief.[47]

2.4.6   Mordecai and Esther in the King's Service (2:19–23)

[19] *When the virgins were gathered a second time, Mordecai was sitting at the King's Gate.* [20] *Esther still did not reveal her family background or her ethnicity, as Mordecai had directed. She obeyed Mordecai's orders, as she always had while he raised her.*

[21] *During those days while Mordecai was sitting at the King's Gate, Bigthan and Teresh, two of the king's eunuchs who guarded the entrance, became infuriated and planned to assassinate King Ahasuerus.* [22] *When Mordecai learned of the plot, he reported it to Queen Esther, and she told the king on Mordecai's behalf.* [23] *When the report was investigated and verified, both men were hanged on the gallows. This event was recorded in the Historical Record in the king's presence.*

2:19–20 The gathering of the virgins "a second time" has presented problems for interpreters.[48] Some wish to emend the text, while others have suggested interpretations raising more problems than they solve. Michael Fox offers a solution which takes the Hebrew text seriously:

---

[47] One such instance is related in Herodotus, *Histories*, 3.67.3.

[48] For a survey of suggestions, see Paton, *A Critical and Exegetical Commentary on the Book of Esther*, 186–87, and Bush, *Ruth, Esther*, 372.

"Second" refers to a gathering into the second harem. . . . We should note that whether "second" in verse 14 refers to "women's house" or is adverbial ("a second time"), there *is* a second harem or a second division of the harem, for the women now have a different keeper. . . . When the women return to the harem they are under the supervision of a different eunuch, Shaashgaz, for they are now officially "concubines," having slept with the king.[49]

The problem with Fox's solution is 2:14 depicts the women entering the second harem individually, not all at once. Another interpretation which understands the Hebrew text of 2:19 as genuine is offered by Frederic Bush: "[W]e interpret the clause as it stands to be a further sarcastic depiction of the king and court by implying that the king continued gathering of concubines even after the choice of queen had been made."[50] This interpretation might explain 4:11 where Esther states she had "not been summoned" to see the king for "thirty days." Perhaps he was too busy with other women—a second group gathered after Esther became queen.

Whatever the reason for the second gathering of young women, the author now tells us Mordecai was "at the King's Gate." The presence of Mordecai at this spot—perhaps synecdoche for the administrative precincts of the palace[51]—presents him as being in service to the royal court in some capacity. This is the second clue Mordecai was not simply a resident of Susa but had access to the royal court by holding some position in the king's administration (see 2:11). It may also explain why once again we are told Esther did not reveal her ethnic or family identity. The text implies she *continued* to keep it a secret even after becoming queen.[52]

2:21–23 The account of the plot by "Bigthan and Teresh" is written with little embellishment. While the reader is told they were furious with the king, the text does not identify the reason for their anger. Given the context, perhaps the author implies they were infuriated the king continued to amass young women for his harem even after naming a queen, weary of his excessive pursuit of pleasure. As palace

---

49 Fox, *Character and Ideology*, 38.

50 Bush, *Ruth, Esther*, 372.

51 Hans Peter Rüger, "'*Das Tor Des Königs'—Der Königliche Hof*," Bib 50 (1969): 247–50.

52 Note the participle 2:20 מַגֶּדֶת, which should be understood as "Esther was still not telling" (see NET, TANAKH).

gatekeepers they would have witnessed the entrance of the second group of women into the harem.

We are not told how Mordecai learned of their assassination plan either. Characteristic of much of his storytelling technique, the author uses a passive construction: "When Mordecai learned of the plot" (*wayyiwwāda' haddābār ləmordŏkay*). No matter how he learned of the scheme, Mordecai passed the information to Esther who conveyed it to the king. Esther's role as intermediary may indicate Mordecai was not of sufficient rank in Ahasuerus's court to gain an audience with him. This becomes the first time in the book where Esther and Mordecai are depicted as working in tandem.

Consequently, the king sentenced the two eunuchs to death by hanging. There remains a difference of opinion, however, concerning the meaning of the Hebrew phrase "hung on a pole/gallows" (*wayit-tālû . . . 'al 'ēṣ*). Some English versions understand this to be execution by hanging (CSB, ESV, NET, NRSV), while others understand it to mean the men were executed and then their bodies were impaled on poles as an example to others (GW, NIV, TANAKH). In fact, there is little evidence the Persians practiced execution by hanging. On the other hand, Herodotus several times mentions Persians, including Ahasuerus, impaling corpses.[53] Moreover, the practice of impalement or otherwise publicly displaying the corpse of an executed person is also mentioned several times in the Old Testament (Deut 21:22–23; Josh 8:29; 10:26; 1 Sam 31:10; 2 Sam 4:12; 21:12; 1 Chr 10:10).

This event in Esth 2:21–23 foreshadows the events in chap. 6. Not only was the incident "recorded" in the official records,[54] but the king was present when it was recorded. Mordecai was not immediately rewarded, however. This is a strange omission not only because Persian kings were known for their generous rewards but also because to this point in the book, Ahasuerus has been portrayed as making an ostentatious display of his largesse.[55]

---

[53] Herodotus, *Histories*, 3.125.3; 3.159.1; 4:43.2; 7.238.1.

[54] This must be the same set of records as mentioned at 6:1. But here the description is abbreviated (סֵפֶר דִּבְרֵי הַיָּמִים, "the scroll of the events of the days"), whereas at 6:1, the full title is given (סֵפֶר הַזִּכְרֹנוֹת דִּבְרֵי הַיָּמִים, "the scroll of the memorials of the events of the days").

[55] Fox, *Character and Ideology,* 40 notes, "Herodotus depicts Persian kings as diligent and generous in rewarding beneficial acts (III 139–41, 153; V II; IX 107). In fact, he knows of an official list of the 'King's Benefactors' in the royal archives (III 140) and reports that these benefactors were called 'Orosangs' in Persian (VIII 85). Thucydides, too, testifies to the practice (I 129)."

THEOLOGY

The rise of Esther to become queen prepares readers for the rest of the story where she will wield great influence over the events to come. While she was not a ruler in the sense Ahasuerus was, by virtue of her position as queen to a pliant king, her actions would carry an authority matched or surpassed only by a few others. According to Paul, such responsibility is bestowed by God (Rom 13:1). Civil authority was instituted by God for the purpose of punishing those who do evil and rewarding those who do good (Rom 13:3–4). Esther would do both. Her words would lead to the execution of "this evil Haman" (Esth 7:6) and the elevation of Mordecai as Haman's replacement in Ahasuerus's administration (8:1). As queen, Esther becomes an example to all Christian magistrates of the proper and effective exercise of their responsibilities as authorities in the civil realm.

While Mordecai's rise is yet to come, the first major incident in Esther involving him demonstrates he was a faithful servant of his master. He looked out for Ahasuerus's welfare. Even when he was not recognized for saving the king's life, he asked for no reward or honor. Mordecai becomes an example to all Christians who serve under the authority of others. They are to do what is right because to serve their superiors is to serve God (Eph 6:7; Col 3:23). Their reward ultimately lies not with their human superiors but with God himself (Eph 6:8; see Ps 62:12), although they acknowledge that they deserve no reward for performing the duties God would have them do (Luke 17:10).

SECTION OUTLINE

3 Mordecai Rises to Become Prime Minister (**3:1–8:17**)
   3.1   Haman Made Prime Minister and Mordecai Refuses to Honor Him (3:1–6)
   3.2   With Ahasuerus's Permission, Haman Issues an Edict against the Jews (3:7–15)
      3.2.1 Haman Casts the Pur (3:7)
      3.2.2 Haman Receives Permission to Issue an Edict (3:8–11)
      3.2.3 Haman Issues the Royal Edict against the Jews (3:12–15)
   3.3   Esther Learns Why Mordecai Is Mourning (4:1–9)
      3.3.1 Mordecai and the Jews Mourn because of the Edict (4:1–3)
      3.3.2 Esther Learns of Haman's Plot (4:4–9)
   3.4   Mordecai Persuades Esther to Approach the King (4:10–17)
      3.4.1 Esther's Reason as to Why She Cannot Intervene (4:10–12)
      3.4.2 Mordecai's Reason as to Why Esther Must Intervene (4:13–14)
      3.4.3 Esther Appeals for Support from the Jews before She Intervenes (4:15–17)
   3.5   Esther's First Banquet for Ahasuerus and Haman (5:1–8)
      3.5.1 Esther Approaches Ahasuerus with an Invitation to a Banquet (5:1–5)
      3.5.2 Esther's First Banquet for Ahasuerus and Haman (5:6–8)
   3.6   Haman's Elation at Being a Guest at Esther's Banquet (5:9–14)
      3.6.1 Haman's Elation Is Tempered by Mordecai's Presence in the King's Gate (5:9–13)
      3.6.2 Haman Advised to Eliminate Mordecai with a Public Display of His Power (5:14)
   3.7   Haman Is Humiliated by Having to Honor Mordecai (6:1–14)
      3.7.1 Ahasuerus Learns He Did Not Reward the Man Who Saved His Life (6:1–3)
      3.7.2 Ahasuerus Orders Honors for Mordecai (6:4–10)
      3.7.3 Mordecai Is Honored while Haman Is Humiliated (6:11–14)

3   MORDECAI RISES TO BECOME PRIME MINISTER (3:1–8:17)

This third section of Esther—the second major section of the book—
chronicles the vicissitudes faced by Mordecai and the threats and
benefits they brought to his fellow Jews in the Persian Empire. At
the beginning of this portion of the book, Esther disappears from
the narrative and only Ahasuerus, Haman, and Mordecai appear as
major characters in the unfolding story. Esther 3 features the acts of
Haman. Ahasuerus does little other than promote Haman (3:1), give
Haman his signet ring (3:10), and authorize him to initiate a pogrom
against an ethnic group within the empire (3:11). Mordecai's actions
are also few: he refused to honor Haman (3:2), refused to listen to the
warnings of Ahasuerus's staff (3:4), and told them that he was Jewish
(3:4). Clearly, the author is focusing readers' attention on Haman "the
enemy of the Jews" (3:10; 8:1; see also 9:10, 24).

    The rest of this section then relates the interplay of the actions of
Mordecai, Esther, Haman, Ahasuerus, and a few other individuals.
The major characters by chapter are these:

Esther 3   Ahasuerus, Haman, Mordecai

Esther 4   Mordecai, Esther, Hathach

Esther 5   Esther, Ahasuerus, Haman, Mordecai, Zeresh

Esther 6   Ahasuerus, Haman, Mordecai, Zeresh

Esther 7   Ahasuerus, Haman, Esther, Harbona

Esther 8   Ahasuerus, Esther, Mordecai

None of the principle persons in this section of Esther—Ahasuerus, Haman, Esther, and Mordecai—appear in every chapter. Yet each is critical for the entire story, and their interactions with one another and their reactions to developing events drive the narrative forward. By choosing to relate these contacts among the major persons, the author skillfully unfolds the dramatic rise of Haman to become prime minister. Moreover, the words of people subtly reveal the workings of the unseen force in the story: God. Haman notes the Jews keep "themselves separate" (3:8), a sign of loyalty to God who had separated them from other nations (Lev 20:24, 26; Num 23:9; 1 Kgs 8:53). Mordecai tells Esther, "[P]erhaps you have come to your royal position for such a time as this" (4:14). In 6:13 Zeresh tells Haman of Amalekite (or more specifically, Agagite descent), "Since Mordecai is Jewish, . . . you won't overcome him, because your downfall is certain." That statement leads perceptive readers to recall God's promise and Moses's prophecy at Exod 17:14, 16.

3.1   Haman Made Prime Minister and Mordecai Refuses to Honor Him (3:1–6)

¹ *After all this took place, King Ahasuerus honored Haman, son of Hammedatha the Agagite. He promoted him in rank and gave him a higher position than all the other officials.* ² *The entire royal staff at the King's Gate bowed down and paid homage to Haman, because the king had commanded this to be done for him. But Mordecai would not bow down or pay homage.* ³ *The members of the royal staff at the King's Gate asked Mordecai, "Why are you disobeying the king's command?"* ⁴ *When they had warned him day after day and he still would not listen to them, they told Haman in order to see if Mordecai's actions would be tolerated, since he had told them he was a Jew.*

⁵ *When Haman saw that Mordecai was not bowing down or paying him homage, he was filled with rage.* ⁶ *And when he learned of*

Mordecai's ethnic identity, it seemed repugnant to Haman to do away with Mordecai alone. He planned to destroy all of Mordecai's people, the Jews, throughout Ahasuerus's kingdom.

3:1–2 The phrase "[a]fter this took place" introduces a temporal clause marking the beginning of a new narrative.[1] It serves to place the promotion of Haman sometime after Esther's coronation in late 479 BC or early 478 BC (2:16) but before Haman's casting the Pur on 1 Nisan 474 BC (3:7), a period of four years and three months. No reason is given for Haman's promotion, but it has been suggested it was part of a reorganization of Ahasuerus's administration in the wake of the assassination plot uncovered by Mordecai (2:21–23).[2] Haman was made Ahasuerus's prime minister: he held "a higher position than all the other officials" (*kis'ô mē'al kol haśśārîm*).

Haman's name and the name of his father, "Hammedatha," appear to be Persian names, though there is no agreement on their meanings.[3] More importantly, Haman is labeled as an *Agagite*, a descendant of Agag, the Amalekite king captured by Saul but executed by Samuel when Saul failed to carry out Samuel's order not to spare any Amalekite (1 Sam 15). To readers familiar with prior biblical history, "Agagite" thus portends a struggle between Haman and Mordecai, a man from Saul's tribe, Benjamin.[4]

Immediately after telling of Haman's promotion, the author once again highlights the officiousness of the protocol of the Persian court, noting the king had ordered everyone to kneel and prostrate themselves before Haman.[5] But Mordecai refused.

---

[1] Literally, "after these things" (אַחַר הַדְּבָרִים הָאֵלֶּה).

[2] Tod Linafelt and Timothy K. Beal, *Ruth and Esther*, Berit Olam: Studies in Hebrew Narrative and Poetry (Collegeville: Liturgical Press, 1999), 44.

[3] A. R. Millard, "Persian Names in Esther and the Reliability of the Hebrew Text," *JBL* 96 (1977), 485, notes that the name *Hammedatha* is attested in Persepolis Fortification Tablets as *ha-ma-da-da*. He believes it is derived from Old Persian *amadāta*, meaning "strongly made."

[4] Fox implies that the identification of Haman as an Agagite might be mistaken and cites 1 Chr 4:42–43 as saying the last Amalekites were killed during the days of Hezekiah (Michael Fox, *Character and Ideology in the Book of Esther*, 2nd ed. [Grand Rapids, MI: Eerdmans, 2001], 42). This, however, is a misreading, since 1 Chr 4:43 says that "the remnant of the Amalekites who had escaped" were killed. This is most likely a reference to 1 Chr 4:41 where some Israelites attacked "Hamites" and "Meunites." Thus, 1 Chr 4:43 is speaking only of the Amalekites who escaped that attack, not all Amalekites.

[5] CSB translates this as "bow" and "pay homage." The Hebrew text, however, indicates kneeling (כֹּרְעִים) and prostrating (וּמִשְׁתַּחֲוִים).

The reason for Mordecai's refusal to honor Haman has prompted much explanation as to why he would not obey him.[6] The best explanation notes 3:4 says, "[Mordecai] had told them he was a Jew." Thus, Mordecai refused to bow to Haman, since as a Jew he would never honor an Agagite/Amalekite, since God had condemned Amalek for attacking Israel in the wilderness (Exod 17:8–16).[7]

3:3–4 Apparently, Haman did not notice Mordecai's refusal, perhaps because he was caught up in the adulation and honor he received from everyone else. Haman's oversight implies at this time Mordecai was a minor official in Ahasuerus's service, so Haman would not have noticed Mordecai's slight.

Ahasuerus's servants at the King's Gate noticed Mordecai, however, and we are told they asked why he was ignoring the royal command. Yet Mordecai provides no clear answer; instead, the reader is told the king's servants repeated their warning "day after day" (*yôm wǝyôm*). This common phrase is reminiscent of Gen 39:10, where Potiphar's wife tried day after day to entice Joseph into committing adultery with her.[8] The author is drawing a parallel with Mordecai's commitment to God's prophecy against Amalek.

Ahasuerus's servants at the King's Gate told Haman about Mordecai's behavior in order to see whether Mordecai's insolence "would be tolerated." Their appeal to Haman seems to be a question as to whether Mordecai could claim an exemption from the king's ruling. The final clause of 3:4, "since he had told them he was a Jew," not only hints at Mordecai's answer to their question (i.e., "Jews don't give honor to Amalekites") but also explains why Mordecai revealed his ethnic identity although he instructed Esther not to reveal her ethnicity to the king. Mordecai needed to explain his behavior. The king's officials, it seems, wanted to know whether this reason provided a valid exemption from the king's order or they should seek to force Mordecai to obey.

---

[6] For a summary of the various reasons proposed, see the discussion in Fox, *Character and Ideology*, 43–46.

[7] Fox, *Character and Ideology*, 44; Frederic Bush, *Ruth, Esther*, WBC 9 (Dallas: Word, 1996), 479. Both Fox and Bush call this "tribal enmity" between Jews and Amalekites. Nevertheless, on Mordecai's part it is not so much tribal enmity as it is a commitment to bless those whom God has blessed and curse those whom God has cursed.

[8] Note the parallel language: כְּדַבְּרָהּ אֶל־יוֹסֵף יוֹם יוֹם וְלֹא־שָׁמַע אֵלֶיהָ ("as she spoke to Joseph day after day, but he would not listen to her"; Gen 39:10) and כְּאָמְרָם אֵלָיו יוֹם וָיוֹם וְלֹא שָׁמַע אֲלֵיהֶם ("as they said to him day after day, but he would not listen to them"; 3:4).

3:5–6 Haman's reaction to being informed of Mordecai's disobedience is "rage." Such emotion overrules good sense. To emphasize this, the author employs a play on words between the name "Haman" and the word "rage" (*hāmān hēmah*). In the book of Esther, only Ahasuerus and Haman are described as enraged (1:12; 2:1; 3:5; 5:9; 7:7, 10). In every instance, the emotion leads to precipitous or ill-advised actions, which is why Proverbs repeatedly warns readers about rage and its consequences (Prov 15:18; 19:19; 22:24–25; 29:22).

Instead of seeking to enforce the king's command as might be expected, Haman's concern is his own honor and glory—a moral failing manifesting itself later in the book (Esth 6:6–9). Nowhere are we told he took legal or administrative steps to enforce the royal order. Instead, he took the matter as a personal affront. Moreover, since Mordecai's reason for refusing to bow before Haman was based in his identity as a Jew, Haman wanted to punish all Jews. After all, if one would not bow to him because he was an Agagite of Amalekite origins, then the rest of the Jews also might refuse him the honor he craved. Thus, his plot was designed to have an empire-wide effect.

Haman's solution to seek to "destroy all" Jews because of an offense committed by an individual is reminiscent of Ahasuerus issuing a decree about all women because of the offense given by one woman (1:19–20).[9] Ahasuerus's previous ill-advised decree led to Esther's replacing Vashti. Haman's ill-considered pogrom against the Jews will lead to Mordecai's replacing him. In each case someone prominent in Ahasuerus's inner circle is replaced by a Jew.

3.2   With Ahasuerus's Permission, Haman Issues an Edict Against the Jews (3:7–15)

The implementation of Haman's plot to destroy the Jews throughout the Persian Empire was dependent on two things: the determination of the most favored day for attacking the Jews and Ahasuerus's general indifference to the details of governing. Haman determined the day by casting lots (3:7, 13). He was able to put his plan into action through Ahasuerus's apathy. Haman presents one ethnic group as a threat to the kingdom in general terms, never identifying them. Ahasuerus never questioned Haman's assertions, nor did he ask which people Haman

---

[9] Berlin, *Esther*, 37–38.

wanted destroyed. Even after the order to destroy the Jews was issued, Ahasuerus remained unconcerned. He went about his leisurely life, sitting down to drink with Haman (3:15).

The balance of chap. 3 took place in one month—"the first month" of the ancient lunar calendrical year, "Nisan" (3:7, 12). The events are told in three vignettes in quick succession with little plot development: Haman's casting the pur, Haman's receiving permission, and Haman's issuing his order.

3.2.1   Haman Casts the Pur (3:7)

⁷ *In the first month, the month of Nisan, in King Ahasuerus's twelfth year, the* pur—*that is, the lot—was cast before Haman for each day in each month, and it fell on the twelfth month, the month Adar.*

Date: 1 Nisan (Friday, April 5), 474 BC

3:7 At the beginning of the year, the lot was cast in Haman's presence. This was a common method of divination, and it was not unknown even among the Israelites.[10] Both Herodotus and Xenophon indicate that lots were used among the Persians.[11] Here we learn the word used for *lot* was *"pur,"* a form of the Old Babylonian word for lot.[12] Since the lot "was cast" in Haman's presence, it is likely the person actually casting lots was a diviner or priest of some sort. The text portrays this event as happening "in the first month." Haman was trying to determine which day or days were most propitious to enact his revenge on Mordecai and the Jews. Thus, it was probably the first day of the year, the first day of Nisan, so every day could be included.

The name "Nisan" for the first lunar month of the Jewish calendar was borrowed from the Babylonian name for this month. It is used

---

[10] Leviticus 16:8; Num 26:52–56; Josh 18:6, 8, 10; 1 Chr 24:31; 25:8; 26:13–14; Neh 10:34; 11:1; Ezek 24:6; Joel 3:3; Obad 1:11; Mic 2:5. Casting lots was used by the apostles after praying that God would choose a successor for Judas (Acts 1:26). This apparently was done with faith that even something as seemingly random as rolling dice is ultimately controlled by God (Prov 16:33).

[11] Herodotus, *Histories*, 3.128.1; Xenophon, *Cyropaedia*, 4.5.55. For an English text of Xenophon's *Cyropaedia*, see volumes 5 and 6 in Walter Miller, *Xenophon in Seven Volumes*, LCL (Cambridge: Harvard University, 1914). Available online at http://www.perseus.tufts.edu/hopper/text?doc=Perseus%3atext%3a1999.01.0204.

[12] William W. Hallo, "The First Purim," *BA* 46 (1983): 21.

here and at Neh 2:1. Before the Babylonian exile, this month was called "Abib" (Exod 13:4; 23:15; 34:18; Deut 16:1). The name given for the twelfth month, "Adar," was also adopted from the Babylonian name for the month and occurs in the Old Testament only in books written after the Babylonian exile (Ezra 6:15; Esth 3:7, 13; 8:12; 9:1, 15, 17, 19, 21).

The last part of this verse is difficult in Hebrew and has been interpreted in various ways.[13] Some English versions, in a fashion similar to CSB, see the text as indicating the lots were cast for each day of the year and the lot chose a particular day in the twelfth month, Adar, which is later revealed to be "the thirteenth day of Adar" (3:13; see NET, NIV, NRSV, TANAKH). Other translations understand the text as saying the lot was cast for each day of the year from the first month to the twelfth month, Adar (see ESV, GW). With that reading, this verse does not designate which month or day was chosen. Instead, the verse says a lot was cast for every day of the year. Considering no day is specified in this verse, it seems the latter interpretation is more likely, and the verse should be understood as saying "The pur . . . was cast for each day and each month up to the twelfth month Adar." If this is the case, the lots may have indicated several days which were key for Haman to implement his plan: the day to approach Ahasuerus with his request (3:8), the day to compose and publish the letter authorizing the destruction of Jews (3:12), and the day when people could attack Jews and confiscate their property with the king's support (3:13).

3.2.2   Haman Receives Permission to Issue an Edict (3:8–11)

⁸ *Then Haman informed King Ahasuerus, "There is one ethnic group, scattered throughout the peoples in every province of your kingdom, keeping themselves separate. Their laws are different from everyone else's and they do not obey the king's laws. It is not in the king's best interest to tolerate them. ⁹ If the king approves, let an order be drawn up authorizing their destruction, and I will pay 375 tons of silver to the officials for deposit in the royal treasury."*

¹⁰ *The king removed his signet ring from his hand and gave it to Haman son of Hammedatha the Agagite, the enemy of the Jews.*

---

[13] The Hebrew reads אֲדָר הוּא־חֹדֶשׁ שְׁנֵים־עָשָׂר לְחֹדֶשׁ וּמֵחֹדֶשׁ לְיוֹם מִיּוֹם, "From day to day, from month to month, twelfth, which is the month of Adar."

¹¹ Then the king told Haman, "The money and people are given to you to do with as you see fit."

3:8–9 Having determined when it was best to put his plan into action, Haman then sought to persuade Ahasuerus to allow him to have them extirpated from the empire. Haman's depiction of the "one ethnic group" he saw as troublesome breaks down into three arguments. First, they are "scattered throughout" the Persian Empire, yet they are "separate." That is, they refuse to assimilate. Second, they have "different" laws from everyone else. This is probably a reference to the various requirements of the law of Moses observed by faithful Jews. Following these most certainly would have set them apart from everyone else and made them seem peculiar. The third argument builds on the second one: they did "not obey the king's laws." Thus, Haman portrays Jews as placing their laws above the imperial law. To many readers this may appear to be slander, since Jews are portrayed as generally disrespectful regarding Persian laws. Indeed, it is an unfair generalization that Haman has presented to the king in order to persuade him. Nevertheless, from Haman's point of view, Jews were disrespectful of Persian law—and his evidence was Mordecai's refusal to give Haman the honor commanded by Ahasuerus. Of course, Haman had already made a prejudicial leap of logic: all Jews needed to be destroyed because they, like Mordecai, would refuse to bow before him, too (see 3:6). Having argued Jews are an insidious threat to the stability of Persian law—and therefore to the crown—and that they constitute a ubiquitous presence in the empire, Haman then states his advice for the king. It is not in the "best interest" of the king to "tolerate" this noncompliant people.

In order to make the appeal more attractive, Haman offered an exorbitant sum to Ahasuerus as an inducement to allow the destruction of this people throughout the empire. The amount he offered—10,000 silver talents ("375 tons" or 340,000 kilograms)—was equivalent to 58 to 68 percent of the annual royal revenue derived from the empire.[14] Haman must have been a very rich man to be able to offer such a sum (5:11). Once again, the author demonstrates his knowledge of Persian

---

[14] Fox, *Character and Ideology*, 51–52. Fox based his figures on information derived from Herodotus, *Histories*, 3.95.1–2, which states that Ahasuerus received 14,560 Euboeic talents in revenue each year.

culture: the word he uses for treasury (*genez*) is a loan word from Old Persian (see also 4:7).

3:10–11 Ahasuerus did not bother to inquire about the accuracy of Haman's statements or to question his advice. As usual, the king left the running of the empire to others. He gave Haman "his signet ring," which Haman could use to seal official royal documents in the king's name. Essentially, Ahasuerus abandoned his responsibility to govern and placed it entirely in Haman's hands. At this point the author takes the unusual step of offering a moral characterization of one of the persons in the narrative: "Haman son of Hammedatha the Agagite, *the enemy of the Jews*" (emphasis added). Normally, the book of Esther's author refrains from making any value judgments himself—though he may quote others as offering such evaluations (e.g., Haman's description of the Jews in the Persian Empire or later, Esther's characterization of Haman as "evil," 7:6). Thus, at this point the author purposely increases the tension in the story.

Ahasuerus, we are told, returned the sum Haman promised to pay back to Haman to use as he wished. The king granted him the power to do what he wanted with the unnamed people Haman had described, too. Many commentators are bothered by Ahasuerus's statement returning the money to Haman (*hakkesep nātûn lāk*), although this is the understanding of many English versions (e.g., CSB, ESV, NRSV, TANAKH) and follows the Hebrew text. A few versions understand this phrase to be an idiom for the king saying, "Keep your money" (GW, NET, NIV), thereby turning down Haman's offer to pay and granting him power to destroy the Jews without incurring personal cost. Some commentators, however, argue the king may have been engaging in polite bargaining over the price to be paid, much as Abraham and Ephron haggled over the price of a field (Gen 23).[15] Their argument is based on the fact Mordecai knew the exact sum Haman had offered (Esth 4:7), and Esther would later say that her people had been "sold" (Hb. root *mkr*; 7:4). But if the king and Haman were negotiating, then the author describes only the beginning of the haggling between Ahasuerus and Haman over the price, which would be a strange storytelling technique. Instead, it is best simply to understand the transaction exactly as stated in the text: Ahasuerus accepted the offer but immediately returned the money to Haman. The people

---

[15] Bush, *Ruth, Esther*, 382; Fox, *Character and Ideology*, 52; Moore, *Esther*, 40.

had indeed been sold, and Ahasuerus once again could appear magnanimous in his generosity toward one of his officials.

3.2.3 Haman Issues the Royal Edict against the Jews (3:12-15)

¹² *The royal scribes were summoned on the thirteenth day of the first month, and the order was written exactly as Haman commanded. It was intended for the royal satraps, the governors of each of the provinces, and the officials of each ethnic group and written for each province in its own script and to each ethnic group in its own language. It was written in the name of King Ahasuerus and sealed with the royal signet ring.* ¹³ *Letters were sent by couriers to each of the royal provinces telling the officials to destroy, kill, and annihilate all the Jewish people—young and old, women and children—and plunder their possessions on a single day, the thirteenth day of Adar, the twelfth month.*

¹⁴ *A copy of the text, issued as law throughout every province, was distributed to all the peoples so that they might get ready for that day.* ¹⁵ *The couriers left, spurred on by royal command, and the law was issued in the fortress of Susa. The king and Haman sat down to drink, while the city of Susa was in confusion.*

Date: 13 Nisan (Wednesday, April 17), 474 BC

3:12–13 Ancient readers of Esther would recognize immediately the importance of the date of Haman's decree to massacre Jews; it was the day before Passover. God had delivered Israel from oppression in Egypt. Would God deliver the Jews from Haman?

The officials addressed in the decree are listed by social status, the most important to the least significant. "[S]atraps" governed the largest administrative districts in the empire.[16] "[G]overnors" were officials over smaller districts within the twenty-two satrapies.[17] Even lower "officials" were selected from various ethnic groups occupying

---

[16] The Hebrew word for "satrap" (אֲחַשְׁדַּרְפָּן) is a loanword from Old Persian. The same Old Persian word was realized in Greek as (ἐ)ξατράπης, which then was translated into English as "satrap."

[17] The Hebrew word for "governor" (פֶּחָה) is a loanword from Aramaic. It occurs only in books whose final form dates from the Babylonian captivity or later (1 Kgs 10:15; 2 Chr 9:14; Ezra 8:36; Neh 2:7, 9; 3:7; 5:14, 15, 18; 12:26; Esth 3:12; 8:9; 9:3; Jer 51:23, 28, 57; Ezek 23:6, 12, 23; Hag 1:1, 14; 2:2, 21; Mal 1:8). The Aramaic word is used in Ezra and Daniel (Ezra 5:3, 6, 14; 6:6–7, 13; Dan 3:2–3, 27; 6:8).

regions within each district. The reference to "ethnic groups" within the empire represents another case of irony, as Fox notes: "An empire that tolerates variety and respects the individuality of its subject peoples (and this was indeed a virtue of the historical Persian empire) is about to destroy one of those peoples because of its distinctiveness."[18]

The decree written in all the languages of the empire recalls the earlier decree issued in Ahasuerus's name (1:22). In fact, Beal points out the parallels between the earlier advice given to Ahasuerus leading to the decree regarding women, and Haman's advice initiating the decree against the Jews.[19] In both cases the act of one person (Vashti, Mordecai) led to a decree concerning an entire category of people (women, Jews). In both instances, the decrees were designed to appease the "rage" (ḥēmâ; 2:1; 3:5) of a single person (Ahasuerus, Haman). The description of the decree employs repetitive legal language to remove any ambiguity ("destroy, kill, annihilate"; "young and old, women and children").

A second reference to Ahasuerus's "signet ring" implies the king abdicated his responsibility to govern sensibly. Instead, using the signet, Haman was able to enact legislation and seal it with the king's seal as if Ahasuerus had personally issued the decree (see 8:8).

3:14–15 The author continues to demonstrate his familiarity with Persian culture, using the Old Persian word for "copy" (Hb. patšegen; Old Persian patšagn; see also 4:8; 8:13). The "couriers" employed to convey official communications throughout the empire are mentioned most famously by Herodotus.[20] He estimated a message conveyed from Susa to Sardis on the westernmost edge of the empire would take ninety days to deliver.[21] While by modern standards this seems slow, by ancient reckoning this was rather quick. Since the decree would not go into effect until the thirteenth day of Adar, the last month of the year, the time of receipt allowed the decree to be disseminated and gave locals time to prepare. The issuance of the decree in Susa would have been on that same day, allowing maximum time. The reaction of the people of Susa—probably the inhabitants of the lower city, not

[18] Fox, *Character and Ideology*, 54.
[19] Linafelt and Beal, *Ruth and Esther*, 55–56.
[20] Herodotus, *Histories*, 8.98.1.
[21] Herodotus, *Histories*, 5.53.1.

of the royal court in the fortress—was "confusion."[22] One can only imagine the questions which arose in the minds of the people. They must have asked things like this: "If one ethnic group can be singled out for persecution and extermination, could this happen to me and my people in the future?" "What have the Jews done to so offend the royal sensibilities?" "Didn't my friend say his people were from Judah?"

No matter how perplexed the general populace of Susa may have been, Haman was obviously pleased as he went "to drink" with the king. Ahasuerus, meanwhile appears unaware of the widespread dismay caused by the decree issued in his name. He continued his life of studied leisure, drinking, and feasting.

THEOLOGY

This chapter raises two important theological issues. One concerns the responsibility of those whom God has placed in authority. By distancing himself from the acts of Haman (3:11) and by carrying on his normal routine as if nothing momentous had taken place for a people within his realm(3:15), Ahasuerus displayed little inclination to rule and govern for good as God intends (Rom 13:1–4). God does not practice "favoritism" (Acts 10:34; Rom 2:11; Gal 2:6; Eph 6:9; Col 3:25; Jas 2:9), and he expects those in authority to use their responsibility as he would— whether they are judges and magistrates, pastors, heads of households, or kings (Exod 23:3; Deut 21:16; 1 Tim 5:21; Jas 2:1). Favoritism results in bigotry and unfair prejudice. By abandoning the responsibilities of his position, Ahasuerus was guilty of allowing Haman's ethnic intolerance to be promulgated in his name. The book of Esther is skillfully illustrating both the evils of bigotry, racism, and unjust discrimination and of failing to carry out responsibilities of a God-given vocation.

The second issue is raised by the mention of dates: the thirteenth day of Nisan when Haman issued his decree and the thirteenth day of Adar when it was to be executed. The time between the two is significant: twelve months.[23] Apparently the decision to delay the attack

---

[22] The Hebrew verb root בּוּךְ (bawak, "to be agitated") occurs only two other times in the Old Testament (Exod 14:3; Joel 1:18). In each case it seems to describe an aimless wandering indicating confusion or a muddled state of mind.

[23] In the lunisolar calendar used throughout most of the ancient Near East, including Persia, a regular year consisted of twelve lunar months, and Adar, the last month, is normally eleven months after Nisan, the first month. A normal lunisolar year, however, falls short of a full solar

on Jews was determined by casting "the pur" (Esth 3:7). Who controlled the timing of these events? From Haman's viewpoint, the pur may have reflected the determination of the mind of the pagan gods. But the Scriptures declare the true God determines the outcome of casting lots (Prov 16:33). Thus, while the events of chap. 3 appear to indicate Haman had gained control of the empire and that the pur was dictating the future, God remains in control of human events. And he always directs them for the good of those who trust and believe in him. He arranged for the pur to indicate the last month of the year, allowing for the events in Esther 4–8 to undo Haman's plot. This principle—God controls history for the benefit of his faithful ones (Rom 8:28)—is expanded in the New Testament, particularly, in the ministry of Christ, whom God the Father sent into human history at the most propitious time, when "the time came to completion" (Gal 4:4; see also Eph 1:9–10).

3.3   Esther Learns Why Mordecai is Mourning (4:1–9)

The crisis for the Jewish community initiated by Haman's decree drives this section of Esther. Mordecai's mourning represents the grieving of his fellow Jews in Susa. Esther learns of the mourning—though it is unclear whether she learns of widespread Jewish mourning or of Mordecai's act of donning "sackcloth and ashes" (4:4). The two are separated by geography and emotional state. The emotional distance between Esther and Mordecai is manifested by the way each tried to bridge their divide. Esther "sent clothes" from the palace to Mordecai in an attempt to bring Mordecai into her environment of luxury and away from his grief and mourning (4:4), but she was unsuccessful (4:5). Mordecai, on the other hand, attempted to bring Esther into his world by commanding her "to approach the king" (4:8). His effort failed to accomplish that (4:10–11). While Mordecai's concern led him to revert to his foster-father role vis-à-vis Esther, she was no longer

---

year by a little over eleven days. In order to adjust the calendar to a solar year, some years would have an extra solar month added at the end of the year—a second Adar (Adar II). In this particular year a second Adar was added from March 24 to April 21, 473 BC (Richard A. Parker and Waldo H. Dubberstein, *Babylonian Chronology 620 B.C.–A.D. 75*, repr. [Eugene, OR: Wipf and Stock, 2007], 31). If the month of Adar mentioned in Esther for this year was Adar II, then Haman's edict declared the attack on Jews to happen twelve lunar months after its initial dissemination. This would be in keeping with modern Jewish practice of celebrating Purim during Adar II in years that have thirteen months on the Jewish calendar.

living in his household and now had a covenant responsibility to her husband—including respecting his office as king and governed by Persian court protocol. She appealed to her position when she informed Mordecai through Hathach that she could not immediately approach Ahasuerus directly with a plea on behalf of the empire's Jews.

When Esther could not understand Mordecai's actions, she resorted to sending Hathach as her intermediary. Hathach performs a vital role for the reader: he emphasizes the distance between Esther and Mordecai. The latter was prevented from entering the King's Gate in his mourning attire and his grief. Esther was in the royal palace where the king and Haman were drinking and enjoying the luxury which only royalty could afford (3:15). Between these two moved Hathach. The author of Esther uses this minor character to emphasize both the physical and situational distance between Esther on the one hand and Mordecai and his fellow Jews on the other. As Grossman notes, "The author chose to draw far more attention to Hathach than seems necessary." For instance,

- Hathach is initially introduced in Esther 4:5;
- The narrator then immediately focuses on Hathach again, while stressing the geographical distance he is expected to bridge (4:6);
- Once Mordecai reports the reason he is mourning, the narrator emphasizes the fact the message was delivered to Esther by Hathach (4:9);
- The author then mentions Hathach again when describing Esther's message for Mordecai (4:10.)[24]

Thus, Esther's alarm at Mordecai's behavior and her accompanying bewilderment is emphasized for the reader by the author's skillful reporting of Hathach's role in shuttling between these two major characters in their attempt to communicate.

3.3.1 Mordecai and the Jews Mourn because of the Edict (4:1–3)

¹ *When Mordecai learned all that had occurred, he tore his clothes, put on sackcloth and ashes, went into the middle of the city, and cried loudly and bitterly.* ² *He went only as far as the King's Gate, since*

---

[24] Yonatan Grossman, "The Vanishing Character in Biblical Narrative: The Role of Hathach in Esther 4," *VT* 62 (2012): 565.

*the law prohibited anyone wearing sackcloth from entering the King's
Gate. ³ There was great mourning among the Jewish people in every
province where the king's command and edict reached. They fasted,
wept, and lamented, and many lay in sackcloth and ashes.*

4:1 The author emphasizes Mordecai learned "all that had
occurred" (*kol 'ăšer na'ăśâ*) in part to demonstrate once more he
enjoyed access to the royal court and its intrigues (2:21–22). He even
knew "the exact amount" of silver Haman offered to Ahasuerus (4:7).

The custom of tearing clothes and donning sackcloth and ashes
was common in Israel as an expression of grief and anguish at the
reception of all kinds of bad news as well as when mourning for the
dead (Gen 37:29, 34; 1 Sam 4:12; 2 Sam 1:2, 11; 15:32; 2 Kgs 18:37;
Isa 3:24; Dan 9:3). But the custom was not confined to Israel; it was
a general practice throughout the ancient Near East (Isa 15:3; Ezek
27:30–33). Herodotus notes the Persians tore their clothes in grief
over losing the battle of Salamis in 480 BC.²⁵

4:2 Mordecai's mourning also prevented him from taking his normal place "at the King's Gate" (2:19; 3:2–3). His approach to the
King's Gate was surely intended to draw the attention of those in the
palace so Esther would learn of his grief.

4:3 Mordecai was not alone in his grief, however. Further signs
of anguish among Jews throughout the empire included fasting and
lamentation. These acts were not only designed to express sorrow;
they were also religious acts. Fasting was often accompanied by prayer
(2 Sam 12:16–22; Ezra 8:23; Neh 1:4; Ps 35:13; Dan 9:3; Luke 2:37;
5:33; Acts 13:3; 14:23). The author of Esther avoided any overt mention of religious practices, suggesting he deliberately omitted any mention of Jewish prayers for deliverance from Haman's plot. Perhaps the
author veils the religious practices of the Jews and Persians in part
to provoke the reader to discover and make the religious connection
implied by the mention of fasting. In some ways this has more powerful effect on the astute reader of Esther than if the author had overtly
mentioned prayer.

---

²⁵ Herodotus, *Histories* 8.99.2.

3.3.2 Esther Learns of Haman's Plot (4:4–9)

⁴ *Esther's female servants and her eunuchs came and reported the news to her, and the queen was overcome with fear. She sent clothes for Mordecai to wear so that he would take off his sackcloth, but he did not accept them.* ⁵ *Esther summoned Hathach, one of the king's eunuchs who attended her, and dispatched him to Mordecai to learn what he was doing and why.* ⁶ *So Hathach went out to Mordecai in the city square in front of the King's Gate.* ⁷ *Mordecai told him everything that had happened as well as the exact amount of money Haman had promised to pay the royal treasury for the slaughter of the Jews.*

⁸ *Mordecai also gave him a copy of the written decree issued in Susa ordering their destruction, so that Hathach might show it to Esther, explain it to her, and command her to approach the king, implore his favor, and plead with him personally for her people.* ⁹ *Hathach came and repeated Mordecai's response to Esther.*

4:4 Esther learned of the unrest among Mordecai and the Jews of Susa through the women and eunuchs who attended to her. This testifies to the cloistered existence of women in the royal harem. Her reaction—one of extreme "fear"[26]—indicates she knew her fellow Jews were in turmoil but did not yet know why. Esther's act of sending clothes to Mordecai has been interpreted in various ways,[27] but it most likely was intended to enable him to come into the palace complex so he could explain the unrest among Susa's Jewish population.

Mordecai's refusal to change clothes is not explained. The most likely reason is he knew his behavior had come to Haman's attention (3:4–5), and Haman was having him closely observed whenever he was in the royal precincts. If he met with Esther, her identity as a Jew might have been exposed, and Haman might have been able to neutralize any influence she had with the king, perhaps even to the point of taking her life. Later Esther told Ahasuerus that along with the rest of the Jewish community, she had been sold "to destruction, death, and extermination" (*ləhašmîd lahărôg ûlə'abēd*; 7:4). If Mordecai's

---

[26] CSB's "overcome with fear" translates the verb וַתִּתְחַלְחַל. This is the only occurrence of this verb in this rare form (*hithpapel*) in the Old Testament. The root denotes to be "in labor or to writhe in pain." Obviously here it denotes great psychic pain for Esther, brought about by the obvious seriousness of the Jewish reaction to Haman's decree.

[27] Baldwin, *Esther*, 77; Bush, *Ruth, Esther*, 394–5; Fox, *Character and Ideology*, 59; Linafelt and Beal, *Ruth and Esther*, 60

refusal was intended to keep Esther safe, then it is matched by Esther's later refusal to approach the king (4:11).

4:5–7 Esther turned to Hathach as her intermediary. Clearly, Hathach would learn of Esther's secret as he conveyed messages between her and Mordecai (see 4:8). Esther must have thought she could rely on Hathach's loyalty to her. Esther wanted to know why Mordecai was in mourning, and Hathach, who was able to go out into the city square" beyond "the King's Gate," could provide that information. This was probably not something the queen or any other member of the royal harem could do.

Mordecai's message to Esther not only explained the situation, but it also demonstrated his intimate knowledge of the inner workings of Ahasuerus's palace—he knew "the exact amount" of silver Haman had offered to the king. The communication of the outrageously large sum of money was surely meant to impress upon Esther the seriousness of Haman's threat.

4:8–9 The decree must have been published in written form, since Mordecai also sent Hathach with a copy of Haman's decree and had Hathach "explain it to her" (*ûləhaggîd lâ*), suggesting he read her the contents of the decree. (On the word "copy," see the comments at 3:14.) Since the decree was published in each region's "own language" (3:12), the copies circulating in Susa were probably written in either Elamite or Old Persian.[28] It is doubtful Esther would have been able to read either language.[29]

Mordecai commanded Esther to do three things in order to save the Jews: "approach the king, [gain] his favor, and plead" for her people. The problem lies in the first of these: Esther could not approach the king without risking her life. She would be able to approach the king *after* gaining his favor, however (5:2).

---

[28] Earlier in history, Susa had been an important Elamite city, though at this time it was serving as the seat of the Persian court. Elamite was an important language in the Persian Empire. The well-known Behistun Inscription in modern Iran was carved on a mountainside to record Darius I's ascent to the Persian throne. It was recorded in four versions: one in Old Persian, two in Elamite, and one in the Babylonian dialect of Akkadian. See Edwin M. Yamauchi, *Persia and the Bible* (Grand Rapids, MI: Eerdmans, 1990), 131–34.

[29] Paton, *Esther*, 218. This is not to say Esther was illiterate. She may have been able to read Hebrew and may have learned this in order to read the Scriptures. Bush contends that the verb וּלְהַגִּיד (i.e., "explain it") does not imply that Hathach read it to her. He believes she read it and then Hathach further explained matters. But this is doubtful since he contends the verb cannot mean "explain" unless there is a direct object. Yet at Gen 41:24 there is no explicitly stated direct object, though the verb must mean "explain." The same is true here. See Bush, *Ruth, Esther*, 395.

3.4   Mordecai Persuades Esther to Approach the King (4:10–17)

In the previous verses (4:1–9) the use of Hathach emphasized the distance—both physical and emotional—between Esther and Mordecai. Hathach continues to serve as a mediator but gradually fades from the narrative. At 4:10 Esther spoke to him with a message for Mordecai. At 4:12, his presence is only implied, as it is also at 4:13 and 4:15.[30] Hathach's disappearance from the narrative is used by the author to signal to readers, despite the physical separation remaining between them, their emotional and situational distance had vanished.[31] This closing of the distance between Esther and Mordecai is also affected by the author's use of direct discourse between the two, their only conversation recorded in Esther (4:11–16). Moreover, 4:13–14 contains the only direct quotation of Mordecai's words in Esther. Significantly, these words mark the closest the book ever comes to mentioning God.

3.4.1   Esther's Reason as to Why She Cannot Intervene (4:10–12)

10 Esther spoke to Hathach and commanded him to tell Mordecai, 11 "All the royal officials and the people of the royal provinces know that one law applies to every man or woman who approaches the king in the inner courtyard and who has not been summoned—the death penalty—unless the king extends the gold scepter, allowing that person to live. I have not been summoned to appear before the king for the last thirty days." 12 Esther's response was reported to Mordecai.

4:10–12 Esther's reply to Mordecai's command serves to inform him of court protocol. No one is permitted to approach the king unless "summoned," a law known among the king's provincial officials.[32] Esther clearly conveys to Mordecai the penalty for ignoring this rule, indicating why she was unable to obey Mordecai's command. The

---

[30] The Hebrew text of 4:12 reads, וַיַּגִּידוּ לְמָרְדֳּכָי אֵת דִּבְרֵי אֶסְתֵּר: "They told Esther's words to Mordecai." Esther 4:13 reads, וַיֹּאמֶר מָרְדֳּכַי לְהָשִׁיב אֶל־אֶסְתֵּר: "Mordecai said to reply to Esther." Esther 4:15 reads, וַתֹּאמֶר אֶסְתֵּר לְהָשִׁיב אֶל־מָרְדֳּכָי: "Esther said to reply to Mordecai."

[31] Grossman, "The Vanishing Character," 567–69.

[32] The phrase וְעַם־מְדִינוֹת הַמֶּלֶךְ, translated in CSB as "the people of the royal provinces" (see also ESV, GW, NET, NIV, NRSV, TANAKH), ought not to be understood as people in general in the provinces. Instead, the phrase most likely denotes the king's top officials of the provinces and ought to be translated "the royal officers of the provinces." Otherwise, the phrase "royal provinces" makes no sense because no special "royal provinces" are known to have existed in the Persian Empire.

rule was most likely adopted to protect the king from assassination attempts and from being besieged by courtiers with petty requests. Since Esther felt the need to inform Mordecai of this royal procedure, it is likely Mordecai was a minor official who was not part of Ahasuerus's inner circle of officials and advisors. In confirmation of this, Mordecai did not have access to the king even to report an assassination attempt but had to communicate with the king through Esther (2:22). Moreover, Ahasuerus had not yet deemed it necessary to reward Mordecai for foiling the plot on his life (2:21–23) and was not aware of him until the official court records were read to him (6:2–3). In addition, Haman did not take notice of Mordecai until Mordecai's behavior was reported to him (3:4–5). All these indicate Mordecai held only a minor position in the royal administration at first.

Esther noted there was an exception to the rule: the king might invite someone into his presence by extending his "gold scepter." The word for scepter, *šarbiṭ* is a loan word from Aramaic, used only in Esther (see 5:2; 8:4). The use of this word instead of the common Hebrew word for *scepter* (i.e., *šebeṭ*) displays another common characteristic of postexilic Hebrew: the use of Aramaisms.[33]

Esther noted she had not been summoned to see the king for "thirty days." Esther gives no reason for this. Had she had fallen out of favor? Was Ahasuerus busy with the rest of the young virgins—the second gathering (2:19)? No matter what the reason, Esther indicates she had no access to the king. We cannot know whether this implies that the king's wives were not permitted to request a royal audience or Esther thought it impolitic to seek one at the time. If she offended the king and fell out of favor or lost her life, what good would she be able to do for her people? Whether Esther was concerned with self-preservation or also with the preservation of her people is not explicitly explained by the text of 4:11. The reader is left to discover through the following narrative Esther eventually managed both self-preservation and the deliverance of her people from the threat of Haman's plot.

3.4.2 *Mordecai's Reason as to Why Esther Must Intervene (4:13–14)*

[13] Mordecai told the messenger to reply to Esther, "Don't think that you will escape the fate of all the Jews because you are in the

---

[33] This word would continue in use in rabbinic Hebrew (*Targum Jonathan* to 1 Kgs 12:11; *Targum Neofiti* to Gen 40:10 and Lev 27:32).

king's palace. ¹⁴ *If you keep silent at this time, relief and deliverance will come to the Jewish people from another place, but you and your father's family will be destroyed. Who knows, perhaps you have come to your royal position for such a time as this."*

4:13 Mordecai's reply warns Esther not to assume she would be immune from Haman's wrath, implying her Jewish ancestry would eventually be discovered. If Haman was to succeed in wreaking his vengeance on the Jews, he would have recognized it foolish to leave Esther in a high position from which she could retaliate.

4:14 This verse is perhaps the most important in the entire book. Nevertheless, it also is one of the most difficult. Most English versions translate the three clauses as in CSB. The first is a protasis of a conditional sentence ("If you . . . "). The second clause is usually understood as a statement forming the apodosis (". . . relief and deliverance . . . "). The third clause is then a second apodosis standing in contrast to the first apodosis (". . . but you . . .").

This reading raises several problems.³⁴ First, what is "another place" (*mimmāqôm 'aḥēr*) to which Mordecai refers? It has been understood to refer to God based on the later rabbinic Hebrew use of the word *place* (*māqôm*) as a circumlocution for *God*.³⁵ Not only does this conclusion rely on a later usage not documented in biblical Hebrew, but if this were the case, then Mordecai is referring to *another god*, which is clearly not in view.

Second, why would Esther and her "father's family" not escape if relief and deliverance came to the Jewish people? The reference to Esther's father's family must include Mordecai himself, since Esther's parents had died (2:7). Was Mordecai implying God would judge Esther and Mordecai if Esther did nothing, and if so, why would Mordecai be held responsible? Is Mordecai implying his fellow Jews would seek vengeance against the two of them for failing to intervene?

The second clause should be understood as a question. While there are explicit markers identifying a question in the Hebrew text, interrogative clauses are often unmarked in biblical Hebrew.³⁶ The

---

³⁴ John M. Wiebe, "Esther 4:14: 'Will Relief and Deliverance Arise for the Jews from Another Place?," *CBQ* 53 (1991): 409–15.

³⁵ Moore, *Esther*, 50; Paton, *Esther*, 22–23.

³⁶ For examples, see Gen 18:12; 27:24; Exod 8:22; Judg 14:16; 1 Sam 11:12; 20:9; 22:7; 24:20; 2 Sam 16:17; 18:29; Job 34:32; Hos 4:16; Jonah 4:11; Zech 8:6; Mal 1:8.

verse could be translated this way: "If you keep silent at this time, will relief and deliverance come to the Jewish people from another place? [Implied answer: No!] You and your father's family will be destroyed!"[37] There is no other place from which deliverance might arise. This rhetorical question makes Mordecai's next statement more poignant: Esther alone can provide deliverance for the Jews, including herself and her father's family.

Mordecai's final statement begins "Who knows . . . " (*mî yôdēaʿ*). James L. Crenshaw notes here, as in some other cases where this phrase occurs in the Old Testament, "*mî yôdēaʿ* implies decisive action may alter the present circumstances in ways that are eminently desirable."[38] Esther, Mordecai is saying, needs to take decisive action because she holds a high position. Moreover, Mordecai suggests Esther was placed in that influential position by God. Crenshaw notes, "Indeed, it seems that such open hostility toward the Jews may be thwarted precisely because God has been at work behind the scenes putting a deliverer in place."[39] Duguid catches well the theological implications of Mordecai's words:

> [W]hen Mordecai said, "Who knows whether you have not come to the kingdom for such a time as this?" he was arguing that there is a meaningful course of history. But who can provide such a meaning, except for God himself? Mordecai was saying essentially what Joseph said to his brothers in Genesis 45:5: "God sent me before you to preserve life"—but once again Mordecai does not mention God.[40]

Finally, Mordecai said Esther had come to her "royal position" (Hb. *malkût*) for just this purpose. This word is also used to describe "her royal clothing" marking her as the queen (5:1). In her regal attire Esther will be admitted by Ahasuerus into his presence. Later, Mordecai will be dressed in royal clothing (*ləbûš malkût*; 6:8; 8:15), and he, too, would come to his position "for such a time as this" (*lə'ēt kāzôt*).

---

[37] Wiebe, "Esther 4:14," 413–15; Bush, *Ruth, Esther*, 395–97.

[38] James L. Crenshaw, "The Expression *Mî Yôdēaʿ* in the Hebrew Bible," *VT* 36 (1986): 277.

[39] Crenshaw, "The Expression," 277.

[40] Iain M. Duguid, *Esther and Ruth,* Reformed Expository Commentary (Phillipsburg, NJ: P&R, 2005), 50.

3.4.3 Esther Appeals for Support from the Jews before She Intervenes (4:15–17)

¹⁵ Esther sent this reply to Mordecai: ¹⁶ "Go and assemble all the Jews who can be found in Susa and fast for me. Don't eat or drink for three days, night or day. I and my female servants will also fast in the same way. After that, I will go to the king even if it is against the law. If I perish, I perish." ¹⁷ So Mordecai went and did everything Esther had commanded him.

4:15–16 Esther's reply, like Mordecai's appeal, comes close to mentioning God. It is characterized by a series of imperatives: "[g]o . . . assemble . . . fast . . . [d]on't eat or drink" (*lēk kənôs . . . wəṣûmû . . . wəʾal tōʾklû wəʾal tištû*). The fast is commanded for "three days, night or day" (*šəlōšet yāmiym laylāh wāyôm*). There are two important aspects of this. First, the three days are counted inclusively, with the day which had already begun beginning one day, and the day when the fast ended the third day, or in our parlance, two days later (5:1). Second, the phrase "night or day" describes fasting that did not end at sundown as it normally did (Judg 20:26; 2 Sam 1:12). Moreover, it describes the Jewish reckoning of a day that began at sundown so night preceded daytime. The fast would not last seventy-two hours but from sometime on the first day to sometime on the third day when Esther went to see the king. It appears at most to have been forty-eight hours, but this would have been a severe fasting.

Fasting could be used to frame a request to God (1 Kgs 21:27; Jonah 3:5–8; Ezra 8:21–23), and this appears to be the case here, since Esther requested the Jews in Susa fast "for [her]." Interestingly, Esther would also impose this fast on her "female servants"—her attendants supplied to her by the Persian court (Esth 2:9)—although they most likely were not Jewish. Esther promised to go to Ahasuerus at the fast's end even if it endangered her life. As Berlin notes, "The grammatical construction, here and in Gen. 43:14 where the same syntax occurs, betokens a fatalistic acceptance of a choice of action to which there is really no alternative."[41] Thus, Esther's "If I perish, I perish" (*wəkʾăšer ʾābadtî ʾābadtî*) acknowledged Mordecai was correct in his assessment of the situation (4:13–14)—inaction on Esther's part was

---

[41] Berlin, *Esther*, 50. At Gen 43:14 Jacob says, "[I]f I am deprived of my sons, then I am deprived," acknowledging he had no choice but to send his sons back to Egypt to buy more grain during the famine which struck Egypt and his own homeland.

not an option since doing nothing meant she and her father's family would perish in Haman's pogrom.

The timing of the fast is also momentous. If Mordecai's lamentations became known to Esther on the same day as the decree was issued in Susa—the day before Passover—then Esther was asking her fellow Jews to fast on Passover and on the day which followed.[42] In essence, they were breaking the law of Moses concerning the Passover meal and risking a curse from God (Num 9:13) in order to call God's attention to their plight. This formed an analogy to Esther, who was asked to break the Persian law and risk death in order to call Ahasuerus's attention to the threat against Esther's people.

4:17 This short verse is easily overlooked, but it reveals three interesting aspects of the story. First, "Mordecai went" is more specifically "Mordecai crossed" (*wayya'ăbōr mordŏkay*).[43] This is probably a reference to the geography of Susa. Mordecai would have left the royal city of Susa and crossed over to the lower city where most of Susa's population lived. Second, this verse depicts Esther commanding Mordecai, signaling a change in their relationship. Esther was no longer the girl Mordecai claimed as his adopted daughter; she was the Persian queen and at least an equal partner with Mordecai in the effort to save the Jewish people from Haman's plot. Finally, this verse marks the last interaction between Esther and Mordecai until after Haman's execution (7:10; see 8:1–2; 9:29–32).

THEOLOGY

Of the ten chapters in Esther, chap. 4 is the most theological in orientation. Mordecai's lament with his fellow Jews has a religious nuance even though the author does not explicitly write of it in terms of appealing to God for mercy. Nevertheless, it is a reminder to readers that, like Mordecai, his fellow Jews are always dependent on God's mercy, especially in times of trouble and sorrow. Mordecai had no claim on God's mercy from his own merit. In fact, his actions triggered their predicament (3:2–4), and now they were completely helpless to change their situation without God's provision of a mediator. This theme prefigures the utter helplessness all humans experience when

---

[42] The day that followed Passover was the first day of the Feast of Unleavened Bread (Exod 12:14–16; Deut 16:1–3).

[43] וַיַּעֲבֹר מָרְדֳּכָי.

faced with their sinfulness and its consequences. Unable to save ourselves, we rely solely on Christ (Rom 3:23–24; Gal 2:15–21; Eph 2:8–9; 2 Tim 1:9).

Mordecai's appeal to Esther recognized God orchestrated events so she was positioned to be God's servant and save her people from annihilation (Esth 4:14). God's intentional placement of Esther in order to accomplish his purpose serves as an example to Christians today. Each has been placed by God into the body of Christ to serve others (Rom 12:3–8) through vocations such as employer or employee, husband or wife, parent or child, magistrate or citizen, pastor or parishioner. Esther's service also reminds us all Christians have a holy calling from God to minister to others through the various stations in life where God has placed them. Although Esther's position as queen of Persia was not an office established or maintained by God's people, it nevertheless afforded her the opportunity to serve God and others honorably. She did this in a God-pleasing way, even at the risk of her own life. In the same way, Christians today are able to act as God's servants in the most secular of circumstances and in a variety of occupations that provide service to their neighbors—thereby becoming God's way of shedding his grace on all humanity, Christians and non-Christians (Job 25:2–3; Matt 5:43–48; Luke 6:35–36).

3.5   Esther's First Banquet for Ahasuerus and Haman (5:1–8)

Esther did not delay in seeking an audience with Ahasuerus. Before "the third day" of the fast was over, she challenged the Persian law, endangering her life to save her people (5:1). Her "royal clothing" was a clear sign to everyone, especially Ahasuerus, she was there in her capacity as queen. Thus, Ahasuerus assumed she had a request (5:3).

It may seem strange Esther did not reveal her real concern either when Ahasuerus first asked her or later at the first banquet she held for the king and Haman.[44] But Esther had earlier indicated she had not

---

[44] Paton, *Esther*, 236, sees Esther as fearful, panicked, timid, and lacking confidence and posits this as the reason for her delay in presenting her request to Ahasuerus. This, however, is not in keeping with Esther's personality in the rest of the book. Since she had already stated that the possibility of death would not deter her, it is hardly believable that she was simply delaying what she surmised might be her undoing. See Joshua Joel Spoelstra, "The Function of the משתה יין in the Book of Esther," *OTE* 27 (2014): 286.

seen the king in "thirty days" (4:11). She may have been proceeding slowly because she was not certain of her standing with Ahasuerus. The first banquet gave her a chance not only to assess the king's attitude toward her but also to observe the relationship between Ahasuerus and Haman. It would have been foolish to challenge Haman if the king favored him greatly while Esther, though queen, was treated as if she were little more than a slightly elevated member of the royal harem. By the end of the banquet, Esther was able to discover the dynamics of the relationship between the king and his prime minister. In addition, she was confident enough in her relationship with Ahasuerus to request a delay of one more day in speaking her concern. By requesting the king and Haman attend a second banquet, Esther allowed herself additional time to plan the best way to broach the subject of Haman's treachery.

3.5.1 Esther Approaches Ahasuerus with an Invitation to a Banquet (5:1–5)

¹ *On the third day, Esther dressed in her royal clothing and stood in the inner courtyard of the palace facing it. The king was sitting on his royal throne in the royal courtroom, facing its entrance.* ² *As soon as the king saw Queen Esther standing in the courtyard, she gained favor with him. The king extended the gold scepter in his hand toward Esther, and she approached and touched the tip of the scepter.*

³ *"What is it, Queen Esther?" the king asked her. "Whatever you want, even to half the kingdom, will be given to you."* ⁴ *"If it pleases the king," Esther replied, "may the king and Haman come today to the banquet I have prepared for them."*

⁵ *The king said, "Hurry, and get Haman so we can do as Esther has requested." So the king and Haman went to the banquet Esther had prepared.*

Date: 15 Nisan (Friday, April 19), 474 BC

5:1–2 Esther's presence in the inner courtyard in royal attire where the king could see her from his throne must have been dramatic. The author tells us once again that "she gained favor with him" (*nāśə'â ḥēn bə'ênāyw*; see 2:9, 15, 17). This expression focuses on what Esther actively did to be in favor with the king. Nevertheless, when Esther spoke with Ahasuerus, she always used the expression *found favor* (5:8; 7:3; 8:5), which focuses on the king's granting favor to Esther.

Ahasuerus's expression of favor was the extending of his scepter, and Esther touching its tip was her way of acknowledging the king's graciousness.

5:3–5 Ahasuerus's question, "What is it?" literally is, "What to you?" (*mah lāk*). This idiom recognizes someone has a need or urgent request (Gen 21:17; Josh 15:18/Judg 1:14; 2 Sam 14:5; Ps 114:5). The closest Old Testament parallel to this situation is David's asking the same question of Bathsheba when she sought to save herself and her son Solomon after Adonijah attempted to assume Israel's throne (1 Kgs 1:16).

Ahasuerus's offer of up to half of his kingdom was an ancient oriental way of expressing royal willingness to grant any reasonable request (see Mark 6:23; Herodotus records Ahasuerus making a similar offer to a certain Artaynte with whom he had an affair).[45] In addition, Ahasuerus indicated his approval of Esther by calling her "Queen Esther," signaling he recognized her importance in the royal hierarchy.

In contrast to Ahasuerus's offer, Esther's reply appears extremely modest. She wanted to host a banquet for the king and his prime minister. Esther's request appears to be cautious and calculated since her true goal was to undermine Haman, and she was treading into unknown territory in doing this. Haman had been elevated to his position by Ahasuerus (Esth 3:1) and was trusted enough by the king that his desire to extirpate an entire ethnic group from the empire had not drawn even a single question about his motives or the wisdom of such an action (3:7–11). Moreover, Haman offered Ahasuerus a ridiculously large sum for the privilege of implementing his plan (3:9). She needed to know whether it was safe to ask the king for a reversal of Haman's decree and determine the best way to bring the threat to her own life to his attention.

Ahasuerus did not question Esther about her motives but immediately accepted Esther's invitation by ordering Haman to be summoned to the banquet. This was not an evening meal since after Haman left the feast he had time on the same day to have a pole erected to display Mordecai's body (5:14), and it was in place by the next day (6:4).

Esther is characterized as a replacement for Vashti and more favored than the former queen. Vashti had been summoned to the

---

[45] Herodotus, *Histories*, 9.109.2.

king's banquet and refused to come (1:10–12). In contrast, Esther invited the king to attend to her banquet, and he readily came.

3.5.2 Esther's First Banquet for Ahasuerus and Haman (5:6–8)

⁶ *While drinking the wine, the king asked Esther, "Whatever you ask will be given to you. Whatever you want, even to half the kingdom, will be done."*

⁷ *Esther answered, "This is my petition and my request:* ⁸ *If I have found favor in the eyes of the king, and if it pleases the king to grant my petition and perform my request, may the king and Haman come to the banquet I will prepare for them. Tomorrow I will do what the king has asked."*

5:6–8 "While drinking the wine" reads literally "in the feast of the wine" (*bəmištēh hayyayin*), indicating a wine course served after the meal had been finished.[46] With the meal concluded, Ahasuerus demonstrated he understood Esther's request for him to attend a meal with her was not her real request. Therefore, he repeated his offer to her.

Esther's reply could be understood in two ways. One is indicated by CSB and most other English versions (ESV, NET, NIV, NRSV). Her request was to hold another banquet for Ahasuerus and Haman where she would present her petition. It is also possible, however, to understand Esther's words as beginning her request, which she then decided to break off and not reveal at this time: "My petition, my request is. . . ."[47] In either case, Esther wanted to delay her request one more time. She may have perceived Haman's good mood (5:9) and wanted to have an opportunity to present her petition when Haman felt less confident. Perhaps she thought an intervening day would change his attitude (which it ultimately did; see 6:12–14).[48]

At the same time, Esther appears to understand she was trying Ahasuerus's patience. Her words are almost fawningly obsequious: "If

---

[46] Fox, *Character and Ideology*, 67.

[47] Berlin, *Esther*, 54; Bush, *Ruth, Esther*, 404; see TANAKH.

[48] The suggestion of Spoelstra, "The Function of: 29, 3–292 ",משתה ין, that Esther was attempting to get the king intoxicated in order to arouse his wrath against Haman is interesting (see 1:10–12) yet speculative. In Spoelstra's view Esther suggested a second feast in hopes that Ahasuerus, who had not come sufficiently under the influence of wine at the first feast, might do so at the second feast. But if that was Esther's plan, what was she to do if Ahasuerus also failed to drink enough at the second banquet? Nevertheless, Spoelstra is correct to point out one recurring motif in Esther: banquets with wine can lead to rage (1:10–12; 5:9; 7:2–7).

I have found favor . . . if it pleases the king. . . ." At the same time, she has maneuvered the king into granting her request no matter what it might be even before revealing it: she said if the king desired to grant her request, he and Haman would attend a second banquet the next day. There she promised to reveal her petition.

3.6 Haman's Elation at Being a Guest at Esther's Banquet (5:9–14)

The balance of chap. 5 and all of chap. 6 chronicle Haman's emotional descent from delight at dining with the king and queen to rage over Mordecai and finally to humiliation (6:12), a prediction of his own "downfall" (6:13). The highpoint for Haman is the private banquet since Persian kings normally dined alone or only with the queen and their own mothers.[49.] The scenes between the two banquets with the king and queen document how Haman unwittingly facilitated his own undoing. (1) His rage led to his erecting a gallows on which to hang Mordecai's body (5:9–14), but instead his body would be hung on it (7:10). (2) His egotistical suggestion to Ahasuerus resulted in his having to oversee Mordecai's royal honors (6:1–11). (3) His despair occasioned his wife's prediction of his downfall (6:12–14).

3.6.1 Haman's Elation Is Tempered by Mordecai's Presence in the King's Gate (5:9–13)

[9] *That day Haman left full of joy and in good spirits. But when Haman saw Mordecai at the King's Gate, and Mordecai didn't rise or tremble in fear at his presence, Haman was filled with rage toward Mordecai.* [10] *Yet Haman controlled himself and went home. He sent for his friends and his wife Zeresh to join him.* [11] *Then Haman described for them his glorious wealth and his many sons. He told them all how the king had honored him and promoted him in rank over the other officials and the royal staff.* [12] *"What's more," Haman added, "Queen Esther invited no one but me to join the king at the banquet she had prepared. I am invited again tomorrow to join her with the*

---

[49] Plutarch, *Plutarch's Lives with an English Translation,* translated by Bernadotte Perrin, LCL (Cambridge: Harvard University Press, 1926), 11 (*Artaxerxes,* 5.3.3): "[N]o one shared the table of a Persian king except his mother or his wedded wife, the wife sitting below him, the mother above him."

*king. [13] Still, none of this satisfies me since I see Mordecai the Jew sit-
ting at the King's Gate all the time."*

5:9 Haman will never be more content than at this point in the
narrative. The middle of the book occurs with the words "[t]hat day"
(*bayyôm hahû'*), with Haman ascending before them and diminishing
after them.[50]

Haman left the feast "full of joy and in good spirits" (*śāmēaḥ
wəṭôb lēb*).[51] His good spirits (*ṭôb lēb*) after the banquet mirrored
Ahasuerus's good feelings when he ordered Vashti to come to his banquet (1:10). Like Ahasuerus, who was enraged when Vashti would
not honor his order, Haman was filled with rage at Mordecai who did
not even acknowledge him. In this case Mordecai not only refused to
bow before Haman; he did not even acknowledge Haman's presence.
At this time Mordecai had nothing to lose—he was already under the
threat of death from Haman's decree. It is also important to observe
Mordecai had ended his fast and his mourning in sackcloth, since he
was once again "at the King's Gate."

5:10–11 Like Ahasuerus summoning his advisors when he was
angry with Vashti (1:13), Haman kept his rage under control and
called "for his friends and his wife." He then set the stage for his
dilemma. He had wealth and many sons, both considered signs of
success (Job 1:2–3).[52] In fact, the author describes Haman's wealth in
such a way as to mirror that of Ahasuerus.[53] The ultimate sign of his
success was his promotion to the highest position in the kingdom.

5:12–13 In addition to all his splendor, Haman bragged he had
been "invited" by Queen Esther not to only one banquet but to two.
Haman's pride in being invited to banquets by Esther, Mordecai's
adopted daughter, provides one of the many ironic subtleties employed
by the author of Esther. As Beal notes, "The irony in this misperception

---

[50] MT Esther contains 4,667 words, and these two are at the center of the book by word
count.

[51] It is not necessary to understand this as if Haman was drunk as do Linafeld and Beal,
Ruth and Esther, 74, and Spoelstra, "The Function of משתה יין," 295. Haman was able to control
his anger (5:10), indicating that while he may have had some wine, he was not to the point of
intoxication.

[52] Herodotus notes that the Persians considered many sons a sign of success (Herodotus,
Histories, 1.136.1). In yet another irony in the book of Esther, Haman—who prided himself as
having wealth, sons, and the king's favor—lost all three: his wealth (8:1), his sons (9:6–10), and
Ahasuerus's favor (7:3).

[53] Ahasuerus's wealth: עֹשֶׁר כְּבוֹד 1:4; Haman's wealth כְּבוֹד עָשְׁרוֹ 5:11.

is due not only to the fact Esther is Mordecai's daughter/cousin (and a Jewish "enemy"; 3:10), but also [that] Mordecai will never be as much a threat to Haman as is Esther."[54]

Yet, as Haman notes, none of his success means anything to him because of Mordecai's presence "at the King's Gate." Haman's obsession with Mordecai, a relatively minor official in Ahasuerus's administration, is signaled partly by his characterization of him as "the Jew," the people hated by Amalekites (see the discussion in the introduction). In turn, because of his fixation on Mordecai, Haman was blinded to the fact that everything he had was imperiled because of Queen Esther.

3.6.2   Haman Advised to Eliminate Mordecai with a Public Display of His Power (5:14)

[14] *His wife Zeresh and all his friends told him, "Have them build a gallows seventy-five feet tall. Ask the king in the morning to hang Mordecai on it. Then go to the banquet with the king and enjoy yourself." The advice pleased Haman, so he had the gallows constructed.*

5:14 While Haman did not directly ask his wife and friends for advice as to what to do about Mordecai, it is obvious he wanted to be relieved of the bad mood brought about by Mordecai so he could enjoy his wealth, honor, and high position. For this reason, Zeresh and his friends offer him advice which leads to unseen consequences favoring the Jews—just as the advice from Ahasuerus's officials and servants led to the unexpected result of a Jewish woman becoming queen (1:19–20; 2:2–4).

The author now mentions Haman's "wife Zeresh" before his friends, signaling she was his principal advisor. Her solution was to eliminate Mordecai as quickly as possible, preparing a pole on which to hang his body (this was not a traditional "gallows"; see the discussion in the introduction). To hasten his good mood, he was advised to obtain permission from Ahasuerus "in the morning" to do this. Then, Zeresh counseled, he would be free to attend the banquet and "enjoy" himself.

The reported height of the pole has caused much discussion among modern commentators, especially those who doubt the historical accuracy of Esther (see the introduction). At fifty cubits, the pole would have been about "seventy-five feet" (twenty-two meters) high.

---

[54] Linafelt and Beal, *Ruth and Esther*, 75.

One explanation is the pole would have been erected on a building or a hill, and the height would have been the total elevation, not simply the height of the pole.[55] This seems unlikely, however, unless Haman's house was extremely grand—on the scale of a palace—or was on a hill in Susa (see 7:9). It is more likely "fifty cubits high" was a well-used hyperbolic expression meaning "extremely high."[56] This would explain how not only Zeresh but also Harbonna, one of Ahasuerus's eunuchs, would have described the pole this way.

THEOLOGY

The events of chap. 5 demonstrate how God often works among people and events. Esther risked her life, but Ahasuerus favored her, offered to grant whatever she wished, and patiently allowed her another day before she revealed her heart to him. While the author does not mention God, it is evident Providence was at work, using Esther's already documented ability to gain the favor of others (2:9, 15, 17). He also used Ahasuerus's predilection to be magnanimously generous with those whom he liked and Haman's overinflated ego and his animosity against Mordecai to accomplish his purposes. The author reveals this to his thoughtful readers without ever mentioning God.

Esther 5 is a fitting narrative for modern readers in highly secularized Western societies. Often we go about our daily lives without perceiving the connection between the actions of persons and the events of our days with the providence of God for his people—just as the author of Esther does not note those connections for his readers. Yet we know the sovereign God controls all of history for the benefit of those whom he has called into his kingdom, and he uses events in their lives to make them his own and to preserve them (Rom 8:28; Eph 1:11–12; 2 Tim 1:9). We see this most of all in Christ Jesus, whom God sent at the right time in history to save sinners (Rom 5:6; Gal 4:4–5; Eph 1:10).

---

[55] Jacob Hoschander, *The Book of Esther in the Light of History* (Philadelphia: Dropsie College, 1928), 20.5

[56] Berlin, *Esther*, 55; Bush, *Ruth, Esther*, 60.

3.7 Haman is Humiliated by Having to Honor Mordecai (6:1–14)

On the advice of his wife, Haman had plans for the next morning. He was going to ask Ahasuerus for permission to execute Mordecai (5:14). But chap. 6 demonstrates human plans are subject to revision by events over which humans have no control—events only God can control (Jas 4:13–17). In addition, Haman's high opinion of himself contributed to his humiliation (Esth 6:6). This chapter serves as an example of why Proverbs warns against self-importance, which leads to the proud person's destruction (Prov 11:2; 16:18; 29:23).

The author of Esther presented the account of Haman honoring Mordecai so it corresponds to the previous account of Haman's actions after his banquet with Ahasuerus and Esther (5:9–14). Note the following parallels:[57]

	ESTHER 5:9–14	**ESTHER 6:1–14**
Takes place immediately after the previous episode	"That day" (5:9)	"That night" (6:1)
Haman to request Mordecai's execution	Plan devised (5:14)	Haman coming to see Ahasuerus (6:4)
Interaction between Haman and Mordecai	Mordecai will not honor or acknowledge Haman (5:9)	Mordecai honored by Haman (6:11)
Haman's high opinion of himself and his success	His wealth, sons, and high position (5:11–12)	His assumption that Ahasuerus wished to honor him (6:6–9)
Mordecai's position at the city gate continues	Mordecai at the King's Gate upsets Haman (5:13)	Mordecai returns to the King's Gate while Haman is in despair (6:12)
Haman receives advice from Zeresh	Prepare to hang Mordecai on a gallows/pole (5:14)	Prepare for your downfall (6:13)

3.7.1 Ahasuerus Learns He Did Not Reward the Man Who Saved His Life (6:1–3)

¹ *That night sleep escaped the king, so he ordered the book recording daily events to be brought and read to the king.* ² *They found the written report of how Mordecai had informed on Bigthana and Teresh, two of the king's eunuchs who guarded the entrance, when*

---

⁵⁷ Expanded from Linafelt and Beal, *Ruth and Esther,* 77.

they planned to assassinate King Ahasuerus. ³ The king inquired, "What honor and special recognition have been given to Mordecai for this act?"

The king's personal attendants replied, "Nothing has been done for him."

Date: 16 Nisan (Friday evening, April 19–Saturday, April 20), 474 BC

6:1–2 The only mention of nighttime activity in Esther results from the king's insomnia. No reason is given for Ahasuerus's inability to sleep that night. Nevertheless, the overall context suggests it relates to Esther, her request, and the two banquets. The Talmud speculated Ahasuerus may have wondered whether Haman and Esther were conspiring against him.[58] It is strange, however, the two would desire to be seen together. It is more likely Ahasuerus could not sleep because he was kept in suspense concerning Esther's request, although we cannot be certain of this, either. Whatever kept Ahasuerus from sleeping that evening, thoughtful readers of chap. 6 may inevitably sense the hand of God at work behind the scenes.

It remains unclear why Ahasuerus wanted to have the official records read to him. Was it to indulge his ego in hearing about his reign? Was it in hope the drone of human voices and the plodding language of bureaucratic writing would prove soporific? Whatever the case, astute readers may conclude it was God's providence which led the courtiers to read the account of the foiled assassination plot.

The "written report" mentioned here is certainly the same as the one in which Mordecai's role in exposing the conspiracy of Bigthana and Teresh was recorded.[59] To emphasize the careful recording of events, the author worded the last thirteen Hebrew words of 6:2 almost exactly the same as the last twelve words of 2:21.[60]

6:3 It is obvious the official record contained Mordecai's name, since Ahasuerus pointedly used his name when asking what had "been done for" him. He specifically asked what "honor and special recognition" (*yǝqār ûgǝdûlâ*) had been given to Mordecai. This phrase

---

[58] *Megillah* 15b.

[59] The description of the book is fuller here, perhaps to emphasize the formal reading before the king: סֵפֶר הַזִּכְרֹנוֹת דִּבְרֵי הַיָּמִים, "The scroll of the memorials of the events of the days" (6:1); סֵפֶר דִּבְרֵי הַיָּמִים, "the scroll of the events of the days" (2:23).

[60] The differences are changes in order to adapt to context (the verbs בִּקְשׁוּ [2:21]/ וַיְבֻקַּשׁ with the addition of 6:2] אֲשֶׁר]) and a slight difference in the name of the first eunuch (בִּגְתָן, Bigthan [2:21]/בִּגְתָנָא, Bigthana [6:2]).

denotes royal dignity given to those whom the king rewarded, since these two words occur together in only one other place in Esther: in the description of the splendor of Ahasuerus's reign at 1:4 (*yɘqār tip'eret gɘdûlatô*, "the magnificent splendor of his greatness"). Such honors were reserved for those who had done a great favor for the Persian king.[61] Yet, as Ahasuerus discovered, nothing had been done for the man who saved his life.

3.7.2   Ahasuerus Orders Honors for Mordecai (6:4–10)

⁴ The king asked, "Who is in the court?" Now Haman was just entering the outer court of the palace to ask the king to hang Mordecai on the gallows he had prepared for him.

⁵ The king's attendants answered him, "Haman is there, standing in the court."

"Have him enter," the king ordered. ⁶ Haman entered, and the king asked him, "What should be done for the man the king wants to honor?"

Haman thought to himself, "Who is it the king would want to honor more than me?" ⁷ Haman told the king, "For the man the king wants to honor: ⁸ Have them bring a royal garment that the king himself has worn and a horse the king himself has ridden, which has a royal crown on its head. ⁹ Put the garment and the horse under the charge of one of the king's most noble officials. Have them clothe the man the king wants to honor, parade him on the horse through the city square, and call out before him, 'This is what is done for the man the king wants to honor.'"

¹⁰ The king told Haman, "Hurry, and do just as you proposed. Take a garment and a horse for Mordecai the Jew, who is sitting at the King's Gate. Do not leave out anything you have suggested."

Date: 16 Nisan (Saturday, April 20), 474 BC

6:4–5 Ahasuerus was eager to bestow honor on Mordecai, so his next inquiry questioned who was in the "court"—perhaps the same area where Esther had come for an audience (5:1)—so he could get that person's help in honoring Mordecai. Haman had arrived early

---

[61] Herodotus recorded three times when Ahasuerus's father Darius had bestowed such rewards (*Histories*, 3.138; 3.140; 5.11) and two times that Ahasuerus also ordered such special recognition (*Histories* 8.85; 9.107).

to request Mordecai's execution (5:14). That fact is an ominous note. After all, to this point in the book and throughout the rest of the story, Ahasuerus never denied a request. If Haman could present his request, the implication is it would have been granted.

Ahasuerus's attendants' reply about Haman's presence imply he was waiting for an audience with the king. Ahasuerus ordered him to be admitted, undoubtedly wanting to put the process of honoring Mordecai into motion without further delay.

6:6 Single-mindedly focused on honoring Mordecai, Ahasuerus preempted Haman before Haman was able to make his request. He did not reveal whom he wished to honor, calling him simply "the man the king wants to honor" (*bāʾîš ʾăšer hammelek ḥāpēṣ*), a phrase repeated three times by Haman (6:7, 9 [twice]).

6:7–9 Since Haman's introduction to the reader (3:1), the author has been revealing the Agagite's character traits. Two related traits are emphasized: Haman's desire for honor and glory and Haman's egotism (3:5–6; 5:9, 11–13). These two come to the fore for the last time in Haman's reply. In the only instance in which the author reveals someone's thoughts to readers, we are told Haman's inflated ego immediately assumed Ahasuerus wanted to honor him (6:6). His desire for even more public honor than he had promptly superseded his longing to be rid of Mordecai, and he did not even ask to be honored by being given permission to hang Mordecai's body on the pole he had erected the previous day. Thus, Haman's ego would be his undoing.

Haman's advice was to treat the man whom the king wished to honor as if that man were king. Adorned with one of the king's personal garments, riding one of the king's personal horses, and requiring a senior royal official to make a proclamation was tantamount to equating the honoree's glory to that of the king. Inadvertently, Haman included himself among the ones who might be selected to declare the proclamation as "one of the king's most noble officials." His ego had blinded him to this possibility.[62]

---

[62] Fox, *Character and Ideology*, 76–77, claims that the author has shaped the royal honor to conform to the honor afforded Joseph in Egypt (Gen 41:42–43). While there are some similarities, the differences between the two contradict the suggestion that the honor was shaped by the author of Esther to match the Genesis passage. As Fox himself notes, "[I]nstead of Joseph's linen garment and gold necklace, Haman prescribes a garment the king has worn (Joseph also gets the royal signet, but Haman already has this). Instead of Joseph's ride in the viceroy's chariot, Haman wants a ride on the king's horse, with the horse itself bedecked in splendor. Instead of the simple call 'abrekh' (an exclamation of obscure derivation), Haman would have himself

As readers suspect prior to this point in the narrative, Haman appears to believe *he deserved to be king*, savoring the notion one of the nobles would publicly declare by Ahasuerus's own orders Haman had been given honor equal to that of the Persian king himself.

As peculiar as it may seem to modern readers, royal horses with various types of headdresses are documented in the reliefs of the Apadana in Persepolis.[63] This large open-air palace was completed during Ahasuerus's reign. One of the horses depicted shows a band holding a tuft of its mane in place between its ears.[64] This may be like the "royal crown" (*keter malkût*) Haman described. Since the horse's crown is not mentioned again, the designation "which has a royal crown on its head" may have been Haman's way of describing a certain horse— perhaps Ahasuerus's favorite ceremonial steed.

6:10 Ahasuerus's reply is recorded by the author in such a way the reader experiences Haman's shock and devastation at the king's instructions. This is accomplished in several ways:

1. Ahasuerus's word "[h]urry" (*mahēr*).[65]

2. A double mention that Haman had suggested this specific honor.[66]

3. Designating Mordecai as "the Jew," thereby unwittingly referencing the reason Haman considered Mordecai his enemy.

4. The instruction to carry out the honor exactly as Haman had proposed. He was not allowed to modify it in any way but was required to give Mordecai complete royal glory.

Ahasuerus, who had no previous interaction with Mordecai, knew not only his name but also his ethnicity, since it probably had been recorded in the official records read to him. This introduces yet another ironic touch. "[Ahasuerus] does not connect Mordecai's Jewishness

---

acclaimed by the cry, 'Thus shall be done for the man whom the king desires to honor!' On top of all this, Haman specifies that the man leading the horse be a nobleman." With all these differences, it is difficult to conclude that the author had Gen 41:42–43 in mind when describing Haman's suggestion.

[63] Margaret Cool Root, "The Parthenon Frieze and the Apadana Reliefs at Persepolis: Reassessing a Programmatic Relationship," *AJA* 89 (1985): 106–9.

[64] See plate 4 in Moore, *Esther* (following page 22).

[65] The only other use of this verb in Esther is at 5:5 where the king wished to immediately attend Esther's first banquet with Haman.

[66] אֲשֶׁר דִּבַּרְתָּ...כַּאֲשֶׁר דִּבַּרְתָּ "just as you suggested . . . you suggested," 6:10.

with the decree of destruction he authorized. The king had not bothered to find out which people he was consigning to destruction."[67]

3.7.3 Mordecai Is Honored while Haman Is Humiliated (6:11–14)

[11] So Haman took the garment and the horse. He clothed Mordecai and paraded him through the city square, calling out before him, "This is what is done for the man the king wants to honor."

[12] Then Mordecai returned to the King's Gate, but Haman hurried off for home, mournful and with his head covered. [13] Haman told his wife Zeresh and all his friends everything that had happened. His advisers and his wife Zeresh said to him, "Since Mordecai is Jewish, and you have begun to fall before him, you won't overcome him, because your downfall is certain." [14] While they were still speaking with him, the king's eunuchs arrived and rushed Haman to the banquet Esther had prepared.

6:11 The author quickly summarized the events, seeing no need for further development of Haman's humiliation or Mordecai's exaltation. Haman's execution of Ahasuerus's order forestalled what Haman had hoped to accomplish that day: Mordecai's execution.

6:12–14 Following the parade in the city square, Mordecai resumed his duty as a mid-level bureaucrat in Ahasuerus's court. Unlike Haman, Mordecai had no overly inflated self-image. Haman, on the other hand, "covered" his head and "hurried" home. Covering one's head was a sign of personal mourning and despair (2 Sam 15:30; Jer 14:3). The narrative's use of words for haste involving Haman leaves readers with the impression events beyond the Agagite's control had overtaken him. He was hurried to Esther's first banquet (Esth 5:5), then hurried to honor Mordecai (6:10). Then he hurried home humiliated (6:12).[68]

The second scene in Haman's home also features his wife and friends (see 5:10–14). Once again, he related what had happened to him. This time his friends and wife reflect his dejection in contrast to the triumphalist advice they had previously given him. Haman's friends are now called "his advisors," in Hebrew, literally *his wise men* (ḥŏkāmāyw). This is another case of irony included by the author.

---

[67] Fox, *Character and Ideology*, 77.
[68] Fox, *Character and Ideology*, 80.

They were not so wise earlier, although they knew Mordecai was Jewish.[69] Now they clearly understand because Mordecai is Jewish, Haman's plan for his enemy is doomed and so is Haman himself. The reason behind their statement is not simply the author placing words in their mouths to highlight the divine protection God had promised to Abraham and his heirs (Gen 12:2–3).[70] Instead, they may have been offering an observation in hindsight that Haman had picked a fight with an ethnic group which now had as its defender someone the king had given the highest honor. Alternatively, from Jews in Susa they may have heard of the Pentateuchal prophecies about God's victory over Amalek and by extension Agag (Exod 17:16; Num 24:20; Deut 25:17–19; see 1 Sam 15). In either case, by Esther's inclusion in the Old Testament canon, readers throughout the church's history understand the words of Haman's friends and wife as unknowingly pointing to God's promise to protect his Old Testament people for the sake of his promises. He pledged to use them to bring the Savior of all humanity into the world. One more time Haman is hurried along, this time to Esther's second banquet where his downfall will be realized.

THEOLOGY

This chapter highlights God's working through seemingly ordinary circumstances (Ahasuerus's insomnia, Haman's pride and arrogance, the advice of Haman's wife and friends). It also promotes several other messages. The contrast between Haman's hubris and Mordecai's humility (compare Prov 16:19; 29:23) is expressed by Haman's arrogance contributing to his own humiliation through his overreach for honor and glory. His ego, which turned him inward toward himself and away from both God and other people, made him oblivious to his social environment and dangerous to himself. Proverbs 30:32–33 speaks advice to anyone who is tempted to follow in Haman's footsteps: "If you have been foolish by exalting yourself or if you've been scheming, put your hand over your mouth. For the churning of milk produces butter, and twisting a nose draws blood, and stirring up anger produces strife."

In contrast, Mordecai neither sought honor from the crown nor thought of himself more highly than he should have (see Rom 12:3).

---

[69] Haman called him "Mordecai the Jew," 5:13.

[70] Berlin, *Esther*, 63; Bush, *Ruth, Esther*, 417.

He accepted his place among Ahasuerus's officials and sought to serve where God had placed him, returning to his position at the King's Gate immediately after having been honored by the king. This does not mean Mordecai was falsely modest. He would eventually accept promotion to become the highest of Ahasuerus's officials. In the meantime, Mordecai was willing to serve with skill, loyalty, and competence, traits leading to advancement and rightful honor (Prov 22:29). He is an example of a person who embodies service to others. The way of such Christian persons was later described by Paul: "Serve with a good attitude, as to the Lord and not to people, knowing that whatever good each one does, slave or free, he will receive this back from the Lord" (Eph 6:7–8).

This chapter also emphasizes a theological theme further developed in the next: the Almighty's will to save the world through Christ cannot be thwarted by humans—not even humans who occupy high positions of great authority and power (Ps 2; Acts 4:24–28). Haman's downfall before Mordecai was necessary to preserve God's promise to bring the Messiah from Israel and specifically from the tribe of Judah. Had Haman succeeded in extirpating the Jewish people from the Persian Empire, God's plan for all humanity may have been frustrated. Yet God's promises are unfailing, and he ensures no circumstances will hinder their fulfillment. In Mordecai's day this meant safeguarding his promise to redeem the world through Israel's Messiah. In our day, this means by God's power the church will continue to bring the message of Christ to our fallen world despite persecution and hardship (Acts 1:8; 1 Pet 2:9).

3.8   Esther's Second Banquet for Ahasuerus and Haman (7:1–10)

This short chapter[71] resolves the tension building in the narrative since Haman was introduced (3:1). It features the second time Ahasuerus's "anger" flared (7:7; see 1:12), that his anger led to someone's removal (7:9; 1:19), and that the king's rage eventually subsided (see 7:10; 2:1). Just as the royal anger of chap. 1 led to a replacement for Vashti in the next chapter, the imperial wrath in this chapter leads to a replacement for Haman in chap. 8.

---

[71] The MT of chap. 7 consists of 293 words and is the second shortest chapter in the book. Only chap. 10 (71 words) is shorter.

3.8.1 Esther Reveals Her Request to the King (7:1–4)

¹ The king and Haman came to feast with Esther the queen. ² Once again, on the second day while drinking wine, the king asked Esther, "Queen Esther, whatever you ask will be given to you. Whatever you seek, even to half the kingdom, will be done."

³ Queen Esther answered, "If I have found favor with you, Your Majesty, and if the king is pleased, spare my life; this is my request. And spare my people; this is my desire. ⁴ For my people and I have been sold to destruction, death, and annihilation. If we had merely been sold as male and female slaves, I would have kept silent. Indeed, the trouble wouldn't be worth burdening the king."

7:1–2 The author transitions effortlessly from Haman's being whisked away from his home (6:14) to his attendance with the king to Queen Esther's banquet. Esther is mentioned eight times by name in the ten verses of this chapter. Multiple times she is called "Queen Esther" to emphasize her royal position, which she will use effectively.

While CSB translates verse 1 "to feast with Esther," the Hebrew text says "to *drink* with Esther" (*lištôt ʿim ʾestēr*). In the following verse "while drinking wine" translates the literal wording, "at the feast of wine" (*bəmištēh hayyayin*). These phrases are intentionally used by the author to draw a parallel with the king and Haman drinking after the decree against the Jews was issued (3:15).[72] Here they drink as the author of the decree is undone. This drinking banquet must have been in the afternoon after the events of the morning (chap. 6) and before the execution of Haman later that day.

Ahasuerus repeated his offer to Esther, pointedly calling her "Queen Esther," thereby making this an official request—not simply the intimate words of a husband to his wife. Key to his words and Esther's reply are the words *ask* and *seek* in parallel.

7:3–4 Esther's reply is full of courtly language intended to disavow any attempt on placing demands on the king: "*If* I have found favor . . . and *if* the king is pleased" (emphasis added). In addition, she maintains the official level on which they are speaking, calling Ahasuerus "Your Majesty" and "the king." Then she employs the language of the king's offer to her: "[S]pare my life; this is my request. And spare my people; this is my desire." The word *request* corresponds to the

---

[72] Berlin, *Esther*, 65; Hoschander, *The Book of Esther*, 219; Moore, *Esther*, 69.

king's *ask* (they are from the same root in Hebrew); the king's word *seek* matches Esther's *desire* (these two words also share the same root in Hebrew). Since the king's *ask* and *seek* are parallel, Esther's *request* and *desire* are parallel, indicating Esther was equating *her life* with *her people*. From her viewpoint, to spare one is to spare the other. Of course, Ahasuerus would want to spare his queen's life. Yet he may have been less interested in the lives of her kinfolk. Esther's skillful words convey to him her life was bound up in that of her people. If Ahasuerus wanted to spare his wife, she said, he needed also to spare them.

Then she explained. Esther's people and she (note the reversed order) had "been sold." This is certainly a delicate reference to Haman's offer of a princely sum for the privilege of destroying the Jews (3:9). While the word *sold* is used in the Old Testament in a metaphorical sense for handing people over to others (Deut 32:30; Judg 2:14; 4:9; Ps 44:12), that is not the case here. Esther refers to the sale negotiated by Haman and the king and its resulting decree, which she quotes verbatim: "to destruction, death, and annihilation" (*ləhašmîd lahărôg ûlə'abēd*; 3:13).[73] Esther deftly avoids directly accusing the king: she uses the passive "have been sold" so the seller (i.e., Ahasuerus) is not mentioned.

Then Esther makes a startling statement. If the Jews had merely been sold as slaves, she "would have kept silent." Enslavement, while being an extremely undesirable state, would not have resulted in the destruction of her people. Moreover, this may be a way for Esther to acknowledge God's messianic promise, even if Ahasuerus would not have grasped the reason for mentioning it. If the Jews continued to live, albeit as slaves, God's pledge of an anointed Savior could still have been fulfilled. In such a case, her silence would not have endangered God's plan. While the full meaning may have been lost on Ahasuerus, those who know of God's Old Testament promise and its fulfillment in Christ will certainly understand.

The last sentence of Esther's request, "Indeed, the trouble wouldn't be worth burdening the king," is perhaps the most difficult in all of Esther. Three words are particularly problematic. The first (*haṣṣar*) is translated "the trouble" but can also mean "enemy." The second

---

[73] The words at 3:13, "to destroy, kill, and annihilate" (CSB), use the identical Hebrew roots translated "to destruction, death, and annihilation" (7:4).

(*šōweh*) is translated "be worth" but literally means "be the same or be equal." The third word (*bэnēzeq*), "burdening" in CSB, is most likely a loanword from Aramaic where it means "damage, harm."[74] Much depends on whether one understands the first word as "trouble" or "enemy." While many English versions agree with CSB in translating it as "trouble" (e.g., ESV, NET, NIV), others translate it as "enemy" (e.g., GW, NRSV, TANAKH).[75] There is good reason to understand this word as "enemy," chiefly because this is what Ahasuerus understood and how Esther would refer to Haman. In response to Esther, he asked, "Who is this and where is he?" (*mî hû' zeh wэ'ê zeh*),[76] indicating he perceived Esther was referring to a person, not a situation (7:5). Esther, likewise, answered Haman was the "enemy" (*ṣar*; 7:6). Therefore, a better translation would be this: "Indeed, the enemy is not equal to the harm done to the king." This enemy of Esther's people is doing more harm to the king than he is worth. Any threat to the queen who had found Ahasuerus's favor as a replacement for Vashti—whether that threat was enslaving the queen or killing her—would do more harm to the king than any benefit derived from that person, no matter what his rank.

3.8.2   *Esther Reveals Who Has Threatened Her Life and the Lives of Her People (7:5–6)*

⁵ *King Ahasuerus spoke up and asked Queen Esther, "Who is this, and where is the one who would devise such a scheme?"*
⁶ *Esther answered, "The adversary and enemy is this evil Haman." Haman stood terrified before the king and queen.*

7:5 The conversation continues as royalty speak to one another: "King Ahasuerus . . . Queen Esther." It is as if Haman has become a mere observer of his superiors. The Hebrew text of this verse repeats the same verb (*wayyōmer*, "spoke up and asked"). Some commentators believe the repetition is *dittography*, an accidental repetition by a careless scribe.[77] But Berlin notes the same type of repetition occurs at Gen 22:7; 46:2; 2 Sam 24:17; Neh 3:34; and Ezek 10:2 for the

---

[74] The verb from the same root meaning *harm something or someone* occurs three times in the Aramaic portions of the Old Testament (Ezra 4:13, 15; Dan 6:3).

[75] See also OG: ὁ διάβολος, "the slanderer, enemy, adversary."

[76] מִי הוּא זֶה וְאֵי־זֶה הוּא, "Who is this, and where is this one," 7:5.

[77] E.g., Moore, *Esther*, 71.

purpose of slowing the narrative. Here it slows Ahasuerus's speech to focus the reader on the indignation he expressed in essentially asking, "Who would dare do such a thing?" Ahasuerus knew what it was like to have a plot against his life (2:21–23; 6:2), and a plot against the queen was almost as grave an offense as a plot to assassinate the king.

7:6 Esther's reply not only accused Haman but almost spit out the words, literally: "A man—an enemy and a foe—this evil Haman!" (*'îš ṣar wə'ôyēb hāmān*). One can almost see her pointing across the room at her enemy, fuming with anger and contempt.

Some believe by pointing to Haman's plot Esther was revealing her identity as a Jew.[78] Yet there is no indication Ahasuerus knew which people Haman targeted. He had never asked who Haman wanted to destroy (3:7–11). Haman had never been able to request Mordecai *the Jew* be hung on the pole he had erected. Nor does Ahasuerus ask Esther, "Which people are we talking about?" In fact, Ahasuerus's ignorance of Esther's identity makes the scene even more powerful. *Her ethnicity did not matter to him* even though it was all that mattered to Haman. What mattered was someone threatening Ahasuerus's queen and, therefore, the stability of his kingdom. No wonder Haman was now "terrified before the king and queen," since the royal offices emphasize the treasonous nature of Haman's plot.

3.8.3   Due to Ahasuerus's Rage, Haman's Appeal for His Life Leads to his Execution (7:7–10)

⁷ *The king arose in anger and went from where they were drinking wine to the palace garden. Haman remained to beg Queen Esther for his life because he realized the king was planning something terrible for him.* ⁸ *Just as the king returned from the palace garden to the banquet hall, Haman was falling on the couch where Esther was reclining. The king exclaimed, "Would he actually violate the queen while I am in the house?" As soon as the statement left the king's mouth, they covered Haman's face.*

⁹ *Harbona, one of the king's eunuchs, said, "There is a gallows seventy-five feet tall at Haman's house that he made for Mordecai, who gave the report that saved the king."*

The king said, "Hang him on it."

---

[78] Baldwin, *Esther*, 93; Mervin Breneman, *Ezra, Nehemiah, Esther*, NAC 10 (Nashville: B&H, 1993, 349.

¹⁰ They hanged Haman on the gallows he had prepared for Morde-cai. Then the king's anger subsided.

7:7–8 The actions of Ahasuerus and Haman are narrated in such a way as to emphasize each man: "*The king* arose . . . and went . . . *Haman* remained . . . *the king* returned . . . *Haman* was falling."[79] No reason is given for Ahasuerus's departure from the room "to the palace garden" (see 1:5). Regardless, Haman should have known better than to stay in the same room with the queen. This would have been a viola-tion of the rules of the king's harem. But Haman perceived Ahasuerus was already determining how to punish him. If there was one certain way to change Ahasuerus, it was to have someone ask him a favor—he delighted in giving favors; and in Esther, he is never recorded denying a request. So Haman hoped Esther would ask his life be spared. Esther, however, would never be given a chance to respond to Haman.

Haman's timing could not have been worse. Ahasuerus entered just as Haman was "falling on" Esther's couch, where like all ancient diners, she would have reclined during the feast. There is another irony here: Haman's friends told him he had "begun to fall before" Mordecai (6:13). Now he is falling on Esther's couch. He has gone from falling before one Jew to falling on another.

Ahasuerus assumed Haman was forcing himself on the queen sex-ually, and Haman had the temerity to do this when Ahasuerus was in residence in his own palace. Taking the king's wife or concubine was usually seen as an attempt to usurp the throne (2 Sam 3:7; 16:21–22; 1 Kgs 2:15–17, 22).[80] Haman was pronounced guilty of treason merely by Ahasuerus uttering his question.

We do not know the meaning of Haman's face covering. The Greeks and Romans covered the heads of those who had been con-demned to death, but there is no information on the practice's signifi-cance among the Persians.

7:9–10 Harbona, one of the seven eunuchs who served as the king's personal attendants (1:10), now offered an observation that functioned as a suggestion: Haman had provided a high pole on which

---

[79] This is achieved in the Hebrew text by beginning each sentence with the subject rather than with the verb, as is normal in narration in Hebrew. See Berlin, *Esther*, 69.

[80] This can be seen especially in Absalom having sex with David's concubines on the roof of David's palace. See also Reuben having sex with his father's concubine as a possible bid for supremacy in Jacob's family (Gen 35:22).

to hang Mordecai's body. The king understood Harbona's suggestion and immediately ordered Haman hung on his own pole.

Harbona identified Mordecai as the man whose report "saved" Ahasuerus's life. This added an additional crime against the throne: Haman wished to kill the man whom the king desired to honor, giving the appearance Haman was in sympathy with Ahasuerus's enemies.[81] The presumed sexual assault on the queen further enraged the king. Haman was executed and then impaled on the pole he had erected for Mordecai (see the discussion in the introduction). Herodotus relates an account of Ahasuerus impaling a man for a sexual crime.[82] How much more serious was the attempted rape of the queen?

When Haman was hanged, "the king's anger subsided," just as it had when Vashti was deposed as queen (2:1). After this bout of anger, the king would need a new prime minister, a position eventually filled by the Jew Mordecai, just as the Jew Esther filled Vashti's vacant position.

THEOLOGY

Haman's downfall in Esther 7 is a case study in God's justice meted out in measure to a person's evil intent, a frequent theme in the Old Testament. Consider these passages from Scripture:

> See, the wicked one is pregnant with evil, conceives trouble, and gives birth to deceit. He dug a pit and hollowed it out but fell into the hole he had made. His trouble comes back on his own head; his own violence comes down on top of his head. (Ps 7:14–16)

> The righteousness of the upright rescues them, but the treacherous are trapped by their own desires. (Prov 11:6)

> The one who digs a pit will fall into it, and whoever rolls a stone—it will come back on him. (Prov 26:27)

> The one who digs a pit may fall into it, and the one who breaks through a wall may be bitten by a snake. (Eccl 10:8)

---

[81] Herodotus, *Histories*, 1.137.1, stated that a Persian king could not have someone executed for one offense. From context, however, this appears to refer to minor offenses. Surely, Bigthan and Teresh had been executed for only one offense (2:21–23), but that offense was a high crime.

[82] Herodotus, *Histories*, 4.43.1–6.

In addition, similar thoughts can be found in Ben Sira, whose wisdom is drawn from the Old Testament:

Whoever throws a stone upwards throws it on his own head, and a treacherous blow opens many wounds. Whoever digs a pit will fall into it, and whoever sets a snare will be caught in it. When a person does evil, it will roll back on him, and he will not recognize where it came from. (Sir 27:25–27)[83]

Moreover, Augustine of Hippo (November 13, 354 –August 28, 430 AD) observed the theme of a person's own evil returning to him is also found in Dan 6, the account of Daniel in the lions' den.[84] Hippolytus of Rome (c. AD 170–235) noted this theme was central to the apocryphal addition to Greek Daniel known as Susannah.[85]

Of course, these are general observations, not rules of divine retribution invariably applied in this life. They are intended to warn those who know and believe in God about the evil that lies in all fallen human hearts and which the believer needs to overcome through the indwelling power of Christ's Holy Spirit. For this reason, James counsels Christians,

But each person is tempted when he is drawn away and enticed by his own evil desire. Then after desire has conceived, it gives birth to sin, and when sin is fully grown, it gives birth to death. Don't be deceived, my dear brothers and sisters. Every good and perfect gift is from above, coming down from the Father of lights, who does not change like shifting shadows. By his own choice, he gave us birth by the word of truth so that we would be a kind of firstfruits of his creatures. My dear brothers and sisters, understand this: Everyone should be quick to listen, slow to speak, and slow to anger, for human anger does not accomplish God's righteousness. Therefore, ridding yourselves of all moral filth and the evil that is so prevalent, humbly receive the implanted word, which is able to save your souls. But be doers of the word and not hearers only, deceiving yourselves. (Jas 1:14–22)

While Haman serves as a lesson in the dangers of unchecked evil desires, Esther serves as an example of courage practiced through skillful use of words and deeds. Her request to Ahasuerus was expertly

---

[83] Author's translation.
[84] Augustine, Letter 93.19 (*NPNF[1]* 1:389).
[85] Hippolytus, *On Susannah*, v. 61 (*ANF* 5:193–4).

worded with the intention of moving the Persian monarch into action so many innocent lives would be saved. Although risking her life, Esther used her royal position as queen not to benefit herself but to benefit others. Her cousin Mordecai caused her to see "relief and deliverance" for "the Jewish people" would come through her and her position as queen (see Esth 4:13–14). In using her access to the king to speak on behalf of those who had no voice, she became an example of acting on the advice given in Scripture:

> Speak up for those who have no voice, for the justice of all who are dispossessed. Speak up, judge righteously, and defend the cause of the oppressed and needy. (Prov 31:8–9)

> Learn to do what is good. Pursue justice. Correct the oppressor. Defend the rights of the fatherless. Plead the widow's cause. (Isa 1:17)

> Hate evil and love good; establish justice at the city gate. Perhaps the LORD, the God of Armies, will be gracious to the remnant of Joseph. (Amos 5:15)

Of course, these directives are intended to lead God's people to be the ones through whom he works to bring relief and deliverance to the downtrodden, to those who have no voice—especially those who are members of his kingdom through faith in Christ Jesus. God is ready to give his people justice and defend them from evil when they cry to him, just as the Jews in Susa fasted for Esther (Esth 4:16)—they prayed that God would use her to free them from Haman's unjust decree. Jesus himself reminds us, "Will not God grant justice to his elect who cry out to him day and night? Will he delay helping them? I tell you that he will swiftly grant them justice." (Luke 18:7–8a)

3.9   Esther and Mordecai Receive Favors from the King (8:1–8)

Haman's execution may have ended the problem of the threat against Queen Esther, and this may have satisfied Ahasuerus (7:10). He gave Haman's estate to Esther and elevated Mordecai to the post of prime minister (8:1–2). These results, however, did not satisfy Esther. In this section Esther "wept" and "begged" (8:3), once again winning Ahasuerus's favor (8:4). Ahasuerus's permission begins with his action against Haman (8:7), indicating he had taken care of the immediate problem, but he was not overly concerned with the Jews' problem. He simply delegated the solution to that predicament to Mordecai (8:8). With the action turned over to Esther and Mordecai, Ahasuerus exits the narrative, no longer an active participant in the rest of chap. 8 or all of chap. 9. His only other act recorded in Esther is the imposition of "a tax throughout" the empire (10:1).

3.9.1   *Esther and Mordecai Are Given Haman's Property and Position (8:1-2)*

¹ *That same day King Ahasuerus awarded Queen Esther the estate of Haman, the enemy of the Jews. Mordecai entered the king's presence because Esther had revealed her relationship to Mordecai. ² The king removed his signet ring he had recovered from Haman and gave it to Mordecai, and Esther put him in charge of Haman's estate.*

8:1 "That same day" marks these events as occurring at the end of a busy day in which Mordecai was honored in the city square (6:4–11), Haman returned to his home (6:12–14), Esther held a banquet for Ahasuerus and Haman (7:1–8), and Haman was subsequently executed (7:9–10). The events in 8:1–2 must have taken place late in the day.

As has often been noted, in Persia the property of those condemned to death reverted to the crown.[86] Ahasuerus gave Haman's to Esther, probably since he saw her to be the aggrieved party as a result of Haman's decree.[87] This was an official act of the state, and the author treats it as such by calling the two parties "King Ahasuerus" and "Queen Esther."

Next, Mordecai "entered the king's presence." This act signifies Mordecai's elevation to being one who had access to the king even without being summoned (see 1:14). It is important to observe Mordecai did not receive his position because of his own merit. Instead, he was admitted to Ahasuerus's inner circle of advisors because of Esther. The phrase, "Esther had revealed her relationship to Mordecai," indicates Esther identified him as her cousin and adoptive father, but it does not stipulate Esther directly revealed she was Jewish. Instead,

---

[86] Herodotus, *Histories*, 3.128.1–129.1; Josephus, *Antiquities*, 11.17 [11.1.3]. The same custom apparently applied in Israel (1 Kgs 21:7–16).

[87] Fox, *Character and Ideology*, 90.

since Mordecai was known to the king as a Jew (6:10), it logically followed Esther, too, was Jewish.[88]

8:2 The king signaled Mordecai was to replace Haman by giving him the "signet ring" taken from Haman. This is a reversal of 3:10, where Haman was entrusted with issuing documents in the king's name. Here Mordecai, the man Ahasuerus could trust with his life (2:21–23; 6:1–3), was now trusted to administer the Persian Empire's affairs in the name of the king.

While Ahasuerus entrusted the royal signet to Mordecai, Esther entrusted her new property—Haman's estate—to his administration. Esther may have done this for practical reasons, since she appears to have been confined to the palace grounds when Ahasuerus was in residence (and may have traveled with him to other royal cities such as Persepolis); moreover, property ownership by women was rare. In addition, the move served to elevate Mordecai's status.

Ironically, the wording of Esther's entrusting Mordecai with Haman's estate employs the Hebrew phrase, "[A]nd Esther placed Mordecai over the house of Haman" (watāśem 'estēr 'et mordŏkāy 'al bêt hāmān). Haman was hung on the pole he had erected over his "house" (7:9), which now belonged to Mordecai. Thus, in a physical sense Haman was "over" his own house while in an administrative sense Mordecai was "over" it.

3.9.2 Esther Appeals to Ahasuerus to Issue a New Edict (8:3–6)

³ Then Esther addressed the king again. She fell at his feet, wept, and begged him to revoke the evil of Haman the Agagite and his plot he had devised against the Jews. ⁴ The king extended the gold scepter toward Esther, so she got up and stood before the king.

⁵ She said, "If it pleases the king and I have found favor with him, if the matter seems right to the king and I am pleasing in his eyes, let a royal edict be written. Let it revoke the documents the scheming Haman son of Hammedatha the Agagite wrote to destroy the Jews who are in all the king's provinces. ⁶ For how could I bear to see the disaster that would come on my people? How could I bear to see the destruction of my relatives?"

---

[88] To this point in the book, Esther has only identified herself as a member of the ethnic group threatened by Haman's decree (see 7:3–4). Neither Haman nor Esther had directly stated that this ethnic group was the Jews.

8:3–4 Esther's first appeal to Ahasuerus (7:3), though he had promised her whatever she desired, had not been granted. The king was concerned about the threat to the throne Haman represented, and he had settled that matter. Haman was dead. His body was a public spectacle designed to deter anyone else who might plot against the king (7:10). Perhaps Ahasuerus thought Esther's double appeal to spare her life and to spare her people was simply a rhetorical device to alert him to the threat Haman posed to her and, by extension, to him.

The scene presenting Esther at the king's feet is the most emotion-laden one for Queen Esther and the only time weeping is mentioned in the book.[89] She "begged him" (*wattithannen lô*), which is exactly what Mordecai told her to do previously (4:8).[90] Her lachrymose appeal is narrated in parallelism: "the evil" (*rāʿat*) and "his plot" (*mahăšabtô*) define each other. Moreover, Haman *the Agagite* is contrasted to his enemies *the Jews*.

When Ahasuerus once again "extended" his scepter to Esther, she knew she could make a formal request. Here the writer does not call Esther "queen," and he does not call Ahasuerus by his name but only by his royal title "king." Thus, the request will be from a subject appealing to the monarch in contrast to the dealings between royals marking 7:1–6 and 8:1. This authorial stratagem allows readers to see Esther not as queen but as a member of her people. Her words are, in effect, the words of the king's subjects who corporately appeal though her.

8:5–6 Esther's request begins with a long conditional preface, three protases with the third one a compound:

First protasis: "If it pleases the king"

Second protasis: "and [if] I have found favor with him,"[91]

Third (compound) protasis: "if the matter seems right to the king *and* I am pleasing in his eyes"

This is the humblest of Esther's requests to the king. At 5:4 she prefaced her request with one protasis. At 5:8 she used two. Later, at 9:13

---

[89] At 4:1 Mordecai "cried loudly and bitterly" (וַיִּזְעַק זְעָקָה גְדֹלָה וּמָרָה). That phrase does not refer to shedding tears but to calling out with one's voice. Here at 8:3 Esther "wept" (וַתֵּבְךְּ).

[90] Both "appeal" in 4:8 (CSB) and "begged" in 8:3 (CSB) translate a *hithpael* form of the verb root חנן, "to seek favor." The *hithpael* functions to denote iterative action.

[91] The Hb. text repeats the word "if" (אִם).

again she will use only one. In this way Esther makes herself like one of the humble Jewish subjects of the empire instead of a queen asking a favor or a demanding wife nettling her husband.

Esther's request was this: "[L]et a royal edict be written" (CSB). The Hebrew text (*yikkāteb*) does not contain the words "royal edict," however, which are added in translation for proper English style and meaning. Esther simply says, "[L]et it be written." Moreover, when referring to Haman's decree, she called them "the documents" (*has-səpārîm*). Her words are carefully chosen. She avoided calling for a "law" (1:13, 15, 19) or "royal decree" (1:8). These are represented by the Hebrew word *dāt*.[92] Such laws, according to Persian custom, cannot be revoked (1:19; 8:8; Dan 6:8, 12, 15). By avoiding the use of the word *dāt*, she was imploring Ahasuerus to find a way around the edict issued by Haman.

Esther also included a long and somewhat awkward description of the decree to be reversed. She introduces it as the one "the scheming Haman son of Hammedatha the Agagite wrote to destroy the Jews who are in all the king's provinces." This descriptor was designed to avoid placing any blame on Ahasuerus. Instead, it accuses one specific individual, Haman, using the title previously employed to identify him when he was given privileges by the crown (3:1, 10). In addition, the phrase characterizes the evil nature of this individual's action, implying they reflected badly on Ahasuerus: He was "scheming" (*maḥăšebet*), he wished to "destroy" (*lə'abbēd*), and it affected Jews in "all the king's provinces" (*bəkol mədînôt hammelek*).

Finally, Esther sought to motivate the king by calling his attention to the pain it would cause her. If Ahasuerus cared at all for his queen, her appeal would certainly move him. In a poetic manner, Esther used two parallel questions, "How could I bear to see . . . ?" The words "disaster" (*rā'â*) and "destruction" (*'ābdan*) stand in parallel to each other and use the classic poetic technique of focusing: the second word narrows the meaning of the first. The words "my people" (*'ammî*) and "my relatives" (*môladtî*) are also parallel to each other. Previously Esther "did not reveal" her people and relatives (2:10, 20).[93] Now for

---

[92] דָּת (*dāt*) is an important word throughout Esther. It is used twenty times in Esther and only once elsewhere (Ezra 8:36). The Aramaic cognate, however, is used fourteen times in Ezra and Daniel (Ezra 7:12, 14, 21, 25, 26 [twice]; Dan 2:9, 13, 15; 6:6 [5], 9 [8], 13 [12], 16 [15]; 7:25).

[93] Though it is not obvious in English versions, the same two Hebrew words are used at 2:10, 20; 8:6.

the first time she directly identified herself as a Jew, although she had indirectly identified herself as such when she told Ahasuerus of her relationship with Mordecai (8:1).

3.9.3 Ahasuerus Grants Permission for a New Edict (8:7–8)

⁷ King Ahasuerus said to Esther the queen and to Mordecai the Jew, "Look, I have given Haman's estate to Esther, and he was hanged on the gallows because he attacked the Jews. ⁸ Write in the king's name whatever pleases you concerning the Jews, and seal it with the royal signet ring. A document written in the king's name and sealed with the royal signet ring cannot be revoked."

8:7–8 The author reverts back to presenting the reader with formal state business by presenting the three parties to the conversation by formal titles: King Ahasuerus, Esther the queen, and Mordecai the Jew. Fox claims "the Jew" is used for Mordecai's title from this point forward, and it lost its main emphasis on his ethnicity.[94] Certainly, when carrying out state duties, he is called "Mordecai the Jew" (9:29, 31; 10:3), but those duties are mostly focused on helping his fellow Jews, so the title seems to serve a dual purpose: both to highlight his ethnicity and to portray him as the supreme royal official.[95]

Ahasuerus appears to believe he has done all he needed to do regarding the matter, stating he gave Haman's estate to Esther and had Haman impaled "because he attacked the Jews."[96] Of course, this is not correct—he had Haman impaled for his supposed attempt to prey on Esther sexually (7:8–9).[97] Yet the claim enabled Ahasuerus to distance himself from Haman's scheme. Neither Esther nor Mordecai

---

[94] Fox, *Character and Ideology*, 94.

[95] In Esther 9 he is only called "Mordecai the Jew" when acting in tandem with "Esther the queen" (9:29, 31).

[96] עַל אֲשֶׁר־שָׁלַח יָדוֹ בַּיְּהוּדִים: "because he stretched out his hand against the Jews." Baldwin, *Esther*, 95, claims this expression is an idiom meaning "conspire against." She cites Hayim Tawil, "Two Notes on the Treaty Terminology of the Sefîre Inscriptions," *CBQ* 42 (1980): 30–7. Tawil coordinates the Hebrew idiom with parallel Assyrian idioms. He then argues that in Ps 55:21; Dan 11:42; Esth 8:7 "stretch out the hand against" does not mean "attack" as it does elsewhere in the Old Testament but that it means "conspire against." The main drawback of Tawil's argument is that at Ps 55:21 and Dan 11:42 there is no reason the idiom must mean anything other than what it means elsewhere. Thus, it is doubtful that it means anything other than "attack" in Esther as well.

[97] Berlin, *Esther*, 75; Fox, *Character and Ideology*, 94.

would see fit to correct the king, and it was to their advantage to have him presented as defender of the Jews.

Never one for the mundane details of running an empire and having done all he was personally going to do, Ahasuerus delegated the undoing of Haman's decree to Mordecai and Esther. His imperative "[w]rite" (*wə'attem kitbû*) contains the unneeded, but in this case emphatic, Hebrew plural pronoun "you." He conferred on them the authority to unravel Haman's edict by whatever means necessary, and they had the royal signet so the reversal would have the effect of an edict issued by Ahasuerus himself.

Ahasuerus's final words on the matter have a retrospective and future quality to them much like the dual-faced Roman god Janus who was the god of both beginnings and endings. His words look back to Haman's edict sealed with the signet ring (3:12) and forward to Mordecai's edict (8:10). Ahasuerus reminded Esther and Mordecai the king's decree sealed with his signet ring "cannot be revoked" (see 1:19). They were reminded they could not directly countermand Haman's edict. Instead, they would have to devise a way to circumvent Haman's plot in place of declaring it null and void.

3.10 Mordecai Issues the Edict (8:9–14)

While both Esther and Mordecai were commissioned to do what was needed to rescue their fellow Jews from Haman's plot, only Mordecai was involved in composing the edict.[98] His solution to the dilemma of reversing Haman's edict was both simple and effective. By authorizing the Jews to conduct a defense against their enemies, Mordecai removed the possibility they would be left unarmed and vulnerable.

This section and the first two verses of the next (8:15–16) parallel the description of Haman issuing his decree (3:12–15). The two passages share identical phrasing with some adaptations for context. Esther 8:9–16 often expands or deletes wording, especially concerning the role of the Jews throughout the empire. In the parallel layout below, changes reflected in the Hebrew text are underlined; expansions (8:9–16) or deletions (3:12–15) are in italics. Regular type signals that

---

[98] Perhaps Ahasuerus's words at 8:8 could be taken to imply that Mordecai consulted with Esther before composing the edict. Esther, however, is explicitly said to have helped Mordecai compose the letter instituting Purim (9:20–21, 29–32). Thus, by her absence here, she apparently had no hand in drafting this edict.

the underlying Hebrew is identical in the two passages. For purposes of translation, the English text may read differently in parallels where the Hebrew is identical.

ESTHER 3:12–15	ESTHER 8:9–16
[12] The royal scribes were summoned <u>on the thirteenth day of the first month</u>, and the order was written exactly as <u>Haman</u> commanded. It was intended for the <u>royal</u> satraps, the governors of each of the provinces, and the officials <u>of each ethnic group</u> and written for each province in its own script and to each ethnic group in its own language.	The king and Haman sat down to drink, while the city of Susa was in confusion. [9] On the twenty-third day of the third month—*that is, the month Sivan*—the royal scribes were summoned. Everything was written exactly as <u>Mordecai</u> commanded *for the Jews*, to the satraps, the governors, and the officials <u>of the 127 provinces from India to Cush.</u> The edict was written for each province in its own script, for each ethnic group in its own language, *and to the Jews in their own script and language.*
It was written in the name of King Ahasuerus and sealed with the royal signet ring. [13] Letters <u>were sent</u> by couriers <u>to each of the royal provinces</u> telling <u>the officials</u>	[10] Mordecai wrote in King Ahasuerus's name and sealed the edicts with the royal signet ring. <u>He sent</u> the documents by *mounted couriers, who rode fast horses bred in the royal stables.* [11] *The king's edict* gave <u>the Jews in each and every city the right to assemble and defend themselves,</u>
to destroy, kill, and annihilate <u>all the Jewish people</u>—*young and old*, women and children—and plunder their possessions	to destroy, kill, and annihilate <u>every ethnic and provincial army hostile to them,</u> including women and children, and to take their possessions as spoils of war. [12] This would take place on a single day *throughout all the provinces of King Ahasuerus*, on the
on a single day,	
the thirteenth day of Adar, the twelfth month.	thirteenth day of the twelfth month, the month Adar. [13] A copy of the text, issued
[14] A copy of the text, issued as law throughout every province, was distributed to all the peoples so that <u>they</u> might get ready	as law throughout every province, was distributed to all the peoples <u>so the Jews</u> could be ready *to avenge themselves against their enemies* on that day. [14] The couriers
for that day. [15] The couriers left, spurred on by royal command,	rode *out in haste on their royal horses* at the king's urgent command. The law was also
and the law was issued in the fortress of Susa.	issued in the fortress of Susa. [15] <u>Mordecai went from the king's presence clothed in royal purple and white, with a great gold crown and a purple robe of fine linen.</u> The city of Susa <u>shouted and rejoiced,</u> [16] *and the Jews celebrated with gladness, joy, and honor.*

3.10.1   The Edict Is Issued for People throughout the Persian Empire (8:9–10)

⁹ *On the twenty-third day of the third month—that is, the month Sivan—the royal scribes were summoned. Everything was written exactly as Mordecai commanded for the Jews, to the satraps, the governors, and the officials of the 127 provinces from India to Cush. The edict was written for each province in its own script, for each ethnic group in its own language, and to the Jews in their own script and language.*

¹⁰ *Mordecai wrote in King Ahasuerus's name and sealed the edicts with the royal signet ring. He sent the documents by mounted couriers, who rode fast horses bred in the royal stables.*

Date: 23 Sivan (Monday, June 25), 474 BC

8:9 The "twenty-third day" of Sivan is two months and ten days after the publication of Haman's edict, a period of sixty-nine days (or seventy days if one counts inclusively). While some have proposed seventy days could be related symbolically to the "seventy years" of Babylon's supremacy over the nations prophesied in Jer 29:10,[99] this proposal suffers from two weaknesses. First, it assumes the date was not historically accurate, an assertion without supporting evidence. Second, as Berlin notes, "[T]he reader must infer this [i.e., that seventy is intended to be symbolic], for the story makes no mention of the number seventy."[100] The name of the third lunar month in the Jewish calendar, "Sivan," was adopted from the Babylonian name for this month and occurs only here in the Old Testament.

It remains unclear why Mordecai waited two months after becoming prime minister to issue this edict. Perhaps he needed time to devise an appropriate response to Haman's decree.

"[T]he royal scribes," we are told, wrote Mordecai's words verbatim. "[F]or the Jews" could be translated "to the Jews," making them the first recipients listed. The reference to "127 provinces" in the empire to which this decree was addressed gives it an explicitly comprehensive scope which Haman's decree did not have (3:12). This is the first mention of Ahasuerus's 127 provinces since the opening

---

[99] See also Jer 25:11–12; 2 Chr 36:21; Zech 7:5. See David J. A. Clines, *Ezra, Nehemiah, Esther*, NCBC (Grand Rapids, MI: Eerdmans, 1984), 316; Bush, *Ruth, Esther*, 444.

[100] Berlin, *Esther*, 77.

verse of Esther. The extent of the empire—"from India to Cush"—is mentioned only here and at 1:1.

The writing of this edict in all scripts and languages mirrors Haman's edict (3:12), except that the language of the Jews is included. During the Babylonian captivity many Jews adopted Aramaic as their first language, although it appears as if Hebrew remained the language of some. For instance, most of Ezra was written in Hebrew except for the letters to and from the Persian court (Ezra 4:9–6:18; 7:12–26). Nehemiah was written entirely in Hebrew, as was Chronicles. Since Aramaic typically served as the official language of correspondence from the Persian court to provinces from Babylon westward, the specific reference to the language of the Jews points to Hebrew.

8:10 Mordecai did not hesitate to use the authority granted to him by Ahasuerus. Although the Persian king did not wish to deal personally with the problem created by Haman, nevertheless the edict bore his "name."

The word used in this verse for the "fast horses" (*rekeš*) occurs only here and at 8:14 and Mic 1:13.[101] Several explanations defining the exact nuance of this word have been proposed.[102] The most cogent of these is the word refers specifically to horses used to transport royal mail.[103] Another Persian loanword is used in this verse to describe these horses (CSB: "bred in the royal stables"). This term, *'ăhaštərānîm*, is usually explained as a compound of the Persian words *ḥšaṣa* ("dominion, rule") and *ana* ("royal").[104]

3.10.2   The Content of the Edict (8:11–12)

[11] The king's edict gave the Jews in each and every city the right to assemble and defend themselves, to destroy, kill, and annihilate every ethnic and provincial army hostile to them, including women and children, and to take their possessions as spoils of war. [12] This would take place on a single day throughout all the provinces of King Ahasuerus, on the thirteenth day of the twelfth month, the month Adar.

---

[101] The more common Hebrew word for horse, סוּס, also is used in this verse and is translated adjectivally in CSB: "mounted couriers" (הָרָצִים בַּסּוּסִים).

[102] See the discussion in Bush, *Ruth, Esther*, 445–6.

[103] Gerald A. Klingbeil, "רכש and Esther 8,10.14: A Semantic Note," *ZAW* 107 (1995): 301–3.

[104] Paul Haupt, "Critical Notes on Esther," *AJSL* 24 (1907–8): 97–186; Moore, *Esther*, 80; Paton, *Esther*, 273.

8:11 When compared to the shorter parallel at 3:13, the words "[t]he king's edict" beginning this verse serve to highlight the royal authority behind Mordecai's action and to emphasize he had been given the authority to eviscerate Haman's edict. The Jews were not only given "the right to assemble" but also the right "to defend themselves" a phrase literally reading, "to stand for their lives" (*wəlaʿămōd ʿal napšām*). This contrasts with the authorization in Haman's decree for Persian officials to kill any Jews they wished. Mordecai's edict defines this self-defense in terms borrowed from Haman's edict: "to destroy, kill, and annihilate" (*ləhašmîd lahărôg ûlə'abēd*). They could attack "every ethnic and provincial army hostile to them," but no one else. This contrasts favorably with Haman's decree in 3:13, which allowed government officials and others to destroy "all the Jewish people" regardless of whether they were deemed a danger to anyone.

For many the most troubling aspect of Mordecai's decree is the authorization to kill women and children. To obviate this concern, it has been suggested the words "children and women" (*ṭap wənāšîm*) should be understood as part of the object of the participle *haṣṣārîm* (*attacking*, CSB: "hostile to").[105] According to this proposal, the phrase might be translated, "[E]very ethnic and provincial army hostile to them, [their] children, and [their] wives . . . ," but such a translation appears to run counter to the syntax of the Hebrew sentence. Bush notes,

> [T]o understand the two nouns *ṭap wenašîm*, "children and women," as further objects of the participle "attacking," they should not only carry the pronominal suffix "their," but the direct object marker *'et* as well. Indeed, the very fact that they are indefinite coordinates them with the equally indefinite "all power of people and province," rather than the definite pronoun "them," which immediately precedes. Finally, as the parallelism also reveals, the final clause,[106] being infinitival and not participial, must coordinate with "to destroy" and not with "attacking."[107]

---

[105] Robert Gordis, "Studies in the Esther Narrative," *JBL* 95 (1976): 49–53; Maggie Low, "To Kill or Not to Kill the Enemies' Women and Children?: The Irony of Esther 8:11," *AsJT* 30 (2016): 145–59.

[106] I.e., "and to take their possessions as spoils of war."

[107] Bush, *Ruth, Esther*, 447.

Esther 8:11 reports the Jews were given permission to attack any hostile force, including women and children. This would not have bothered ancient readers since family members were often considered extensions of the head of the clan and suffered for any offenses committed by him. Berlin notes, "From a literary point of view, the mention of women and children parallels the mention of Jewish women and children in Haman's decree (3:13). This is part of the reversal of Haman's decree and so the stipulations are the same."[108]

No women or children were explicitly reported to have been killed, however (see 9:11–16). In Susa only "men" (*'îš*; 9:12, 15) are said to have been killed. Since the author specifically notes the Jews took no "plunder" (9:10, 15, 16), the text may be implying they also killed only men among those who were hostile to them—their "enemies" (*'ōybêhem*; 9:1, 5, 16, 22), "those who hated them" (*śōnə'êhem*; 9:1, 5, 16)—not women and children, suggesting that while the decree allowed the Jews to do to their enemies what Haman had authorized done to the Jews, the Jews intentionally targeted only those who remained openly hostile to them. (Many groups, in fact, appear to have self-identified as Jews "for fear of the Jews" in order to escape any threat to their lives. See 8:17.) Fox concludes, "The permission to take spoil allows the Jews to *refuse* to do so."[109] Perhaps the same was true of permission to kill women and children—it allowed the option of refusing to do so, though the text leaves the question unanswered.

8:12 The permission for Jews to defend themselves applied for one day only—"the thirteenth day of . . . Adar," the same day Haman had authorized the provincial authorities to attack the Jews (3:13). The choice of this date was significant, highlighting the defensive nature of the Jews' actions. They were not to attack anyone, but only to defend themselves against any who attacked them. Moreover, any Jewish action against their enemies was limited to "a single day." This

---

[108] Berlin, *Esther*, 77. Berlin also notes that the practice of the "ban" (חֵרֶם), the Pentateuchal authorization to kill all the people of Canaan including women and children as well as livestock, is not applicable here, and those who reason that this is the motivation behind this provision in Mordecai's edict are incorrect (e.g., Fox, *Character and Ideology*, 100). Furthermore, Mordecai's decree is not repeating Samuel's authorization to Saul to attack and kill the Amalekites (1 Sam 15:3). That instruction to Saul, like the Pentateuchal ban, not only included women and children but also livestock, which are not mentioned in Mordecai's authorization of his fellow Jews.

[109] Fox, *Character and Ideology*, 100.

limitation kept the violence to a minimum so it would not escalate into a vendetta.[110]

3.10.3   The Edict Is Promulgated throughout the Persian Empire (8:13–14)

[13] A copy of the text, issued as law throughout every province, was distributed to all the peoples so the Jews could be ready to avenge themselves against their enemies on that day. [14] The couriers rode out in haste on their royal horses at the king's urgent command. The law was also issued in the fortress of Susa.

8:13 The distribution of the text "throughout" the empire is once again emphasized. The author indicates the Jews who were scattered throughout much of the kingdom knew they had the right to defend themselves (see 8:9; on the word "copy," see comments at 3:14.) The publishing of this decree to "all the peoples" functioned to counteract Haman's edict, also addressed to "all the peoples" (3:14). The word translated "to avenge" (*ləhinnāqēm*) denotes "meting out punishment for a wrong." Fox comments this verbal root "never refers to a simple defense or rescue, but everywhere designates a punitive action and presupposes a prior wrong, that is, some offence to which the avenging party is responding."[111] The document reinforces the concept the Jews were not initiating any attack on their enemies but only responding to the wrong done to them by those who would attempt to carry out Haman's plot. As Fox notes,

> The scope of this edict implies that the Jews would otherwise be forbidden to defend themselves. Without Mordecai's edict, the army would have prevented effective Jewish resistance, since Haman's edict made the massacre of Jews legal. Now that the Jews are guaranteed the right to defend themselves, the army can, and indeed must, stand aside.[112]

8:14 The mention of couriers on horses, previously referred to in 8:10, emphasizes not only the official nature of Mordecai's edict but also the urgency of delivering the message. To reinforce this urgency,

---

[110] Baldwin, *Esther*, 98.

[111] Fox, *Character and Ideology*, 101.

[112] Fox, *Character and Ideology*, 103.

the author notes the couriers left "urgently and hastily" (*məbōhālîm ûdəḥûpîm*) whereas Haman's earlier edict was sent out "hastily" (*dəḥûpîm*). Special mention of the distribution of the decree in Susa anticipates the next chapter's emphasis on the Jews' defensive activities in the Persian capital (9:8–15).

3.11   Mordecai's Elevation Leads to Rejoicing Among the Jews and Fear Among Others (8:15–17)

¹⁵ Mordecai went from the king's presence clothed in royal blue and white, with a great gold crown and a purple robe of fine linen. The city of Susa shouted and rejoiced, ¹⁶ and the Jews celebrated with gladness, joy, and honor. ¹⁷ In every province and every city where the king's command and edict reached, gladness and joy took place among the Jews. There was a celebration and a holiday. And many of the ethnic groups of the land professed themselves to be Jews because fear of the Jews had overcome them.

8:15–16 Following the issuance of the decree we are told Mordecai left "the king's presence." The contrast with Haman is stark. When the Agagite issued his royal edict, he followed it with a round of drinking with the king. Mordecai, in contrast, carries the royal symbols out of the palace to "[t]he city of Susa." His clothing is in the Persian royal colors, as he was clothed in white and violet (*təkēlet;* "blue" CSB) and had "a purple (*'argāmān*) robe of fine linen." The colors, as well as the fabric, were all part of the royal trappings of the palace during Ahasuerus's feast (1:6). Mordecai's headdress (*'ăṭārâ*) is not the same as the "royal crown" mentioned elsewhere in Esther (*keter;* 1:11; 2:17; 6:8). Nevertheless, his "great gold crown" is also a symbol of his rank and authority granted by the king. The word used for Mordecai's "robe" (*takrîk*) is a loanword from Aramaic and occurs only here in the OT. Such Aramaic loanwords became increasingly common in Hebrew during and after the Babylonian captivity.

The reaction of the city of Susa to Mordecai also contrasts its reaction to Haman's absence following the publication of his edict against the Jews. Mordecai's presence brought shouting and rejoicing whereas Haman's absence produced "confusion" (3:15). The rejoicing engendered by Mordecai's regal position, which coincided with Haman's downfall, provides a fitting example of the truth of Prov

11:10: "When the righteous thrive, a city rejoices; when the wicked die, there is joyful shouting."

In addition, Susa's Jews experienced four things: light (see CSB footnote a), "gladness, joy, and honor." The rather strange way light is introduced by the author calls the reader's attention to it.[113] Light can signify joyfulness and prosperity (Ps 97:11; Job 22:28; 30:26). More importantly, light comes as a gift from God and brings salvation and life (Ps 27:1; 36:9). Esther's author, who avoided mentioning God or his work in the narrative, may be hinting to his readers God's work through Mordecai's acts saved his ancient people.

The use of "honor" (yəqār) to describe one of the things the Jews of Susa received is noteworthy. This word is used frequently in Esther—ten times out of a total of sixty-one occurrences in the OT. In 1:4 the word describes Ahasuerus's honor and in v. 20 expresses the honor wives were commanded to give their husbands. In Esther 6, "honor" was bestowed on Mordecai by Ahasuerus (vv. 3, 6 [twice], 7, 9 [twice], 11). Now it was extended to all the Jews in Susa. Through Mordecai's triumph, they have honor instead of mourning (4:1–3).

8:17 The description of the consequences of Mordecai's decree for the provincial Jews compares to that of Susa's Jews with important distinctions. Like the Jews in Susa, the Jews in the provinces experienced "gladness and joy." In contrast to Susa's Jews, they participated in "a celebration and a holiday." The word for "celebration" (mišteh) is the same as used for feasts and banquets throughout Esther. For "holiday," the Hebrew expression is "good day" (yōm ṭōb), a phrase also used in 9:19, 22 and 1 Sam 25:8. In postbiblical Hebrew, the phrase frequently denotes a holiday. Once again, Esther's author draws a contrast between the effect of Haman's decree and the decree from Mordecai by wording this verse similarly to 4:3:

There was great mourning among the Jewish people in every province where the king's command and edict reached. They fasted, wept, and lamented, and many lay in sackcloth and ashes. (4:3)

In every province and every city where the king's command and edict reached, gladness and joy took place among the Jews. There was a celebration and a holiday. And many of the ethnic groups of the land

---

[113] The Hebrew construction is unique: לַיְּהוּדִים הָיְתָה אוֹרָה, "the Jews had light."

professed themselves to be Jews because fear of the Jews had overcome them. (8:17)

The reaction of Jews to Haman's edict was lamentation. The reaction of non-Jews to Mordecai's edict was "fear." This is not reverential fear[114] but fear for their lives and well-being.[115] Motivated by this fear, they "professed themselves to be Jews."[116] The statement has significant importance since the Jewish community in every town and village would know the ethnicity of its residents. It may indicate these Gentiles adopted Jewish customs and practices and at times may have converted and begun to worship the God of Israel.[117] For other instances in the OT where Gentiles converted, see Ruth (Ruth 1:16) and Naaman (2 Kgs 5:15–19).

THEOLOGY

Esther 8 provides three distinct opportunities for theological reflection. The first is Esther's persistence in asking for deliverance for the Jewish people from Haman's edict. It was clear Ahasuerus considered the matter ended when he had dealt with the threat to Esther's life and had Haman executed. Esther was safe, but she was not content with her own self-preservation. She risked Ahasuerus's wrath a second time by falling at his feet and begging him to do more so her people would be spared. In this way, Esther was fulfilling God's law: "Love your neighbor as yourself" (Lev 19:18; Matt 19:19; 22:39; Mark 12:31, 33; Rom 13:9; Gal 5:14; Jas 2:8). Esther risked her relationship with Ahasuerus in order to help her people, providing an example of loving others even when there is a potential cost to one's own well-being.

The second theological message is found in Mordecai's decree. He tailored his declaration narrowly, targeting only those who would attack the Jewish people. This contrasts with Haman, who wished to kill many innocent people because he took offense at Mordecai.

---

[114] As argued, for instance, by Clines, *Ezra, Nehemiah, Esther*, 318–19.

[115] H. G. M. Williamson, "Review of *The Esther Scroll*, by D. J. A. Clines," *JTS* 37 (1986): 146–52. Williamson notes that the idiom נפל פחד על regularly denotes fear of a calamity, and the calamity is often military action (Exod 15:16; 1 Sam 11:7; Ps 105:38; Job 13:11).

[116] The verb מִתְיַהֲדִים is a denominative verb in the *Hithpael* stem. Some verbs in the *Hithpael* stem take an estimative-declarative or reflexive meaning, as here. See *IBHS* §26.2f.

[117] Berlin, *Esther*, 80–1; Mervin Breneman, *Ezra, Nehemiah, Esther*, NAC 10 (Nashville: B&H, 1993), 356; Bush, *Ruth, Esther*, 448; Fox, *Character and Ideology*, 105.

Yet Mordecai's provision the Jews could not only defend themselves against those men who would attack them but also kill women and children if provoked certainly bothers many modern readers. Nevertheless, a contemporary perspective represents an instance of imposing modern Western sensibilities onto a text from antiquity. Moreover, there is no evidence the Jews killed Persia's women and children (see commentary on 8:11). Mordecai serves as an example of a good magistrate, one who imitates God and rules fairly and with justice (Deut 10:18; 16:20; Ps 33:5; 37:6, 28; 45:4; 48:10; 82:3; 89:14; 97:2; 99:4; 103:6; 106:3; 111:7; Prov 29:4; 31:8; Isa 1:17; 5:16). Christians who serve in government can look to Mordecai as an example of one who governed rightly and sought justice for all people.

Third, the work of God to bring Gentile people to the truth of his gospel is implied at the end of this chapter. Many "professed themselves to be Jews" because of "fear of the Jews" (Esth 8:17). While this is not an ideal motivation for associating oneself with God's people, it nevertheless may have exposed many to the promises of God in the coming Messiah. These persons may have associated with the Jews throughout the Persian Empire as a result, hearing the promises of a Savior in the words of the OT Scriptures. Certainly, there were many who may have professed themselves to be Jews only out of worldly fear and were insincere in their claim. Yet it is also likely some took their new profession earnestly. This concept reminds us that God can use events to bring people into churches, and while their original motive for attending may be questionable, their church attendance provides God's New Testament people with opportunities to deliver the gospel to them at an appropriate moment in their lives.

SECTION OUTLINE

4   THE JEWS ARE VICTORIOUS OVER THEIR ENEMIES (9:1–32)

This last major section of Esther occupies the entirety of chap. 9 and centers on two main foci: the victory of the Jews over their enemies and the institution of Purim. The author maintains the distinction between the Jews in Susa and the provincial Jews at the end of chap. 8. Since he is more knowledgeable about the events in Susa (9:6–15) than in the provinces (9:16–17), it is likely he either received his information about the events during Ahasuerus's reign from Jews in Susa or was himself a resident of the royal Persian city.

4.1   Mordecai's Edict Takes Effect (9:1–2)

[1] *The king's command and law went into effect on the thirteenth day of the twelfth month, the month Adar. On the day when the Jews' enemies had hoped to overpower them, just the opposite happened. The Jews overpowered those who hated them.* [2] *In each of King Ahasuerus's provinces the Jews assembled in their cities to attack those who intended to harm them. Not a single person could withstand them; fear of them fell on every nationality.*

Date: 13 Adar II (Thursday, April 5), 473 BC

9:1 This chapter begins with one of the most ponderous sentences in the entire book. In Hebrew the entire verse is one extended sentence, though it has been divided into several sentences in translation to accommodate good English style. The verse begins with two temporal clauses. The first temporal clause identifies the date on which the king's edict went into effect. It is not clear from the context which edict is referenced—the one issued by Haman or the one published by Mordecai. Both mentioned "the thirteenth day of Adar" (3:13; 8:12). The next temporal clause ("On the day when the Jews' enemies had hoped to overpower them") refers to the same day in a different way— by what was anticipated by the Jews' enemies—they would overpower them. The verb translated "overpower" is a loanword from Aramaic occurring only in this verse.[1]

The main clause of the sentence notes the ironic twist in the narrative: "[J]ust the opposite happened," literally the edict "was overturned" (*wənahăpôk hû'*).[2] The second temporal clause defines what "overturned" means: when "[t]he Jews overpowered those who hated them."[3] This is the first use of "who hated them" (*śōn'êhem*), which occurs again at 9:5, 16. It appears to be another way of referring to those who had hostile intent toward the Jews (see 8:11).

9:2 The assembling in "their cities" (*'ārêhem*) implies only certain cities throughout the empire are in view. While by this time there was a Jewish Diaspora outside of the Persian province of Yehud (Judah), it was mainly confined to Mesopotamia. In those cities they assembled the Jewish population. The idiom translated "to attack" is literally "to stretch out a hand against" (*lišlōaḥ yād bə*). This is the final use of this idiom in the book; it occurred earlier to describe the plot of Bigthan and Teresh, the two eunuchs who sought to assassinate Ahasuerus (2:21; 6:2), and the scheme of Haman to exterminate the Jews in the empire (3:6; 8:7).

The inability of anyone to withstand the Jews' self-defense is explained by the "fear" experienced by various ethnic groups in the Persian Empire, incapacitating them. Such paralysis occurs several other times in the OT (1 Sam 11:7; Esth 8:17; 9:3; Job 13:11;

---

[1] It occurs elsewhere in the OT at Neh 5:15; Ps 119:133; Eccl 2:19; 5:18; 6:2; 8:9.

[2] וְנַהֲפוֹךְ הוּא. This phrase employs a rare use of a *Niphal* infinitive absolute in place of a finite verb.

[3] אֲשֶׁר יִשְׁלְטוּ הַיְּהוּדִים הֵמָּה בְּשֹׂנְאֵיהֶם, "[T]he Jews overpowered their enemies."

Ps 105:38; Isa 24:18; Jer 48:44), but the closest parallel is found with Exod 15:16 in Israel's song to the Lord after the Israelites' deliverance from the Egyptians at the Red Sea. The song prophesied the peoples of Canaan would be paralyzed by "terror" of Israel. The author of Esther may be hinting the deliverance of the Jews in Esther is the work of the same God who delivered Israel from Egypt and gave them the land of Canaan.

4.2 Persian Officials Aid the Jews (9:3–4)

³ All the officials of the provinces, the satraps, the governors, and the royal civil administrators aided the Jews because they feared Mordecai. ⁴ For Mordecai exercised great power in the palace, and his fame spread throughout the provinces as he became more and more powerful.

9:3 While the peoples of the empire were paralyzed with fear of the Jews (9:2), the officers of the empire were spurred into action by fear of Mordecai. Unlike the list of officials at 3:12 and 8:9, these "officials" are not listed from highest in authority to least in rank. Instead, the local officers are listed first: the provincial officials. In addition, this list of royal officers is the longest in Esther, including four offices. The "royal civil administrators" (*'ōśê hammələā'kâ 'ăšer lammelek*, "doers of the kingdom which are the king's") may be the same "officials" (*'ōśê hammələā'kâ*, "doers of the kingdom") which Haman had mentioned when he offered to transfer money to the royal treasury (3:9). These officials were now caught in a conflict of interest: they had been ordered to "destroy" the Jews (3:13), and they had been ordered to allow the Jews to "defend themselves" (8:11). It seems because of Mordecai many of these officials decided to ignore Haman's decree and "aided the Jews" in keeping with Mordecai's decree.

9:4 Mordecai's increasing influence in the palace and the spread of his "fame" throughout the empire engendered fear among the population.[4] The use of the participle *hôlēk* to describe the process of the spread of Mordecai's fame indicates this took some time to reach all the provinces, suggesting the entire nine months between Moredecai's

---

[4] The suggestion of Moore, *Esther*, 86, that the phrase בֵּית הַמֶּלֶךְ "house of the king" refers not to the palace but to the entire city of Susa is doubtful. See Bush, *Ruth, Esther*, 462, as well as Esth 2:8–9, 13; 4:13; 5:1; 6:4.

edict and the thirteenth of Adar is in view. The end of the verse, "as he became more and more powerful," literally reads, "For the man Mordecai continued to become great."[5] This phrase is similar to Exod 11:3: "The man Moses was very great."[6] The author may be making another one of his subtle connections to Israel's earlier history. Mordecai was a deliverer of his people from oppression in the mode of the great deliverer Moses. Moreover, he may be implying Mordecai came to his office by God's silent-to-the-reader call, thereby hinting at the unseen hand of God at work in delivering his people from Haman.

4.3   The Enemies of the Jews are Executed (9:5–10)

[5] The Jews put all their enemies to the sword, killing and destroying them. They did what they pleased to those who hated them. [6] In the fortress of Susa the Jews killed and destroyed five hundred men, [7] including Parshandatha, Dalphon, Aspatha, [8] Poratha, Adalia, Aridatha, [9] Parmashta, Arisai, Aridai, and Vaizatha. [10] They killed these ten sons of Haman son of Hammedatha, the enemy of the Jews. However, they did not seize any plunder.

9:5 The report of Jewish action is direct and short. The phrase "They did what they pleased," might strike readers as referencing wanton destruction of the enemies. But Baldwin suggests it simply means the Persian authorities did not interfere.[7] In support of this theory, the same expression occurs at 1:8 where everyone was allowed to drink as much as he pleased at Ahasuerus's banquet: no royal restriction interfered with each guest's desire for wine.

9:6–10 We are told "five hundred men" in "the fortress of Susa" (bǝšûšan habbîrâ) were killed. Some believe this number represents an exaggeration.[8] Others believe the king would not have allowed such slaughter within the palace precincts.[9] Nevertheless, if Haman had supporters and allies that posed a threat to the Jews in Susa, most of them would have been cloistered in the fortress of Susa. There is no need to doubt the text's accuracy here. Paton notes, "This slaughter

---

[5] .כִּי־הָאִישׁ מָרְדֳּכַי הוֹלֵךְ וְגָדוֹל

[6] .גַּם| הָאִישׁ מֹשֶׁה גָּדוֹל מְאֹד

[7] Baldwin, *Esther*, 104.

[8] E.g., Fox, *Character and Ideology*, 110.

[9] Moore, *Esther*, 87.

took place in the palace-quarter under the King's very eyes. It indicates the presence of a considerable body of Jews in Susa (cf. 4[16])."[10]

Men killed in the fortress included Haman's "ten sons," indicating they likely served in Ahasuerus's court. All their names appear to be Persian. The name of the first son, *Parshandatha*, is a genuine Persian name attested on a cylinder seal now in the possession of the British Museum.[11] This list of ten sons by name not only demonstrates the thoroughness of the Jews' annihilation of their enemies, but also reinforces the total downfall of Haman: he previously lost his life and his estate. Now he has lost his progeny.

Finally, the author notes the Jews took no "plunder" (see also 9:15, 16). This is another of the author's understated ways of referring to previous Israelite history. Saul, who was not supposed to take plunder from the Amalekites, disobeyed God's instructions given through Samuel and seized plunder (1 Sam 15:17–23). The Jews in Esther, who were allowed to take "spoils of war" (Esth 8:11), did not. They, in effect, reversed Saul's sin. In addition, by abstaining from plundering their enemies, they demonstrated their action was purely in self-defense and not performed out of avarice or hatred.

4.4 The King Receives a Report and Authorizes Further Action (9:11–19)

The action of the Jews on the thirteenth of Adar occurred only "[i]n the fortress of Susa," the palace precincts (9:11). Yet there were others in the lower city of Susa who were hostile to the Jews. After Ahasuerus received a report of the number killed in the fortress, Esther asked him to extend the law for another day in Susa only so the Jews would be able to defeat their enemies there also. The author records the actions of the provincial Jews, maintaining the distinction between the Jews in Susa and those in the provinces that he introduced in 8:15–16.

4.4.1 The Report and Ahasuerus's Reaction to It (9:11–12)

[11] *On that day the number of people killed in the fortress of Susa was reported to the king.* [12] *The king said to Queen Esther, "In the*

---

[10] Paton, *Esther*, 283–4.

[11] Henry Snyder Gehman, "Notes on the Persian Words in the Book of Esther," *JBL* 43 (1924): 327; Millard, "Persian Names in Esther," 484.

fortress of Susa the Jews have killed and destroyed five hundred men,
including Haman's ten sons. What have they done in the rest of the
royal provinces? Whatever you ask will be given to you. Whatever you
seek will also be done."

9:11 The king received a report of the number killed in Susa even
though he had taken little interest in what would be done to defend
the Jewish people, leaving the details to Esther and Mordecai (8:7–8).
Perhaps during the months Mordecai served as prime minister he had
come to respect Esther's cousin and developed an interest in the welfare of the Jewish people. This may be why Mordecai "became more
and more powerful" (*hôlēk wəgādôl*; 9:4).

9:12 Ahasuerus's concern for Esther and his close relationship
with her is signaled by his report of the number of men killed "[i]n the
fortress of Susa." He must have still had vivid recollection of Haman
falling on Esther's couch and the threat he perceived to the queen (and
his throne) because of that memory, so he included a report about
Haman's sons. The question that follows, "What have they done in the
rest of the royal provinces?" is most certainly not asking for a report
from Esther. Moreover, it would have been too soon to receive reports
from distant provinces. Instead, this must be a rhetorical question.[12]
Berlin understands it as the king cheering for the Jews and their victory.[13] Fox interprets the question as the king expressing admiration for
the Jews' success.[14] Perhaps the king's question also reveals a certain
astonishment the Jews had such a large number of enemies within his
own palace.[15]

The king's offer to Esther mirrors his previous offers except it does
not use the rhetoric of offering up to "half of the kingdom" to her (see
5:3, 6; 7:2). Moreover, as Beal comments, "Unlike any of these previous speeches . . . Esther does not come before the king to make her

---

[12] This is understood by several English versions that punctuate the question with an
exclamation point instead of a question mark. See ESV, GW, NET, TANAKH.

[13] Berlin, *Esther*, 96.

[14] Fox, *Character and Ideology*, 112; see also the discussion in Bush, *Ruth, Esther*, 475–6.

[15] The suggestion of Bruce W. Jones, "Two Misconceptions about the Book of Esther," *CBQ*
39 (1977): 180, that the king's question is expressing his humor at the situation is doubtful. He
appears utterly serious about the deaths of Haman's sons. In addition, his question to Esther
concerning further requests as to what ought to be done are not the words of a jokester, nor
are they intended to be humorous to readers and play on their sense of schadenfreude as they
rejoice in the slaughter of so many. Instead, these are sobering words, noting that so many died
because of their hatred engendered by ethnic strife.

request (5:1; 8:3); rather, he comes before *her* for direction."[16] Earlier, Ahasuerus seemed to care only that his queen was safe from Haman's threat. His action caused Esther to have to beg for the lives of her people (7:10–8:2). Here he seems to have grown in his appreciation for her and her sensibilities. We may surmise the king and queen have developed a more intimate emotional relationship due to the threat posed against both by Haman.

4.4.2   Esther Receives Permission for Further Action (9:13–15)

   [13] Esther answered, "If it pleases the king, may the Jews who are in Susa also have tomorrow to carry out today's law, and may the bodies of Haman's ten sons be hung on the gallows." [14] The king gave the orders for this to be done, so a law was announced in Susa, and they hung the bodies of Haman's ten sons. [15] The Jews in Susa assembled again on the fourteenth day of the month of Adar and killed three hundred men in Susa, but they did not seize any plunder.

9:13 Esther's address to Ahasuerus is formal: "If it pleases the king" (*'im 'al hammelek ṭôb*). When making a request, Esther always uses this formal opening, though here it is unadorned with other conditional phrases as previously (5:4, 8; 8:5). The change once again signals a growing intimacy between the king and queen, showing her comfortable enough to make her request. The fighting on the thirteenth of Adar was concentrated in the fortress of Susa where the Jews eliminated their enemies from the king's palace precincts. Apparently, the Jews had no time to deal with those who were hostile to them in the lower city of Susa. Esther's request sought to extend their permission to deal with their enemies so they could defend themselves there. This would lead to their feeling secure within the larger lower city.

   Royal permission was needed to hang "the bodies" of those executed, as exhibited in Haman's intended request to hang Mordecai's body (5:14). The reason for the request was to discourage others from any aggression against the Jews. The display of bodies of the vanquished was often used to demonstrate victory and discourage further resistance (Josh 8:29; 1 Sam 31:10).

   9:14 True to his word, Ahasuerus gave the order. The resulting decree—which applied only "in Susa"—is the only one mentioned

---

[16] Linafelt and Beal, *Ruth and Esther*, 112.

in Esther published there alone. Since Esther contains a number of echoes of the story of Israel's King Saul, Berlin sees the hanging of the bodies of Haman's sons as a reversal of the fate of Saul's body, which the Philistines hung "on the wall of Beth-Shan" (1 Sam 31:10).[17] If this is what the author of Esther intended, it is only a faint echo, since the enemies in this case are Amalekites, not Philistines, which are not paralleled elsewhere in Esther.

Date: 14 Adar II (Friday, April 6), 473 BC

9:15 The action of Susa's Jews on "the fourteenth" of Adar is important for the telling of the rest of the story of the institution of the feast of Purim (9:17, 18, 19, 21). Ahasuerus asked for no report of the casualties in this case since throughout Esther he seems only interested in events directly affecting the royal court. The author provides the number killed: 300, seeming to indicate the percentage of enemies of the Jews in the more populous lower city was far less than those in the palace precincts. The author is eager to demonstrate the Jews were not taking this action for personal gain since he once again notes they took no "plunder" (see 9:10, 16).

4.4.3   The Differences between Jews in the Provinces and Those in Susa (9:16–19)

[16] *The rest of the Jews in the royal provinces assembled, defended themselves, and gained relief from their enemies. They killed seventy-five thousand of those who hated them, but they did not seize any plunder.* [17] *They fought on the thirteenth day of the month of Adar and rested on the fourteenth, and it became a day of feasting and rejoicing.* [18] *But the Jews in Susa had assembled on the thirteenth and the fourteenth days of the month. They rested on the fifteenth day of the month, and it became a day of feasting and rejoicing.* [19] *This explains why the rural Jews who live in villages observe the fourteenth day of the month of Adar as a time of rejoicing and feasting. It is a holiday when they send gifts to one another.*

---

[17] Berlin, *Esther*, 86.

Date: 13–15 Adar II (Thursday, April 5–Saturday, April 7), 473 BC

9:16–17 The separate accounting of those killed in the provinces answers Ahasuerus's rhetorical exclamation at 9:12, yet this notice is not a direct response to his question to Esther. The number killed, 75,000, appears to be large and has occasioned speculation as to its accuracy.[18] Nevertheless, the ancient Syriac and Vulgate versions contain the same number. Josephus also affirms this figure.[19] The OG reads 15,000, but that must be a late modification, since both Josephus and the Syriac version relied on the OG.[20] The Alpha Text of Esther 8:46 (roughly corresponding to MT 9:16) reads 70,100, a total which appears to include all the men killed in both Susa and the provinces. For the final time, the author emphasizes no spoils were taken (see 9:10, 15).

The author also emphasized the provincial Jews followed their legally given rights by noting they "defended themselves" on the thirteenth day of Adar. The mention of rest, "feasting and rejoicing" on the fourteenth day of Adar in the provinces anticipates his comment in 9:19.

9:18–19 The assembling of Jews in Susa to defend themselves on both the thirteenth and fourteenth of Adar repeats they took advantage of the extension granted by Ahasuerus (9:15). It is mentioned here for contrast to the action of the provincial Jews (9:16–17) and anticipates the explanation in the following verse. The announcement assigning "the fifteenth day" of Adar as "a day of feasting and rejoicing" is identical in wording to the announcement at the end of 9:17 except for the date. The author, who has maintained a distinction between the provincial Jews and those of Susa, now unites them in feasting and rejoicing, albeit on different days. David J. A. Clines observes, "The Jews celebrate not their victory but the absence of cause for blood or victory in the future."[21]

The mention of rest (*nô'aḥ*) after victory is important. God is said to grant rest throughout the OT (Deut 25:19; Josh 21:44;

---

[18] Breneman, *Ezra, Nehemiah, Esther*, 361, speculates that the "thousand" (אֶלֶף) might mean "clans," making the total killed seventy-five clans. This, however, seems too small a number. Berlin, *Esther*, 87, understands the number to be an exaggeration.

[19] Josephus, *Antiquities* 11.291 [11.6.13].

[20] Moore, *Esther*, 89.

[21] David J. A. Clines, *The Esther Scroll: The Story of a Story.*, JSOTSup 30 (Sheffield: JSOT, 1984), 161–2.

2 Sam 7:11; 1 Kgs 5:4; 1 Chr 23:25; 2 Chr 14:6–7; 20:30). Despite the author's apparent avoidance of mentioning God or divine action throughout Esther, he may be hinting to his readers God is the ultimate reason behind the Jewish victory over their enemies.

The note about rural Jews celebrating on "the fourteenth day" of Adar is intended to explain why their celebration of Purim was a day earlier than that of the Jews in Susa. This note is an important clue as to when the book of Esther was written (see the discussion in the Introduction). Beal remarks,

> Note that this verse does not simply acknowledge the different dates for observing Purim, but links those dates with what are assumed to be contemporary practices within different regions of the Persian empire. It appears that this note assumes a Persian-period audience, and thus provides support for dating the composition of this version of Esther to the Persian period rather than to the later Hellenistic period.[22]

We can go further than Beal's observation, since not only does 9:19 provide a rough date for the composition of Esther (mid-fifth century BC), but it also implies a place of composition and the location of the original intended audience for the book: the city of Susa. Esther 9:19 does *not* say, "The Jews in Susa celebrate one day but the rural Jews another day." Instead, it only explains why the rural Jews celebrate a particular day. The author assumes his audience knows which day his audience celebrates and that it is not the fourteenth of Adar. He is writing from Susa for Jews in Susa and felt the need to explain why the provincial Jews celebrated a day different from that celebrated by them.

The provincial Jews here are called *happərāzîm*, translated as "rural" in CSB.[23] This is a little-understood term. It has been suggested the word refers to Jews living in wall-less cities as opposed to

---

[22] Linafelt and Beal, *Ruth and Esther*, 114, n. 14.

[23] הַפְּרָזִים is the reading of the Qere (what is read). The Ketiv (what is written) is הַפְּרוֹזִים. The Ketiv has been explained as a deliberate introduction of assonance with the previous word הַיְּהוּדִים by the author of Esther. (Hans Striedl, "*Untersuchung Zur Syntax Und Stilistik des Hebräischen Buches Esther*," *ZAW* 55 (1937): 90–91.) This, however, is dubious (Bush, *Ruth, Esther*, 477). Indeed, if the author was introducing assonance, one might expect the Ketiv to be הַפְּרוֹזִים. Instead, the Ketiv is likely a scribal error of dittography of either the ר or the ז and resulting graphic confusion leading to the substitution of ו for the repeated ר or the ז.

walled cities like Susa.[24] This is unlikely, since the author has been consistently contrasting the Jews in Susa with the Jews elsewhere in the Persian Empire. Certainly, the Jews outside of Susa were living in many places, including both walled cities and wall-less villages. It is more likely the word derives from the concept of being *outside* instead of *inside*, thereby referring to Jews outside the jurisdiction of Susa, the Jews in the provinces (8:5; 9:2, 16, 20, 30).[25]

The exchange of "gifts" (*mānôt*) marks this day as especially festive. Berlin believes the gifts mentioned here are specifically food, marking a continuation of the feasting found throughout the book.[26]

This first celebration of Purim marks the first Jewish "holiday" to be celebrated in the last five months of the year (according to the Jewish calendar). Later, Jews would institute two other holidays in the last months of the year. The first was the Festival of Dedication (Hannukah; see 1 Macc 4:52–59; John 10:22). They would also institute Nicanor's Day on the thirteenth of Adar to commemorate the victory of Judas Maccabeus over the Seleucid general Nicanor (1 Macc 7:43–50). While Hannukah continues to be an annual celebration among Jews, Nicanor's day ceased to be celebrated sometime in the second century AD.

4.5   Mordecai Commands Future Celebrations of Purim (9:20–28)

Mordecai established the permanent celebration of Purim (9:21), and his fellow Jews agreed to this (9:23). With this action Mordecai became the only person in the OT other than Moses to establish feast days for Israel. Thus, the author's unobtrusive comparison of Moses and Mordecai continues (see commentary at 9:4), providing another subtle hint to readers God was with Mordecai in his leadership role just as he was with Moses.

This section also presents a summary of the events related in Esther 3:1–8:17. It serves as an etiology—an origin story—for the feast of Purim. Although this is an etiology, that does not imply it is a fictional

---

[24] Fox, *Character and Ideology*, 113; Moore, *Esther*, 85.
[25] Hermann Michael Niemann, *"Das Ende des Volkes der Perizziter: Über Soziale Wandlungen Israels im Spiegel Einer Begriffsgruppe,"* ZAW 105 (1993): 234–43; Bush, *Ruth, Esther*, 477.
[26] Berlin, *Esther*, 88.

one.[27] After examining the various alternative suggestions for the origin of the feast of Purim, Hallo concluded,

> [T]he terminology and the underlying technique [for using lots] remain the same: one casts the lots called *pūr* or, in the plural, *pūrīm*. And the festival of the fourteenth of Adar (originally the fifteenth, observed today as Shushan Purim) takes its name, we are told, from this very word for lots. That explanation will have to do for us too, for none of the many alternatives offered during a century of the most ingenious scholarly detective work is more convincing. Such alternatives include various far-fetched comparisons as those with the Greek festival of Pithoigia, with the Hittite festival of *purulli*, and with the Roman festival of Feralia (Greek *phournikália*), as well as the inherently more plausible theory of Julius Lewy, described as "probably the most skillful" of these constructions, which derives the festival from the Persian festival of Farwadigan. The problem is that each of these alleged precedents rests on little more than a dubious assonance, and none of them has anything in the least to do with the casting of lots. . . . [T]hat text [i.e., Esther] is robbed of its raison d'être if it is not seen as the necessary and sufficient justification for the institution of the festival. The only solid evidence (outside the Scroll of Esther) for the observance of a festival having anything in common with Purim is the allusion in II Maccabees (15:36) to "Mordecai's Day" which is celebrated on the fourteenth of Adar. Thus the biblical derivation of the name of the festival from the lots called *pūr* remains the best available.[28]

4.5.1 Moredcai's First Letter (9:20–22)

[20] *Mordecai recorded these events and sent letters to all the Jews in all of King Ahasuerus's provinces, both near and far.* [21] *He ordered them to celebrate the fourteenth and fifteenth days of the month of Adar every year* [22] *because during those days the Jews gained relief from their enemies. That was the month when their sorrow was turned into rejoicing and their mourning into a holiday. They were to be days*

---

[27] Contrary to many critical scholars, e.g., Berlin, *Esther*, 88.
[28] William W. Hallo, "The First Purim," *BA* 46 (1983): 22.

of feasting, rejoicing, and of sending gifts to one another and to the poor.

9:20 Mordecai's recording of the "events" was understood by medieval rabbis to mean he was the author of the book of Esther.[29] This is probably not what is meant.[30] Instead, the reference is probably to a brief recounting of the events from the issuance of Haman's decree up to the Jews' victory, similar to what is recorded in 9:24–25 but perhaps not as brief. These "letters" might have explained the events in Susa for Jews in the distant part of the empire which had little knowledge of the reasons for either Haman's edict or the edict issued by Mordecai.

9:21–22 While CSB says Mordecai "ordered" his fellow Jews to celebrate two days in Adar, the Hebrew is less forceful. The word *ləqa-yyēm* (an Aramaism) means "confirm or authorize" and occurs in vv. 27, 31 to note the Jews adopted the celebration of Purim.[31] It is used in vv. 29, 32 to speak of Esther and Mordecai confirming the celebration of Purim. Mordecai's authorization for celebration does not mean he enjoined all Jews to celebrate both the fourteenth and fifteenth days of Adar, which would be a contradiction of what was previously stated v. 19. Instead, he probably was authorizing the celebration on either day. Bush notes,

> [O]ne of the main purposes of Mordecai's letter may well be to adjudicate the differences in the dates of celebration by calling upon both groups to celebrate both days, since each day has been made legitimate by the experience of one of them. On the other hand, the language of vv 21–22 may also plausibly be taken to mean that there is to be one day of celebration for each of the two groups, the Jews of Susa and the Jews of the provinces.[32]

The celebration was one of "relief," not the defeat of the enemies nor of their deaths, so the celebration was confined to the days *after*

---

[29] Clines, *The Esther Scroll*, 177 n. 12; Bush, *Ruth, Esther*, 478.

[30] Fox, *Character and Ideology*, 117, allows the possibility that the sentence means Mordecai wrote the book, but that does not mean he finds the claim credible.

[31] See the discussion in Fox, *Character and Ideology*, 118. לְקַיֵּם (piel infinitive construct of the root קוּם) is an Aramaism that is used mainly in Hebrew texts from late in the Judahite monarchical period onward (see Ps 119:28, 106; Ezek 13:6). Prior to this time the more common piel stem formation for this verbal root was *polel* (Isa 44:26; 58:12; 61:4; Mic 2:8).

[32] Bush, *Ruth, Esther*, 479–80; see also Fox, *Character and Ideology*, 114.

the Jewish victories, not the days *of* the victories.[33] The turning of sorrow and mourning into rejoicing and a holiday is a brief summary of the events from 4:1–3 and 9:16–18. The word for "relief" is literally "rest" (*nāḥû*). Beal comments on the irony introduced here by the use of this word: "Whereas Haman had recommended that the king not let this matter of the Jews rest (i.e., he should not tolerate them but should have them destroyed), now the Jews have found 'rest' from that intolerance."[34]

The future celebrations are to be festive—with feasting, rejoicing, and gifts—but also a time to remember the poor. Two words for "gifts" are used in this verse. The first, *mānôt*, is usually reserved for portions of food (Exod 29:26; Lev 7:33; 8:29; 1 Sam 1:4; 9:23; 2 Chr 31:19; Neh 8:10, 12) and refers to the general exchange of gifts on Purim. The second word, *mattānôt*, often denotes gifts of nonfood items (Num 18:6–7; 2 Chr 21:3; Ezek 46:16; Sir 3:17; 26:3). This is the word for the gifts to be given "to the poor." Sending gifts to the poor is mentioned elsewhere in postexilic Jewish writings in connection with feast days (e.g., Tob 2:2).

4.5.2   The Jews Agree to Celebrate Purim (9:23–28)

²³ *So the Jews agreed to continue the practice they had begun, as Mordecai had written them to do.* ²⁴ *For Haman son of Hammedatha the Agagite, the enemy of all the Jews, had plotted against the Jews to destroy them. He cast the* pur—*that is, the lot—to crush and destroy them.* ²⁵ *But when the matter was brought before the king, he commanded by letter that the evil plan Haman had devised against the Jews return on his own head and that he should be hanged with his sons on the gallows.* ²⁶ *For this reason these days are called Purim, from the word* pur. *Because of all the instructions in this letter as well as what they had witnessed and what had happened to them,* ²⁷ *the Jews bound themselves, their descendants, and all who joined with them to a commitment that they would not fail to celebrate these two days each and every year according to the written instructions and according to the time appointed.* ²⁸ *These days are remembered and celebrated by every generation, family, province, and city, so that*

---

[33] Linafelt and Beal, *Ruth and Esther*, 115.
[34] Linafelt and Beal, *Ruth and Esther*, 115.

these days of Purim will not lose their significance in Jewish life and their memory will not fade from their descendants.

9:23 The acceptance by Jews of a perpetual holiday is attributed to Mordecai's letter. Thus, Mordecai became the founder of a new Jewish holiday, and this is probably the reason 2 Macc 15:36 calls it "Mordecai's Day."

9:24–25 These verses appear to be a summary of the events based on the text of Mordecai's letter, perhaps a paraphrase of Mordecai's text.[35] Some of the summarizing is evident; for instance, the statement the lot was cast to destroy the Jews, although in actuality it was cast to determine the date of their destruction. The plot of Haman is said to be against "all the Jews," without any mention of the plot targeting Mordecai specifically. The hanging of Haman was combined with the hanging of his sons, although they were two separate events.

Regardless, other features of these verses point to this decree as an official letter, and the events are portrayed so the king is presented in the most favorable light: credit is given to "the king" for the foiling of Haman's plot, and there is no mention of the roles of Esther and Mordecai. The decree to counter Haman's plot is specifically said to be the king's decree, not Mordecai's. The king is characterized as a defender of the Jews and more decisive in ordering Haman's execution immediately upon learning of his plot, although 7:6–10 portrays him as delaying the execution and later ordering it in defense of Esther. The king's countermanding of Haman's plot and his order to execute Haman are merged into one act. This summary of events drawn from Mordecai's letter departs in strategic ways from the manner in which the story is told in 3:1–9:19 in order to glorify Ahasuerus, a clear sign this summary was written to be royal propaganda in an official letter. Mordecai understood his position as prime minister was to serve the interests of the throne. Therefore, he avoided glorifying himself or Esther (contrast Haman, 6:6–9) and was obligated to present Ahasuerus as protector of the Jews in order to reinforce their loyalty to the crown.[36]

---

[35] Bush, *Ruth, Esther*, 480–1; Fox, *Character and Ideology*, 119–20; Berlin, *Esther*, 89, sees these verses as an intentional retelling for the purpose of explaining the holiday.

[36] Paton understands 9:20–32 as derived from the Chronicles of the Kings of Persia and Media (Paton, *Esther*, 58–59). This is less likely, but it would also explain the elevation of the role of Ahasuerus and the lack of mention of the actions of Esther and Mordecai in 9:24–25.

There are two interesting features of these verses. One is the introduction of the image of Haman attempting "to crush" the Jews (9:24).
Since this image is not used elsewhere to describe Haman's motives,
it most likely was used in order to form a pun between "to crush"
(*ləhummām*) and the name *Haman*. Another interesting feature is the
phrase behind CSB's "when the matter was brought" (9:25), which
is literally "when she/it came" (*ûbəbô'āh*). Traditionally this was
understood as an indirect reference to Esther's alerting Ahasuerus to
Haman's plot.[37] But Esther's role in bringing the plot to the king is not
part of the immediate context of these verses. Indeed, it has not been
mentioned since 8:3–6. It is more likely that the third-person feminine
pronoun refers to the feminine noun "plot" (*mahăšbtô*), justifying the
CSB's rendering.[38]

9:26–27 The origin of the name *Purim* is directly tied to the word
for *lot*, namely *Pûr* (from Akkadian *pūr[u]*). Earlier at 3:7, the author
included this word deliberately in anticipation of this explanation. The
plural form *pûrim* is explained by the author in that it commemorates
the "days" (*yāmim*; pl.) when Jewish deliverance is celebrated.[39] This
name is shorthand for "days of the lots," making a satirical reference
to Haman's reliance on the lots in pagan divination. The perpetual
commemoration of Purim is motivated not only by Mordecai's letter
but also by what the Jews "witnessed" and experienced. Three groups
were bound to this perpetual remembrance: "the Jews" (i.e., those
who experienced these events), "their descendants," and "all who
joined with them." The participle "those who joined" (*hānnilwîm*) is
from the verbal root used elsewhere for converts (Isa 14:1; 56:3, 6; Jer
50:5; Dan 11:34; Zech 2:15) and appears to be a reference to genuine
converts among those who had professed to be Jews (Esth 8:17).

The pledge "they would not fail to celebrate" these days introduces
another irony to the book: the words for "not fail" (*wəlō' ya'ăbôr*) are
the same as the words describing the Persian law that cannot change
(1:19). The changeless royal law failed since Mordecai was able to
counteract its effects. But the celebration of Purim continued without

---

[37] See, for instance, 9:25 in NRSV and TANAKH: "when Esther came before the king." See
also Moore, *Esther*, 92.

[38] See also ESV, GW, NET, NIV, as well as Bush, *Ruth, Esther*, 481–2.

[39] Many critical scholars see the explanation as a strained, false etiology (e.g., Berlin,
Esther, 26). For this reason they ignore or downplay the deliberate reference to the two days of
celebration as the reason for the plural form.

fail. The Jews' celebration of "these two days"—one or the other depending on their location (see 9:17–21)—is according to the "written instructions and . . . time appointed" (*kiktābām wǝkizmannām*). This makes the celebration of Purim comparable to the celebration of other Jewish holy days such as Passover, First Fruits, Pentecost, and the Day of Atonement. They, too, are celebrated according to written instructions (the Pentateuch) at the appointed times. Thus, once again, Mordecai is cast in the mold of Moses (see commentary on 9:4).

9:28 This verse appears to skip to the current day of the author and his original intended readers. Purim was still being celebrated some years after the events the book describes, and in a comprehensive way among Jews: by "every generation, family, province, and city."[40] The emphasis on the days maintaining their "significance" and not fading from memory functions as an appeal to those readers to continue the days of Purim as established by Mordecai's letter.

4.6   A Letter from Esther and Mordecai (9:29–32)

   [29] *Queen Esther, daughter of Abihail, along with Mordecai the Jew, wrote this second letter with full authority to confirm the letter about Purim.* [30] *He sent letters with assurances of peace and security to all the Jews who were in the 127 provinces of the kingdom of Ahasuerus,* [31] *in order to confirm these days of Purim at their proper time just as Mordecai the Jew and Esther the queen had established them and just as they had committed themselves and their descendants to the practices of fasting and lamentation.* [32] *So Esther's command confirmed these customs of Purim, which were then written into the record.*

The Hebrew text of these verses contains several difficulties making it problematic for interpreters, especially since it might be construed as contradicting earlier passages in Esther. For this reason, some scholars held this description of a letter from Esther is a later insertion into Esther 9.[41] A less radical view held by others believes there are several late insertions into this section making it awkward and difficult to understand.[42] In particular, there are three phrases some believe

---

   [40] בְּכָל־דּוֹר וָדוֹר מִשְׁפָּחָה וּמִשְׁפָּחָה מְדִינָה וּמְדִינָה; the repetition of terms is a way of expressing a distributive sense.

   [41] Samuel E. Loewenstamm, "Esther 9:29–32: The Genesis of a Late Addition," *HUCA* 42 (1971): 117–24; Moore, *Esther*, 95; Paton, *Esther*, 57–60.

   [42] Fox, *Character and Ideology*, 123–7; Bush, *Ruth, Esther*, 469–71.

should be excised as later glosses: "along with Mordecai the Jew" (*ûmordăkcay hayyɘhûdî*; 9:29), "second" (*haššēnit*; 9:29), and "and Esther the queen" (*wɘ'estēr hammalkâ*; 9:31).

The first supposed addition in 9:29 makes a compound subject with both Esther and Mordecai writing the letter. This is said to contradict 9:32, which reports that Esther alone "confirmed" the Purim custom.[43]

The second alleged addition in 9:29, referring to a *second* letter, is explained as a later intrusion into the text because "without it 'this letter about Purim' would naturally refer to the previous letter written by Mordecai" (i.e., 9:20–22).[44] Moreover, it is held Esther's letter mentioned here is the second letter, and "[i]t surely makes little sense to state that they are writing a letter to confirm the letter they are writing."[45] Also it is noted the syntax of the Hebrew text is peculiar at this point since the attributive adjective "second" ought to be followed by the demonstrative pronoun "this": *haššēnit hazzô't,* not as the text has it: *hazzô't haššēnit.* Finally, the word *second* does not appear in either OG (which is a highly paraphrastic translation at this point) or in the ancient Syriac version, which exhibits a formal correspondence to the Hebrew text.[46]

Finally, the third suspected addition, "and Esther the queen" in 9:31, seems to contradict 9:20–23 where Mordecai alone "sent letters" establishing the festival of Purim—not Mordecai and Esther. According to this view Esther's role was only in confirming the Purim customs, not in establishing them.

While these arguments claiming insertions in the text of 9:29, 31 at first blush appear most persuasive, they are conjectural and, except for the missing word *second* in OG and Syriac, are unsupported by text critical evidence suggesting their absence from the Hebrew text of Esther. Moreover, the text of 9:29–32 can be understood without them. The inclusion of Mordecai at 9:29 is probably because he—not Esther—had access to scribes who would write the letter, and he

---

[43] Paton, *Esther*, 302; Clines, *Esther Scroll*, 56, and Baldwin, *Esther*, 100, hold that the mention of Mordecai as part of the subject of the feminine verb וַתִּכְתֹּב (lit. "then she wrote") is grammatically problematic. But as Bush, *Ruth, Esther*, 471, observes, "The agreement of the fem sg verb [ותכתב, "and she wrote"] with the fem 1st person noun ["Queen Esther"] of a fem sg + masc sg compound subject is perfectly acceptable BH [see Num 12:1]."

[44] Bush, *Ruth, Esther*, 470.

[45] Bush, *Ruth, Esther*, 469.

[46] Fox, *Character and Ideology*, 287; Bush, *Ruth, Esther*, 470.

controlled the means of distribution of the letter, the Persian royal mail. Even then, however, Esther is the main author. She alone is listed by her title and her lineage. The verb "wrote" is second-person feminine singular, pointing to her as the primary writer. As Baldwin comments, "Despite the plural subject the first word of the verse in Hebrew is a feminine singular verb, indicating Esther is the effective subject: 'she decreed.'"[47]

The problem of the use of "second" in 9:29 is not as difficult as it has been made to seem. Concerning the observation that if "the second" (haššēnit) modifies "this letter about Purim" ('ēt 'igeret happûrîm hazzô't), it is out of place grammatically: this should have been a clue that it is not a modifier for that phrase.[48] The phrase, "the second" ought to be understood as the direct object of the main verb "she wrote" (wattiktōb), so the main clause reads, "Queen Esther, daughter of Abihail, along with Mordecai the Jew, wrote . . . the [= this] second letter" (see CSB).[49] In addition, the reference to Mordecai's previous letter is mentioned in the infinitival phrase "to confirm [this] letter about Purim" (ləqayyēm 'ēt 'igeret happûrîm hazzô't). Therefore, when it is correctly construed, 9:29 says Esther (and Mordecai) wrote a second letter confirming Mordecai's previous letter about Purim.

Finally, the inclusion of "Esther the queen" at 9:31 is also not a later intrusion into the text. Instead, Ahasuerus gave authority to Esther and Mordecai to write "whatever pleases [them] concerning the Jews" ('al hayyəhûdîm kaṭṭôb bə'ênêkem; 8:8). They established Purim jointly, though Mordecai alone was responsible for communicating this in his first letter.

The purpose of 9:29–32 is to confirm the Purim customs by means of the royal authority of Esther, who wrote this letter with the assistance of Mordecai. It is noteworthy Esther's royal position as queen is used at 9:29, 31 to lend weight to the letter written "with full

---

[47] Baldwin, Esther, 110.

[48] Nevertheless, it appears that both OG and Syriac did not understand this and likely omitted the word second since it was thought to be problematic.

[49] It might be objected that there is no direct object marker on this determined direct object. Yet at times the direct object marker (אֵת) is omitted not only in poetry but also in prose. See, for instance, Gen 25:25: וַיִּקְרְאוּ שְׁמוֹ עֵשָׂו, "They called his name Esau," where neither direct object ("his name" and "Esau"), though determined, is preceded by the direct object marker. In this case the direct object marker may have been omitted to avoid confusion since it precedes the previous phrase "this letter about Purim," which is the direct object of the verb of the infinitive "to confirm" (לְקַיֵּם).

authority" (*kol tōqep*). Moreover, in the final verse in chap. 9, she alone is mentioned as giving the "command" (*ma'ămar*) concerning Purim customs.

9:29 This verse asserts Esther and Mordecai had complete authority concerning the establishment of customs for Purim. This is surely a reference to Ahasuerus's authorization of them at 8:8. The noun translated "authority" is *tōqep*. It appears to be another Aramaism in Esther. This noun occurs in the Hebrew text of the Old Testament only here and in 10:2 (where it is translated "powerful . . . accomplishments" in CSB). The verb from the same root occurs at Job 14:20; 15:24; Eccl 4:12; 6:10. The cognate noun in Aramaic means "power" or "might" (Dan 2:27; 4:30 [Hb. 4:27]).[50]

9:30–31 The letter assures Jews in every Persian province of "peace and security" (*šālôm we'emet*). It has been suggested this phrase was drawn from the letter's greeting.[51] In a study of Aramaic letters, however, Joseph A. Fitzmyer noted while "peace" is often used in a letter's salutation, "security" (or truth) is never used this way.[52] Esther and Mordecai were assuring their fellow Jews they now had nothing to fear since the queen and prime minister had thwarted Haman's plot and their continuing presence in the royal court would ensure the safety of Jews throughout the empire.

The letter also confirmed the days of Purim "at their proper time" (*bizmannêhem*). In this way they authorized two different days of Purim: the fourteenth of Adar in the provinces and the fifteenth of Adar in Susa. The word for "proper time" (*zəmān*; see also 9:27) is another Aramaism. As such, this word occurs only in late biblical Hebrew (Ezra 10:14; Neh 2:6; 10:35; 13:31; Eccl 3:1).

The commitment was not only to the celebration of Purim but also to "fasting and lamentation." While this might be interpreted as a reference to the earlier fasting when facing the threat of Haman's decree (4:3, 16), this verse instead seems to be speaking of a more permanent practice enjoined on future generations. For this reason, the medieval Jewish commentator Abraham ben Meir Ibn Ezra (AD 1089–c. 1167) suggested this verse was an allusion to Zech 8:19 (see also Zech 7:5).[53]

---

[50] For the cognate verb in Aramaic (תקף, "grow strong"), see Dan 4:11, 20, 22 [Hb. 4:8, 17, 19]; 5:20; 6:7 [Hb. 6:8].

[51] Robert Gordis, "Studies in the Esther Narrative," *JBL* 95 (1976): 57–8.

[52] Joseph A. Fitzmyer, "Some Notes on Aramaic Epistolography," *JBL* 95 (1974): 201–25.

[53] Berlin, *Esther*, 93.

There the prophet references several fasts: "The fast of the fourth month, the fast of the fifth, the fast of the seventh, and the fast of the tenth." These fasts commemorated events associated with the destruction of Jerusalem's temple by the Babylonians. The fast of the fourth month recalled the breach of Jerusalem's walls (Jer 39:2–5). The fast of the fifth month remembered the burning of the temple (Jer 52:12–13). The fast of the seventh month ostensibly refers to the anniversary of the assassination of Gedaliah, governor of Judah (Jer 40:13–14; 41:1–3). The fast of the tenth month commemorated the beginning of the siege of Jerusalem (2 Kgs 25:1). Berlin notes,

> As Ibn Ezra explains (at Esther 9:31 and Zech. 8:19), just as the Jews had adopted these fasts that had not been commanded by the Torah, so they will here, for the first time, adopt a new non-Torah holiday commemorating their deliverance. In other words, the author of Esther has found in the Zechariah passage a precedent for the institution of a new festival.[54]

The link between the "practices of fasting and lamentation" (*dibrê haṣṣōmôt wəzaʿăqātām*) and Purim is strengthened by the similar construction to the earlier phrase "assurances of peace and security" (*dibrê šālôm we'emet*).[55]

9:32 Esther's command was of such authority it was officially recorded. The use of the word "command" (*maʾămar*), which only occurs in the Old Testament in Esther (1:15; 2:20; see Sir 3:8; 13:16), is probably a deliberate comparison with Ahasuerus's command (1:15). In another touch of irony, the king's command failed to produce results and was not officially recorded, but the queen's command was effective and permanent.

THEOLOGY

This longest chapter in Esther records the Jewish acts of self-defense and emphasizes the Jews did not take any plunder (9:10, 15). Their acts were taken to preserve their own lives and the lives of their families. Moreover, they were not being attacked or persecuted because of

---

[54] Berlin, *Esther*, 93.
[55] Sandra Beth Berg, *The Book of Esther: Motifs, Themes, and Structure*, SBLDS 44 (Missoula, MT: 1979), 44.

their faith in God but because of their ethnic identity. This distinction is important for Christians today.

When believers are persecuted for their faith, they are forbidden to use violence in their defense. Instead, they are to rejoice that they are worthy of bearing the scorn Christ also bore and use persecution as an opportunity to bear witness to the gospel (Matt 5:10–12; Luke 21:12–13; John 15:20; Acts 5:40–41; 1 Cor 4:12–13; see Matt 24:9). They are to respond with prayer and blessing for the persecutors (Matt 5:44; Rom 12:14). Nevertheless, believers may seek to defend themselves and others when attacked for reasons other than their faith in Christ. In fact, God has instituted human government to punish those who do wrong (Rom 13:3–4). Christians who are public servants may use their authority as magistrates to defend the lives of the innocent and may even authorize others to conduct such defense, just as Mordecai did for his fellow Jews.

The latter part of Esther 9 is devoted to the establishment of Purim by which the Jews celebrate their deliverance from their enemies. For Christian readers this evokes thoughts of a greater annual celebration of deliverance from eternal enemies—sin, death, and Satan—through faith placed in the death and resurrection of Jesus. Good Friday and Easter commemorate the great liberation from bondage to sin and Satan and the release from eternal death: an event whose timing was not chosen by lot (as was Purim) but was determined by God to take place at the correct time in human history (Rom 5:6; Eph 1:9–10). While the celebration of Purim rightly led to joy over lives saved in this world, the celebration of Christ's resurrection brings the joy of knowing God has saved the faith-filled for eternal life in the coming resurrection of all people that will result in everlasting joy for those who trusted in Christ (Job 19:25–27; Dan 12:2; John 5:28–29; 11:25–26; 14:19; 1 Cor 15:42–43; 1 Thess 4:16–17).

SECTION OUTLINE

5   CONCLUSION: AHASUERUS'S KINGDOM UNDER THE LEADERSHIP OF MORDECAI (10:1–3)

¹ King Ahasuerus imposed a tax throughout the land even to the farthest shores. ² All of his powerful and magnificent accomplishments and the detailed account of Mordecai's great rank with which the king had honored him, have they not been written in the Book of the Historical Events of the Kings of Media and Persia? ³ Mordecai the Jew was second only to King Ahasuerus. He was famous among the Jews and highly esteemed by many of his relatives. He continued to pursue prosperity for his people and to speak for the well-being of all his descendants.

The conclusion of the book of Esther corresponds with its beginning. The extent of Ahasuerus's taxing authority corresponds to his empire of 127 provinces (1:1). His magnificence and accomplishments parallel his resplendent banquet displaying his power (1:2–4). Yet there is a difference: at the book's opening there was no Mordecai, protector and advocate for the empire's Jews. The book's concluding note corrects this and signals a period of relative calm for Jews throughout the ancient Near East under the remaining years of the Persian Empire.

10:1–2 The Hebrew word for the "tax" imposed on the empire is *mas*. Elsewhere in the OT, the word denoted forced labor for service of royal projects (e.g., 1 Kgs 5:13). But in later Hebrew it came to denote a tax, which is surely its meaning here. It is difficult to understand it as forced labor from the farthest reaches of the empire, especially since there is no hint in the text that *mas* was used for grand imperial building projects. Instead, throughout Esther Ahasuerus's great wealth is emphasized: much of it probably came from tax revenue. Imperial taxes were often heavy and unpleasant. Yet the point of the text here is not the burden placed on the empire's subjects but on the magnificent power of Ahasuerus to impose such levies.

The mention of "the land even to the farthest shores" speaks especially about the distant western edge of the empire. The words for "farthest shores" (*'iyyēy hayyām*) denote the Mediterranean coast and its islands (Isa 42:4, 10). Herodotus reports Ahasuerus's father received income "from Asia and a few parts of Libya. But as time went on he drew tribute also from the islands and the dwellers in Europe, as far as Thessaly."[56]

The author ties the greatness of Ahasuerus with Mordecai's great rank and notes both were recorded in a historical record "of the Kings of Media and Persia." There is some debate among commentators regarding whether this refers to the official Persian records or Jewish records about the Persians.[57] Yet it would appear the author is not referring simply to Jewish records since he is speaking of Mordecai's general greatness (gəd ûlat) in contrast to his fame among the Jews (wəgadôl leyyəhûdîm) mentioned in the next verse.[58] The mention of official records of kings is frequent in 1 Kings (e.g., 1 Kgs 14:19, 29 and thirty-one more times; see also 2 Chr 25:26). The effect of the author's mention of the Persian records is to place Mordecai on a level similar to that of the kings of Judah and Israel.

10:3 Mordecai's rank as "second" to the king also creates a favorable comparison to Joseph, who rode in Pharaoh's "second chariot" (Gen 41:43). Mordecai's fame and esteem among his relatives extends that comparison, since the esteem Joseph had among his brothers and subsequent generations was evident in the care they took to carry out his wishes to be interred in Canaan (Gen 50:25; Exod 13:19). The book ends by noting Mordecai's continued concern "for his people," hinting once again of God's providence and protection for his ancient people. This also points toward his ultimate care for the entire human race since from the Jews would come the world's Savior (John 4:22).

---

[56] Herodotus, *Histories*, 3.96 (translation from Godley).

[57] Moore, *Esther*, 99; Breneman, *Ezra, Nehemiah, Esther,* 369–70, believes it was unlikely that a Jewish prime minister would receive mention in the official records of Persia. Nevertheless, history often records what might be considered unlikely. Baldwin, *Esther*, 115, believes it is a reference to the official Persian records.

[58] The phrase for the historical records here is דִּבְרֵי הַיָּמִים לְמַלְכֵי מָדַי וּפָרָס ("the book of the historical events of the kings of Media and Persia"). This mirrors the references to the official Persian records elsewhere in Esther: דִּבְרֵי הַיָּמִים דִּבְרֵי ("the book recording daily events," Esth 6:1).

BIBLIOGRAPHY

Baldwin, Joyce G. *Esther: An Introduction and Commentary*. TOTC. Leicester: Intervarsity, 1984.

Bar-Efrat, Shimon. *Narrative Art in the Bible*. JSOTSup 70. Sheffield: Sheffield Academic, 1989.

Barucq, André. *Judith, Esther*. 2nd ed. La Sainte Bible. Paris: Cerf, 1959.

Berg, Sandra Beth. *The Book of Esther: Motifs, Themes, and Structure*. SBLDS 44. Missoula, MT: Scholars, 1979.

Bergey, Ronald L. "Late Linguistic Features in Esther." *JQR* 75 (1984): 66–78.

———. "Post-Exilic Hebrew Linguistic Developments in Esther: A Diachronic Approach." *JETS* 31 (1988): 161–8.

Berlin, Adele. *Esther: The Traditional Hebrew Text with the New JPS Translation*. The JPS Bible Commentary. Philadelphia: Jewish Publication Society, 2001.

Berquist, Jon L. *Judaism in Persia's Shadow: A Social and Historical Approach*. Reprint. Eugene, OR: Wipf and Stock, 2003.

Bickerman, Elias J. *Four Strange Books of the Bible: Jonah, Daniel, Koheleth, Esther*. New York: Schocken, 1967.

Breneman, Mervin. *Ezra, Nehemiah, Esther*. NAC 10. Nashville: Broadman and Holman, 1993.

Brighton, Louis A. "The Book of Esther—Textual and Canonical Considerations." *ConJ* 13 (1987): 200–18.

Bush, Frederic. *Ruth, Esther*. WBC 9. Dallas: Word, 1996.

Cameron, George Glenn. "Persepolis Treasury Tablets Old and New." *JNES* 17 (1958): 161–76.

Clines, David J. A. *The Esther Scroll: The Story of a Story.* JSOTSup 30. Sheffield: JSOT, 1984.

———. *Ezra, Nehemiah, Esther.* NCBC. Grand Rapids, MI: Eerdmans, 1984.

Craig, Kenneth. *Reading Esther: A Case for the Literary Carnivalesque.* Literary Currents in Biblical Interpretation. Louisville, KY: Westminster John Knox, 1995.

Crenshaw, James L. "The Expression *Mî Yôdēaʿ* in the Hebrew Bible." *VT* 36 (1986): 274–88.

Day, Linda. *Three Faces of a Queen: Characterization in the Books of Esther.* JSOTSup 186. Sheffield: Sheffield Academic, 1995.

Dempster, Stephen G. *Dominion and Dynasty: A Biblical Theology of the Hebrew Bible.* New Studies in Biblical Theology 15. Downers Grove, IL: Intervarsity, 2004.

De Troyer, Kristin. "On Crowns and Diadems from Kings, Queens, Horses and Men" Pages 355–67 in IX Congress of the International Organization for Septuagint and Cognate Studies, Cambridge, 1995. Edited by Bernard A. Taylor. Atlanta: Scholars, 1997.

Duguid, Iain. *Esther and Ruth.* Reformed Expository Commentary. Phillipsburg, NJ: P&R, 2005.

Dumbrell, William. *The Faith of Israel: A Theological Survey of the Old Testament.* 2nd ed. Grand Rapids: Baker Academic, 2002.

Fitzmyer, Joseph A. "Some Notes on Aramaic Epistolography." *JBL* 93 (1974): 201–25.

Fox, Michael. *Character and Ideology in the Book of Esther.* 2nd ed. Grand Rapids, MI: Eerdmans, 2001.

Friedberg, Albert D. "A New Clue in the Dating of the Composition of the Book of Esther." *VT* 50 (2000): 561–5.

———. and Vincent DeCaen. "Dating the Composition of the Book of Esther: A Response to Larsson." *VT* 53 (2003): 427–9.

Gardner, Anne E. "The Relationship of the Additions to the Book of Esther to the Maccabean Crisis." *JSJ* 15 (1984): 1–8.

Gaster, Theodor Herzl. "Esther 1:22." *JBL* 69 (1950): 381.

Gehman, Henry Snyder. "Notes on the Persian Words in the Book of Esther." *JBL* 43 (1924): 321–8.

Godley, A. D. *Herodotus, with an English Translation*. LCL. Cambridge: Harvard University, 1920.

Goldman, Stan. "Narrative and Ethical Ironies in Esther." *JSOT* 15 (1990): 15–31.

Gordis, Robert. *Megillat Esther: The Masoretic Hebrew Text with Introduction, New Translation and Commentary*. New York: Ktav, 1974.

———. "Studies in the Esther Narrative." *JBL* 95 (1976): 43–58.

Grossman, Yonatan. "The Vanishing Character in Biblical Narrative: The Role of Hathach in Esther 4." *VT* 62 (2012): 561–71.

Hallo, William W. "The First Purim." *BA* 46 (1983): 19–26.

Hamilton, Victor P. *Handbook on the Historical Books*. Grand Rapids, MI: Baker Academic, 2004.

Hanhart, Robert, ed. *Esther*. Septuaginta: Vetus Testamentum Graecum VIII, 3. Göttingen: Vandenhoeck & Ruprecht, 1983.

Haupt, Paul. "Critical Notes on Esther." *AJSL* 24 (1907–8): 97–186.

Horbury, William. "The Name Mardochaeus in a Ptolemaic Inscription." *VT* 41 (1991): 220–6.

Hoschander, Jacob. *The Book of Esther in the Light of History*. Philadelphia: Dropsie College, 1923.

House, Paul R. *Old Testament Theology*. Downers Grove, IL: Intervarsity, 1998.

Howard, David M., Jr. *An Introduction to the Old Testament Historical Books*. Chicago: Moody, 1993.

Hubbard, Robert L. "Vashti, Amestris and Esther 1,9." *ZAW* 119 (2007): 259–71.

Huey, F. B., Jr. "Esther" *The Expositor's Bible Commentary with the New International Version*. Edited by Frank E. Gaebelein. Grand Rapids: Zondervan, 1988.

Humphreys, W. Lee. "Life-Style for Diaspora: A Study of the Tales of Esther and Daniel." *JBL* 92 (1973): 211–23.

Jacobs, Jonathan. "Characterizing Esther from the Outset: The Contribution of the Story in Esther 2:1–20." *JHebS* 8 (2008); doi: 10.5508/jhs.2008.v8.a16.

Jobes, Karen. *The Alpha-Text of Esther: Its Character and Relationship to the Masoretic Text*. SBLDS. Atlanta: Scholars, 1996.

Jones, Bruce W. "Two Misconceptions about the Book of Esther." *CBQ* 39 (1977): 171–81.

Klingbeil, Gerald A. "רכש and Esther 8,10.14: A Semantic Note." *ZAW* 107 (1995): 301–3.

Kolb, Robert. "Called to Milk Cows and Govern Kingdoms: Martin Luther's Teaching on the Christian's Vocations." *ConJ* 39 (2013): 133–41.

Koller, Aaron. "The Exile of Kish: Syntax and History in Esther 2.5–6." *JSOT* 37 (2012): 45–56.

Lacocque, André. "The Different Versions of Esther." *BibInt* 7 (1999): 301–22.

Larsson, Gerhard. "Is the Book of Esther Older Than Has Been Believed?" *VT* 52 (2002): 130–1.

Lee, Peter Y. "Esther" Pages 475–94 in *A Biblical-Theological Introduction to the Old Testament: The Gospel Promised*. Edited by Miles V. Van Pelt. Wheaton, IL: Crossway, 2016.

Lees, David. "Hapax Legomena in Esther 1.6: Translation Difficulties and Comedy in the Book of Esther." *BT* 68 (2017): 88–108.

Levenson, Jon D. *Esther: A Commentary*. OTL. Louisville, KY: Westminster John Knox, 1997.

Linafelt, Tod and Timothy K. Beal. *Ruth and Esther*. Berit Olam: Studies in Hebrew Narrative and Poetry. Collegeville: Liturgical Press, 1999.

Loader, J. A. "Esther as a Novel with Different Levels of Meaning." *ZAW* 90 (1978): 417–21.

Loewenstamm, Samuel E. "Esther 9:29–32: The Genesis of a Late Addition." *HUCA* 42 (1971): 117–24.

Low, Maggie. "To Kill or Not to Kill the Enemies' Women and Children?: The Irony of Esther 8:11." *AsJT* 30 (2016): 145–59.

Martin, R. A. "Syntax Criticism of the LXX Additions to the Book of Esther." *JBL* 94 (1975): 65–72.

Merrill, Eugene H. "The Book of Esther," in *The World and the Word: An Introduction to the Old Testament*. Edited by Eugene H. Merrill, Mark Rooker, and Michael A. Grisanti. Vol. Series 354–61. Nashville: B&H Academic, 2011.

Millard, A. R. "Persian Names in Esther and the Reliability of the Hebrew Text." *JBL* 96 (1977): 481–8.

Miller, Walter. *Xenophon in Seven Volumes*. LCL. Cambridge: Harvard University, 1914.

Moore, Carey A. "Archaeology and the Book of Esther." *BA* 38 (1975): 62–79.

———. *Daniel, Esther and Jeremiah: The Additions.* AB 44. New York: Doubleday, 1977.

———. *Esther: Introduction, Translation, and Notes.* AB 7B. Garden City, NY: Doubleday, 1971.

———. "On the Origins of the LXX Additions to the Book of Esther." *JBL* 92 (1973): 382–93.

———. ed. *Studies in the Book of Esther.* New York: KTAV, 1982.

Murphy, Roland E. *Wisdom Literature: Job, Proverbs, Ruth, Canticles, Ecclesiastes, and Esther.* FOTL XIII. Grand Rapids, MI: Eerdmans, 1981.

Niemann, Hermann Michael. *"Das Ende des Volkes der Perizziter: Über Soziale Wandlungen Israels im Spiegel Einer Begriffsgruppe."* ZAW 105 (1993): 233–57.

Noss, Philip A. "A Footnote on Time: The Book of Esther." *BT* 44 (1993): 309–20.

Olmsted, A. T. *History of the Persian Empire.* Chicago; University of Chicago, 1948.

Parker, Richard A. and Waldo H. Dubberstein. *Babylonian Chronology 620 B.C.–A.D. 75.* Reprint. Eugene, OR: Wipf and Stock, 2007.

Paton, Lewis Bayles. *A Critical and Exegetical Commentary on the Book of Esther.* ICC. New York: Charles Scribner's Sons, 1916.

Paul, Shalom M. "Adoption Formulae: A Study of Cuneiform and Biblical Legal Clauses." *Maarav* 2 (1980): 173–85.

Pierce, Ronald W. "The Politics of Esther and Mordechai: Courage or Compromise?" *BBR* 2 (1992): 75–89.

Pietersma, Albert and Benjamin G. Wright, eds. *A New English Translation of the Septuagint and the Other Greek Translations Traditionally Included under That Title.* New York: Oxford University, 2007.

Plutarch. *Plutarch's Lives with an English Translation.* Translated by Bernadotte Perrin. LCL. Cambridge: Harvard University Press, 1926.

Polzin, Robert. *Late Biblical Hebrew: Towards a Typology of Biblical Hebrew Prose.* Missoula, MT: Schoarls, 1976.

Provan, Iain. "Hearing the Historical Books." Pages 254–76 in *Hearing the Old Testament: Listening for God's Address.* Edited by Craig G. Bartholomew and David J. H. Beldman. Grand Rapids: Eerdmans, 2012.

Redditt, Paul R. "Esther, Book Of." Pages 194–6 in *Dictionary for Theological Interpretation of the Bible*. Edited by Kevin J. Vanhoozer, Craig G. Bartholomew, Daniel J. Trier, and N. T. Wright. Grand Rapids: Baker, 2005. Reprinted as "Esther" Pages 142–8 in *Theological Interpretation of the Old Testament*. Edited by Kevin J. Vanhoozer, Craig G. Bartholomew, and Daniel Trier. Grand Rapids: Baker Academic, 2008.

Root, Margaret Cool. "The Parthenon Frieze and the Apadana Reliefs at Persepolis: Reassessing a Programmatic Relationship." *AJA* 89 (1985): 103–20.

Rüger, Hans Peter. "'*Das Tor Des Königs'—Der Königliche Hof*. *Bibit* 50 (1969): 247–50.

Salvesen, Alison. "Keter (Esther 1:11; 2:17; 6:8): 'Something to Do with a Camel'?" *JSS* 44 (1999): 35–46.

Schreiner, Thomas R. *The King in His Beauty: A Biblical Theology of the Old and New Testaments*. Grand Rapids: Baker Academic, 2013.

Shea, William H. "Esther and History." *ConJ* 13 (1987): 234–48.

Spoelstra, Joshua Joel. "The Function of the יין משתה in the Book of Esther." *OTE* 27 (2014): 285–301.

Steinmann, Andrew E. *From Abraham to Paul: A Biblical Chronology*. St. Louis: Concordia, 2011.

———. *The Oracles of God: The Old Testament Canon*. St. Louis: Concordia, 1999.

Striedl, Hans. "*Untersuchung Zur Syntax Und Stilistik des Hebräischen Buches Esther*." *ZAW* 55 (1937): 73–108.

Talmon, Shemaryahu. "'Wisdom' in the Book of Esther." *VT* 13 (1963): 419–55.

Talshir, David and Zipora Talshir. "The Double Month Naming in Late Biblical Books: A New Clue for Dating Esther?" *VT* 54 (2004): 549–55.

Tawil, Hayim. "Two Notes on the Treaty Terminology of the Sefire Inscriptions." *CBQ* 42 (1980): 30–7.

Walfish, Barry. *Esther in Medieval Garb: Jewish Interpretation of the Book of Esther in the Middle Ages*. Albany: SUNY, 1993.

Waltke, Bruce K. *An Old Testament Theology: An Exegetical, Canonical, and Thematic Approach*. Grand Rapids: Zondervan Academic, 2007.

Weiland, Forrest S. "Historicity, Genre, and Narrative Design in the Book of Esther." *BSac* 159 (2002): 151–65.

Wenham, Gordon J. "*Betûlāh*, a Girl of Marriageable Age." *VT* 22 (1972): 326–48.

Wiebe, John M. "Esther 4:14: 'Will Relief and Deliverance Arise for the Jews from Another Place?'" *CBQ* 53 (1991): 409–15.

Winitzer, Abraham. "The Reversal of Fortune Theme in Esther: Israelite Historiography in Its Ancient Near Eastern Context." *JANER* 11 (2011): 170–218.

Wright, J. S. "The Historicity of the Book of Esther." Pages 37–47 in *New Perspectives on the Old Testament*. Edited by J. Barton Payne. Waco, TX: Word, 1970.

Yamauchi, Edwin M. "The Archaeological Background of Esther: Archaeological Backgrounds of the Exilic and Postexilic Era, Pt 2." *BSac* 137 (1980): 99–117.

———. "Mordecai, the Persepolis Tablets, and the Susa Excavations." *VT* 42 (1992): 272–5.

———. *Persia and the Bible*. Grand Rapids, MI: Eerdmans, 1990.

Zadok, Ran. "Notes on Esther." *ZAW* 98 (1986): 105–10.

———. "On Five Biblical Names." *ZAW* 89 (1977): 266–8.

———. "On Five Iranian Names in the Old Testament." *VT* 26 (1976): 246–7.

———. "On the Historical Background of the Book of Esther." *BN* 24 (1984): 18–23.

NAME INDEX

183

SCRIPTURE INDEX